Profiles
of
Preservice Teacher Education

SUNY Series in Teacher Preparation and Development
Alan R. Tom, Editor

Profiles
of
Preservice Teacher Education

Inquiry into the Nature of Programs

Kenneth R. Howey and Nancy L. Zimpher

State University of New York Press

The work reported herein was funded in part by the North Central Regional Educational Laboratory, a non-profit organization supported in part by the Office of Educational Research and Improvement, U.S. Department of Education. The opinions expressed in these materials do not necessarily reflect the position or policy of the Laboratory or the funding agency, and no official endorsement should be inferred.

Published by
State University of New York Press, Albany

©   1989 State University of New York

For information, address State University of New York Press, State University Plaza, Albany, N.Y., 12246

Library of Congress Cataloging in Publication Data

Howey, Kenneth R.
    Profiles of preservice teacher education : inquiry into the nature of programs / Kenneth R. Howey and Nancy L. Zimpher.
        p.   cm.—(SUNY series in teacher preparation and development)
    Includes index.
    ISBN 0-88706-973-8.   ISBN 0-88706-974-6 (pbk.)
    1. Elementary school teachers—Training of—United States—Case studies.   I. Zimpher, Nancy L.   II. Title.   III. Series.
LB1715.H73   1989
372.11'46—dc19   88-19995
                                                              CIP

10 9 8 7 6 5 4 3 2

Contents

Acknowledgments

These authors wish to acknowledge the support of the North Central Regional Educational Laboratory and Judson Hixson in the design and conduct of this study. To Karen Fellows and Sharon Strom, then doctoral students at The Ohio State University and the University of Minnesota respectively, we owe a debt of gratitude not only for their technical assistance but also for their curiosity and keen observations as members of the research team.

Introduction

THE CURRENT CONTEXT

Little exists in the way of comprehensive descriptions of teacher preparation programs beyond the impersonal, prescribed documentaries gathering dust on the shelves of regulatory and accrediting agencies. While relatively brief narratives have been published in education journals, more exhaustive accounts incorporating the multiple perspectives of faculty, students, administrators, and those in schools who work with these programs cannot be found. This book addresses this void and provides in-depth, personal accounts of initial teacher preparation as conducted in six different types of institutions of higher education ranging from a small liberal arts institution to major research-oriented universities.

The book is timely in that teacher education is currently the source of considerable ferment. Recent concerns over our nation's schools and the quality of teaching within them have been translated into questions of who prepares our teachers, in what manner, and how well. Critics of teacher education, always plentiful, now have the floor. "Reform" proposals abound. Before we review the nature of the research that informed our descriptive portrayals of different teacher preparation programs, we examine briefly the nature of the current debate over teacher education in order to provide some perspective for the questions we focused on in these field studies.

Assumptions about the general quality of teacher preparation programs, the faculty attached to them, and students enrolled in them are at the root of the current debate about needed reform in teacher education. Critics vary both in terms of their assessment of the current quality of these programs as well as in terms of how they should be changed. Also, various changes proposed for teacher preparation address different purposes. The Holmes Group (1986), for

1

example, in advocating postbaccalaureate teacher preparation, focuses on the enhanced professional status of teachers, an expanded empirical base for guiding teaching and learning how to teach, and the development of a career ladder as one means of retaining our best teachers. It hopes in its ambitious agenda to contribute ultimately to better conditions in schools. It is therefore an agenda with major political as well as programmatic implications. On the other hand, many advocates for alterations in and extensions to undergraduate programming focus more squarely on questions of curriculum change in programs of teacher education. These critics focus in part on the nature of pedagogy, informed now by several decades of research on teacher effectiveness and on appropriate methodologies to increase student learning and retention in school. They are also concerned with optimal timeframes or the "life" space needed for the development of a teacher and the matter of access to teacher education, especially in terms of how this relates to what many predict will be an impending teacher shortage.

To illustrate further, two eminent scholars in teacher education, David Clark and Alan Tom, both view the quality of teacher preparation as a major problem yet call for quite different approaches to improve it. And, as indicated above, they address somewhat different purposes. Clark (1984) proposes that entrance to teacher preparation programs be limited to students who hold a bachelor's degree with a subject-matter major and who have demonstrated a commitment to service and achievement appropriate to a professional field. This advocacy for a postbaccalaureate-only approach emanates from the following contention on his part:

> More than 70 percent of the four-year colleges and universities in the U. S. operate state-approved teacher training programs. A few of these programs are dreadful on all counts—liberal arts education, subject-matter major, and professional preparation. Many are substandard in one or more of these areas. This proliferation of teacher training programs dilutes the human and financial resources available to the field, impedes reform efforts that require additional funding or staff, and divorces the bulk of the training programs from the centers that produce knowledge about education. The fact that teacher education programs exist in so many institutions of higher education does not represent a commitment to preparing excellent teachers on the part of the participating colleges. It represents instead a commitment to serving the vocational needs of their undergraduate populations. The majority of these institutions are bachelor's-degree-granting colleges caught up in teacher education because they wish to compete for students with other colleges. Their faculty members are typically not involved in the production of knowledge about education. (p. 117)

Thus, he supports postbaccalaureate preparation because he assumes it will eventually place teacher education only in institutions which are capable of offering "professional" level training, staffed by faculty who engage in scholarly inquiry to support the nature and direction of that training. As a result of fewer institutions currently preparing teachers, greater resources would be attached to these programs. Beyond this, Clark sees a confederation such as Holmes as a more viable strategy for improving teacher preparation than single institutions moving independently of one another—a strategy, he reminds us, that has been less than effective in the past.

Similarly, Tom (1986) acknowledges major shortcomings in teacher preparation but suggests that, rather than moving to postbaccalaureate teacher education, we need basically to redesign general education, as well as professional education, at the baccalaureate level:

> . . . the problem with general education is its quality and coherence, not its length. Further, additional academic study is not as important as reorganizing this study so its focus is more on core disciplinary ideas and inquiry processes. Thus, a reasonable case can be made that the rethinking of general education and subject matter preparation is a far more significant reform than the expansion of either of these areas of study. Similarly, the present size of the professional curriculum is sufficient for the inclusion of pedagogical knowledge which has been developed in recent years, providing redundant and unnecessary professional content is removed from the current professional curriculum. At the same time, there is no reason to believe that housing professional education in an autonomous postbaccalaureate professional school is a wise idea. Establishing an autonomous professional school structure is not likely to augment the status of the occupation of teaching. Moreover, such a professional school of education tends to artificially separate the academic and professional aspects of teaching. Instead of disassociating itself from undergraduate arts and sciences instruction, the department or school of education ought to support the reform of the arts and sciences curriculum and seek to regenerate the professional aspects of teacher preparation. (p. 31)

Tom assumes that needed curricular reform carried out concurrently in general education and professional education will lead to better teachers. Such coordinated changes, he argues, are more likely to occur in programs at the baccalaureate level. He sees little potency in a strategy of attempting to upgrade the profession of teaching by moving to postbaccalaureate professional schools.

There are other thoughtful advocates for both what are basically baccalaureate as well as extensive postbaccalaureate approaches to teacher preparation. Additionally, there are many who apparently view the problem as less severe than critics such as Tom or Clark and who suggest rather that the appropriate courses of action are more modest extensions of current preparation programs. Such advocates assume a primary problem is a crowded teacher preparation curriculum (Scannell, 1984; Smith, 1984). They advocate either fifth-year or extended baccalaureate programs which begin at the undergraduate level and continue into graduate level work, adding a year or so of postbaccalaureate study. These advocates reflect a more moderate stance than the one the Holmes Group has assumed. The American Association of

Colleges for Teacher Education (AACTE), for example, calls for serious consideration of extended programs and has identified seven alternative models of *extended* teacher preparation to promote involvement in this direction. As we have observed (Howey and Zimpher, 1986), these models for change are explicated largely at the structural level. Although there is increasing advocacy for the integration of the expanding "knowledge base" on teaching in the curriculum of teacher education, rarely do the debates about reform and redesign focus on alternative frameworks for program design. As a result, there continues to be an overreliance on rather technical conceptions of teacher competence, with little regard for the discipline-related properties of teaching or more phenomenological or critical perspectives on teaching.

This trend to extend the length of initial preparation is also manifested in the growing number of designs for the induction of first-year teachers. In these arrangements, beginning teachers typically are released from their classrooms periodically and assigned to "mentors" (experienced teachers) who provide both personal support and continuing educative experiences. In other instances, there is more of an emphasis on monitoring and evaluating the progress of these novitiates. And in yet other situations the support and evaluative functions are combined in various ways. These *entry-year* or *induction* arrangements are the most prevalent extension of baccalaureate-level teacher preparation at present. More than one-third of the states have legislatively derived rules and regulations in this regard (AACTE, 1987).

There are also many who see no compelling reason to make any major changes in current practice. This position is represented in the views of a dean of a well-regarded, state-supported college of education we recently interviewed, who opined:

> We are very pleased with our program. We get positive feedback year after year from those who employ our students. Students who want to teach in this state seek us out. We begin our program in the freshman year and we provide a wide variety of opportunities in schools for our teacher candidates. By the time they are in their senior year [and] student teaching, they are ready to teach. These young people go out with considerable confidence and skill. I can't imagine why we would want to expand our present efforts.

There are also many who take the position that teacher educators should be more realistic in terms of what can be done initially in teacher preparation. These observers suggest that there are phases in the career of a teacher which call for more powerful teacher education interventions spread out over a longer period of time. This argument is made in at least two ways. Some argue, for instance, that current undergraduate patterns already address this phasing problem. Another dean stated:

> The vast majority of teaching jobs are going to be in blue collar areas and particularly in areas where there are high minority populations. And so we're trying to

recruit people who can hack it in these places and our best hope is to give them a bachelor's degree and some degree of ability to teach well at the outset. Somebody's got to do that. . . . See, I'm convinced because I think I was a pretty good teacher after four years of college. I believe I was effective. And I believe I became a better teacher when the state made me go back to school and get a master's degree *after I had some experience* and I felt it was a relevant experience for me. I don't know about anybody else, but I think this is a pretty good pattern.

Others, such as the Holmes Group, call for a more interrelated pattern of teacher preparation than that suggested above. Its report, *Tomorrow's Teachers* (1986), outlines a three-tiered hierarchical structure of teacher roles and responsibilities. In order for teachers to move up this ladder, they would have to proceed through rather continuous professional development tied to specific testing and credentialing while accruing experience in the classroom.

Finally, many view the positive effects of any teacher education effort, however well-conceived and however protracted, as problematic. They take the position that change or reform efforts must focus primarily on changing basic conditions in schooling in terms of such factors as smaller class size, improved curricular and instructional resources, redefined teacher roles, or achieving extended amounts of time for study by students in schools. For these advocates, decisions made closest to the children are the most important and they believe the impact of teachers will be enhanced more by altering conditions in schools than by expanding their initial preparation (Kirst, 1986). While many advocates for change in teacher education, including the Holmes Group, call for concomitant changes in schools, these latter critics argue that such advocacy only represents an even more unrealistic view of what can be accomplished via programs of teacher preparation and by those in higher education.

We disagree. We believe that teacher education does foster more positive conditions in schools and could make an even greater contribution. However, before new paths for change can be charted for the various institutions that prepare teachers, we need to be clearer about current policy and practice. For us, a fundamental constraint to the dialogue and debate concerned with projected changes in teacher preparation is the lack of a clear understanding of the nature and quality of various programs of teacher education. As a case in point, Koehler's (1985) review of 220 studies on preservice teacher education concludes with the assertion that, "there are lots of studies, but they do not add up to anything; they are piecemeal and particularistic" (p. 23). Certainly, major problems are assumed by many. Yet given a lack of assessment data, let alone clear and relatively complete descriptions of similarities and differences across various types of institutions which prepare teachers, the validity of these assertions remains largely a matter of conjecture. Little, in fact, is known in a fine-grained manner about the nature of teacher preparation curricula, the instructional activities of faculty attached to these curricula, and the frequency, timelines, and quality of opportunities which prospective teachers have for learning how to teach.

It should not be surprising, then, that many "reform" efforts tend to stress more general and structural changes concerned, for example, with adding a fifth year or increasing the number of hours of "field" experiences. Surely problems of various types exist and improvements can and should be made. Nonetheless, as we attempted to illustrate at the outset, there is hardly consensus on the nature and scope of these problems, let alone the most efficacious means of resolving them.

It was our intent that the six descriptive portrayals which follow and the insights garnered from our study which led to these descriptions would begin to address basic data gaps about the education of teachers. It is the lack of understanding about many aspects of this most important endeavor—the education of our nation's teachers—that prompted our inquiry. Our major aim was to describe in an indepth, yet personal, manner how preservice teacher education is conducted in quite different contexts in six institutions of higher education.

BACKGROUND AND PURPOSES OF THE STUDY

Again, the major purpose of the case studies reported herein has been to provide a more in-depth picture than currently exists of how teachers are prepared in preservice programs, namely programs which prepare elementary teachers. Specifically, we selected six sites for our comparative cases that reflect similarities and differences in teacher education programs housed in different types of institutions, from liberal arts colleges to major research-oriented universities. Furthermore, we selected institutions from among those viewed by state-level stakeholders, described in national journals, and designated as national award recipients, to be distinctive, if not exemplary. The programs identified through this informal nominating process were elementary education programs. Historically, these are the programs that have received the most faculty attention in terms of curriculum innovation and program variation. Further, we selected only institutions located in the midwest region of the country.

Our focus on the midwest is not coincidental. The interests and involvement of the authors in the study of teacher education predate this study considerably. Both of us have been housed as faculty members and program administrators in colleges of education for a combined total of more than thirty years. In 1984, our institutions (the University of Minnesota and the Ohio State University) became involved in a consortium composed of the Big Ten institutions and the University of Chicago (through the Council for Inter-Institutional Cooperation or CIC) in the founding of a regional educational laboratory in Elmhurst, Illinois. Today, the North Central Regional Educational Laboratory (NCREL) is one of nine such regional laboratories in the United States. This network of labs has been in operation for more than two decades and is supported in large part by funds from the U. S. Department of Education, Office of Educational Research and Improvement. NCREL serves the seven-state midwest region of Illinois, Indiana, Iowa, Michigan, Minnesota, Ohio, and Wisconsin under the general charter of helping to improve education for students in the region's elementary and secondary schools.

Early on in the evolution of the lab's broader agendas, member institutions in NCREL's region contributed time in formulating platforms from which the lab could serve its various constituencies, including elementary and secondary school personnel and pupils; state agencies and association representatives; and schools, colleges, and departments of education (SCDEs) in higher education. One such effort was to define more generally the nature of the continuing professional development of teachers. A monograph (Howey, Matthes, and Zimpher, 1985) was subsequently produced, describing issues and problems cited in the empirical and expository literature on teacher education. It delineated the continuum of teachers' professional growth and development, from recruitment and selection into teacher education programs to the nature of preservice, induction, and inservice programs for teachers. Out of this analysis grew agendas that allowed the lab to help its constituents set priorities for identifying timely and appropriate research-based information, encouraging its development, and demonstrating its use. One such area of focus was to probe in-depth the nature and quality of preservice programs in the region; thus, this study was initiated.

A parallel development that also warrants explanation here is the evolution of what is now designated by AACTE as the Research About Teacher Education (RATE) project. This effort began with the designation of an ad hoc information and planning group in 1984 to study the data collected from AACTE member institutions about their preservice preparation programs. The evolution of this group to a standing committee of AACTE on Research and Information resulted in the formulation of a longitudinal data collection effort to greatly enhance the quality of information obtained from a stratified random sampling of ninety of the more than 700 AACTE member institutions. Now in its fourth year of data collection, the RATE project's initial report (AACTE, 1987) presents institutional profiles and data on programs, faculty, and students from which generalizations can be drawn about the nature and quality of preservice efforts across the country.

Along with a small group of teacher education researchers, we have served on this committee since its formation. As such, we have contributed to the conceptualization of this longitudinal study, designed survey instrumentation and analyzed results for three annual studies, focusing in 1986 on secondary education, in 1987 on foundations courses, and in 1988 on elementary education and field experiences. Particularly relevant to our report of the case studies has been the opportunity to complement the highly objective, quantitative format of the AACTE effort with the more qualitative portrayals that resulted from our multisite studies reported herein. The coincidence of the two efforts has allowed us to pose questions drawn from the case studies in questionnaire form to a national probability sample for confirmation of descriptively derived observations. In turn, we were able to add, as a result of our case studies, explanatory data to inform survey responses. The interplay of these two data bases will become apparent in the summary chapters of this text.

Thus, these case studies have benefited in conceptualization by the larger agenda of a federally funded regional laboratory to foster the professional development of teachers and by the research and information needs of the major member organization for SCDEs in the United States. When these studies were initiated, no other studies of teacher education of this scope were being conducted. Our efforts had been preceded by the data base efforts of AACTE, which it admittedly was seeking to improve, and by a previous federally sponsored initiative by the former U. S. Department of Health, Education and Welfare (HEW) in 1973 to conduct research into teacher education (known as the RITE project). This initiative, conducted by David Clark and Egon Guba (1977), resulted in reports on knowledge production and utilization in SCDEs (Guba and Clark, 1978) and also included case studies of a dozen teacher education sites which were never published. However, data and design features of these studies were made available to us as this study was formulated.

Our first site visitations were begun in November 1985. Since 1986, two national studies of teacher education have been initiated, one by the federally funded National Center for Research on Teacher Education at Michigan State University; the other by John Goodlad in an Exxon-funded study at the University of Washington on the education of educators. At this writing, only preliminary executive summaries of the Goodlad effort are available. The center's agenda and design are more widely distributed (Kennedy, 1988) and a twelve-site initiative has been launched. We have reported at the center regarding the nature of our study and have been informed as well by the work of the center.

These antecedent events provide a rich context for conceptualizing a long-overdue and greatly needed series of studies on the nature of preservice teacher education programs. Obviously there is, at long last, somewhat of a groundswell of interest in the topic. Our efforts have been enhanced accordingly. From the beginning of our study four years ago to this writing, we continue to refer to this set of case studies as preliminary or pilot in nature and certainly exploratory. As the report of our findings and analysis of these data subsequently shows, we have raised many more questions than we have answered. As such, we could be characterized in Krathwohl's (1987) typology as "synthesizers"; that is, we are primarily concerned with description and explanation rather than prediction or evaluation.

We have not judged the programs we studied to be effective based on data which indicate that teachers graduating from them have acquired desired knowledge, skills, and dispositions at a specified criterion level or, beyond that, that these teachers have demonstrated themselves to be effective by enabling some set of pupil outcomes when they have assumed teaching positions. Our effort has been modest. Our observations rest rather on the perceptions of the persons most closely involved in these programs; that is, the faculty and the prospective teachers themselves. Their perceptions were further examined in light of those who receive these beginning teachers; that is, supervising teachers and administrators in schools which cooperated with these programs. Neither do we suggest these programs we have studied are representative of most programs nor that we can generalize from our observations. We selected them because of nominations from multiple sources which indicated that they were *distinctive* and/or *exemplary* in some ways. While we designed our studies carefully in order to examine specific conditions and practice and to observe instruction in a variety of contexts, nonetheless we were limited by the brief periods of time we actually spent on each campus. Our work is typified by an effort to pose questions, to enter a setting through a process of analytic induction (Robinson, 1951), and ultimately to seek to derive generalizations or develop theory about the phenomenon under study. To this end, our study has been guided by the following four objectives:

1. To provide contextually framed descriptive documentation of the scope, nature, and quality of teacher education *curricula* reported as distinctive or exemplary of good practice.
2. To provide descriptive documentation of the conceptual orientations and instructional or pedagogical practices of the *faculty* as exhibited for prospective teachers in their professional preparation.
3. To provide descriptive documentation of the nature of the preservice *students* with regard to their background, orientation to teaching as a career, and their opportunities to exhibit good teaching practices.
4. To identify preliminary indices of the extent to which *programs* of teacher preparation are conceptualized and implemented and to reflect attributes of a cohesive design for relating didactic and applied experiences to teacher preparation.

These four objectives were further specified into a set of questions that guided our inquiry into the nature of preservice preparation and that we believe are the key questions in the dialogue and debate we briefly reviewed at the outset of this chapter. These questions are as follows:

1. Curricula
   1.1 What does the scope and sequence of courses look like across different elementary programs?
   1.2 What conception(s) of teaching, learning, and schooling appear in the curricular design of the programs?
   1.3 To what extent does a laboratory component exist in which simulated, microteaching, and/or peer teaching opportunities are afforded in the prospective teachers' programs?
   1.4 What opportunities are provided for prospective teachers to explore

and employ instructional approaches in school settings? How consonant are the goals of the preservice programs studied with those of schools where students practice teaching?

1.5 What type of expectations and intellectual challenge does the curriculum represent?

1.6 What type or level of research and evaluation has been conducted into the preservice programs studied?

2. Faculty

2.1 What is the general sociodemographic profile and background and experience of the faculty who devote their efforts to teacher preparation?

2.2 How do faculty describe their attitudes toward and commitment to teaching, research, and service across the institutions?

2.3 What is the nature of faculty contribution to program design, implementation and evaluation?

2.4 How do faculty relate to students in and out of classrooms?

2.5 What conceptions of teaching, learning, and schooling are held by the faculty?

3. Students

3.1 What is the general sociodemographic profile of students enrolled in these programs?

3.2 What motivated students in these programs to select teaching as a career and to enroll in this institution for a teaching degree?

3.3 How do students matriculate through these programs?

3.4 What is the nature of work and travel, cultural and informal activities of the students?

3.5 How do students perceive the nature and quality of their preparation for teaching, their achievement in the program, and their subsequent role as teachers?

4. Program

4.1 To what extent do the curricula studied reflect not only relatedness across courses and experiences in the preservice program, but also articulation with the institution's general studies or arts and sciences curricula?

4.2 To what extent are explicit conceptions of teaching and learning and the mission of schooling filtered throughout the totality of the students' preservice program?

4.3 To what extent are courses and experiences structured in some developmental sequence?

4.4 To what extent does the program accommodate faculty collegiality and student cohort groups?

4.5 How are schools and supervising teachers selected and prepared? To what extent are their philosophies about teaching, learning, and schooling consistent with that of the program studied?

4.6 What has been the extent of change over time in the programs studied? What are sources of leadership for the development and maintenance of the programs studied?

DESIGN OF THE STUDY

The design for the descriptive portrayals presented in this book is that referred
to as an observational case study (Bogden and Biklen, 1982), usually including observations of a particular place (such as a classroom or a school), of a
specific group of people (such as a group of students or a department), and of
some activity in this place (such as a curriculum planning effort). In some
instances, such as our study, all three of these perspectives apply in combination. Such studies are also guided by the selection of key informants in a
purposeful sampling of sites. As Bogden and Biklen observe, "You choose
particular subjects [or sites] to include because they are believed to facilitate
the expansion of the developing theory" (p. 67).

The institutions selected for study on-site represent three types of institutions preparing teachers including: (1) schools and colleges of education in
major universities with a knowledge production mission; (2) state universities
where teaching is emphasized over research; and (3) smaller institutions with
a liberal arts orientation. As a result, the regional sites selected for study included two "Big Ten" research-oriented institutions (Indiana University and
Michigan State University); three state-supported institutions with a rich history of teacher education (Ball State University, the University of Wisconsin-
Eau Claire, and the University of Toledo); and one liberal arts institution in
Iowa (Luther College). We selected baccalaureate-level programs because
we wanted to describe as fully as possible what exists now, and what primarily exists now are baccalaureate-level programs in a variety of institutional
contexts.

The rationale for this project and the objectives which define the dimensions of this study were based on the premise that a better understanding about
teacher education requires both quantitative and qualitative methods of inquiry. As such, our attention was to generate rich descriptions of the "lived
experience of teacher education" through intensive site visitations. Such portrayals required inquiry not only about the faculty and students who participated in the selected programs, but also teachers and other school personnel
who support these programs through providing a context for field experiences. Accordingly, we evolved a set of rough definitions and explanations of
the phenomenon under study, which became our research questions listed earlier. Subsequently, after we entered the sites, we held these questions up to
the data collected, and modified the questions to some degree as each new
case was analyzed. We also looked for contradictions in order to redefine and
reformulate explanations until, ultimately, new relationships between the

questions and the data were formed. This process complies with the modified analytic induction process described by Bogden and Biklen (p. 67).

These case studies were guided, as well, by a set of principles for conducting a naturalistic qualitative study (Lincoln and Guba, 1985). First, we entered into the natural setting of teacher education; that is, the college and university setting, using as the tools for our inquiry our own insights as researchers on site. We studied both the history of the selected programs and the behaviors which influence and are influenced by these settings. In order to discover how the work of teacher education occurred in these institutions, data collection procedures depended largely on verbal accounts (transcribed), observations, document review, and anecdotal records, guided by the questions shared earlier. As accounts or events were described and abstractions were translated into words and actions, interpretations were made in light of the multiple perspectives of the various role groups in the study and the researchers. Themes or understandings that were perceived by the researchers were validated against the perceptions of faculty and students. Data compilation included taped interviews, field notes, and the collection and study of several artifacts such as curriculum reports, research reports, and course syllabi. A standard procedure was to make preliminary contact with site personnel to request pertinent documents prior to the visit and to coordinate observations and interviews during the site visits. Accordingly, each case study required multiple visits or, in the case of the University of Wisconsin-Eau Claire, an extended single visit.

For purposes of verifying the credibility of our study, we have relied heavily on the Lincoln and Guba (1985: 301–16) analysis of the "trustworthiness" of qualitative data. Consequently, we have applied to the degree possible techniques that are likely to make our findings and interpretations more credible through the use of: (1) prolonged engagement (spending enough time on-site to arrive at data saturation or redundancy in our data); (2) triangulation (seeking perceptions from multiple sources); (3) peer debriefing (sharing preliminary analyses with other informed teacher education researchers through an advisory committee structure); (4) negative case analysis (continuing to list our findings against new information that caused a redefinition of results); and (5) member checks (by asking all interviewed respondents to attest to the adequacy of the portrayal, to correct factual error and to inform the analysis). This, then, we believe serves our larger purpose, and that proposed by Krathwohl as well, of "creating a consensus about the interpretation of evidence" (1987, xii) with respect to the knowledge claims evidenced in this study.

We acknowledge, as well, that there may be some concern by our readers as to the degree of "objectivity" exercised in these portrayals; a concern fueled perhaps by our decision to personally identify faculty members in the interview excerpts we cite. On the one hand, participant observation assumes that events are best understood from the multiperspectives of key informants in exchange with the researcher in situ. This we believe to be a well-established tradition of naturalistic inquiry. As to the personal identification of respondents, we take our lead from the highly acclaimed work of Grant and Reisman (1978) called the *Perpetual Dream*, which received the American Council on Education Award for the Outstanding Book in Education. They, as well as we, determined that the key informants in a university setting are unique. Professors are most known for their persona. We attach our names to everything, and particularly to our ideas. To attempt to camouflage a university profile seemed contrived to us. Again, these are studies to illustrate good practice. By definition, these are "known" programs, thus we wanted to resist an after-the-fact guessing game. So we sought the permission of key faculty informants to release their comments. Students and school personnel are not, on the other hand, identified by name. Still it remains to the reader to decide if the portrayals we present belie a kind of trustworthiness that could have been garnered by anonymity. Beyond these personal accounts, however, we do offer in the critical analyses provided in chapters seven and eight, a more objective review of issues and concerns accumulated during the course of these case studies.

ORGANIZATION OF THE TEXT

This book has been organized into eight chapters. In this introduction, we provide a context for the reform climate that prompted our investigation of preservice teacher education programs and the research questions and methodology that allowed and guided our inquiry. In chapters one through six, we present the institutional portrayals generated from our multisite case studies. In chapter seven, we present a description of the findings across sites, answering in a critical, analytic and comparative fashion the research questions originally posed with regard to curricula, faculty, and students. Then, in chapter eight, we address the fourth objective, discussing in detail the degree to which we found *programs* of teacher education and the attributes we believe, at this point in our analysis, define the nature of a program. Here, too, we offer recommendations for improving the quality and character of teacher education which appear to be suggested by the nature of our findings. We also offer, in conclusion, a discussion of unanswered questions prompted by this investigation.

Recall again that our primary goal has been to illustrate through multiple but personal accounts examples of good, if not "best," practice. While these portrayals are largely descriptive in nature, they were designed to accentuate the positive. As promised, critical, cross-institutional analyses of these programs follow these narrative accounts in chapters seven and eight. In this vein, we wish to underscore here that in developing these portrayals we in no sense wish to be viewed as proponents for the status quo. We believe that changes are needed in teacher education—in some instances major ones—

and we have been involved for many years in working for improved practice. For example, we are currently working with key faculty and administrators in the nineteen institutions of the Midwest Regional Holmes Group in the hopes of effecting needed changes in teacher preparation.

The portrayals begin with life in a teacher preparation program in a small liberal arts institution, Luther College in Decorah, Iowa, proceed through the relatively large state-supported institutions with a history of preparing teachers, namely Ball State University, the University of Toledo, and the University of Wisconsin-Eau Claire, and culminate with descriptions of student and faculty activity in the large research-oriented universities, namely Indiana University and Michigan State University.

Common themes flow across these institutions, including the labor-intensive nature of these programs, the pride in and apparent commitment of these young people to teaching, and, perhaps surprisingly, the pervasive personal affection for these students exhibited by the faculty we visited. There are many distinctive conditions and practices manifested across these campuses as well: the Paideia experience at Luther College, the historical impact of Teachers College on the arts and sciences at Ball State University, the modular approach to instruction at Toledo, the "block" experience at the University of Wisconsin-Eau Claire, the Center for Excellence in Education at Indiana University, and the alternative programs at Michigan State University. Also, strong personalities dominate these different landscapes, allowing the reader to become familiar firsthand with diverse views of teacher education as reflected in the portrayals. While these institutions are all nestled in the midwest, we believe that many of the situations we describe will have a ring of familiarity wherever the reader's experience with teacher education might be. We first visit Decorah, Iowa, a place students suggest "that while it isn't the end of the earth, you can see it from here."

1

Teacher Education and Liberal Study in a Conservative Setting: Paradox and Promise

LUTHER COLLEGE

Paideia is the ancient Greek word for education. It is the process of acquiring knowledge. It is also the result of that process; that is, learning and culture. A common cultural tradition is created and renewed by generations of persons who have learned. Luther College adopted the term Paideia for the core curriculum taken by all students, which recognizes that life and community depend on centuries of shared wisdom. Paideia is comprised of three semester courses, two of which are required for all freshmen, including an integrated course in English and history. A third interdisciplinary course taken the following year concentrates on the process of making ethical decisions. Accordingly, the Paideia program is described in the college bulletin as "a prologue to the total educational experience at Luther [College]." It is intended to provide "a foundation for a liberal arts education, for the continuous learning of Luther students, and for patterns of thinking and raising questions about the values vital to a healthy society." The students we interviewed referred repeatedly and with respect for the high quality of their experience in Paideia. In many ways, Paideia captures the essence of both the academic experience at Luther and the quality of life in this small, liberal arts college.

The brochures which present Luther College to prospective students have repeated references to what characterizes the liberally educated graduate of the college as follows, "Luther's graduates succeed because they are what John Stewart Mill might have called 'capable and cultured human beings.' . . . To understand life on Luther's campus, it is imperative first to understand what is important to the college. Music is important. So are sports. And religion. And quality. And heritage. And being a community. And having the right to be different."

People who live at Luther reflect on the quality of life there. Particularly, we recall an observation made by Dr. Roger Anderson, who chaired the Department of Education for twenty years prior to the recently appointed chair, Edgar Epperly. When asked what was distinctive about Luther College, now Registrar Roger Anderson responded:

> Well, our major strengths are as follows: a very strong student body. I think we get the finest young people not only in terms of academic preparation, but their background—their moral background and so forth. I can't imagine that anybody could have nicer young people. That isn't to say we don't have problems. We also have a very strong faculty; a dedicated faculty. We have a good administration. The President and the Dean are strong people who are listeners and very supportive. We have a tradition not only for excellence but for caring. We have a very loyal alumni group. Our college has accomplished a lot. Many colleges don't have this support. Our constituency is there because this is still a college of the church. That means we have support from many congregations. That doesn't always mean financial support, but they send their sons and daughters. And that's very important. We have a reasonably good physical plant and we have a very attractive location. Once we get people on campus and they see the beauty of this setting, that's a good selling point. At one time, we thought we had a handicap being somewhat isolated from major metropolitan areas. But we're not so sure that's a handicap anymore. A lot of people are anxious to get away from the hustle and bustle, even of suburbia, to come to a place like this.

Chuckling softly, Anderson asks: "Is that a long enough list?"

Where do the students come to? Luther College is a small denominational, liberal arts college, located in Decorah, a pastoral community in the scenic Oneota River valley in the northeast corner of Iowa. Our intention in this descriptive portrayal of the teacher education program at Luther is to describe the academic experience and the quality of life we observed.

ACADEMIC EXCELLENCE AND QUALITY OF LIFE

Luther College As a Place to Be

Toward the end of one of our visits to Luther College, while we were browsing in the bookstore, we stopped to look at the variety of campus t-shirts and sweat shirts. One of the most popular selling t-shirts proclaimed boldly, "Decorah may not be the end of the earth, but you can see it from here. . . ." On our first visit, we experienced a bit of the veracity of this expression. It was December. The day before, the thermometer recorded $-27°F$, with a wind chill factor of $-50°F$, at 4 p.m. in the afternoon. The term *very cold* does not aptly describe that day, and we were a long way from the main highways that wind through Rochester, Minnesota, and ultimately back to the Twin Cities and civilization. Yet the beauty of Luther College and the surrounding valley did not escape us—even though more than two feet of snow lay on the ground. Our initial observations were reinforced when we returned to a blooming and lovely campus in the springtime. Luther College ambassadors like to recall an observation by Eric Sevareid of CBS news, who rhapsodized after visiting Luther, "There is a corner of America here where spring is lovely beyond belief, the land is rolling and green like the center of France, the river small between oak-covered bluffs and crossed by quiet bridges where boys still sit with pole and line, hook and worm. . . ."

Luther College was built on rolling wooded hills and rugged limestone cliffs in what is called the northeast Iowa bluff country. The Upper Iowa River flows through the lower portion of the 800-acre campus; the main section is composed of stately older buildings like old Main Hall and lovely contemporary facilities such as the Center for Faith and Life, a 1,500-seat auditorium and performance center. Some two dozen buildings dot the Luther College campus.

In the midst of these buildings stands the imposing figure of Martin Luther. When you come to Luther College, you cannot help but encounter this man, for embedded in the warp and woof of this college are tenents espoused by Martin Luther. Noticeable, for example, in publications of the college are statements by Martin Luther. One in particular, published in the *Freedom of a Christian* (1520), reads, "A Christian is the perfectly free lord of all, subject to none. A Christian is a perfectly dutiful servant of all, subject to all."

The self-contained nature of the campus in a relatively remote area surely contributes to a sense of community, what Luther calls "at once a community of faith and a community of learning." This blend we saw in the mixture of academic and spiritual buildings, of worship settings and work settings, spaces given over to the work of the mind and others to the work of the spirit.

Luther's history dates back to October 1857, when a newly organized body of Norwegian Lutherans voted to found a college and began to solicit donations for buildings. At this time, Luther's first students were sent to a university in St. Louis; next the college moved to Halfway Creek, near LaCrosse, Wisconsin, in 1861 and finally to Decorah a year later. The first main building was completed in 1865 and the first class graduated in 1866.

Many of Decorah's early settlers were from Norway, people who brought with them the traditions, foods, and arts and crafts of that country. Decorah's Norwegian heritage is so much a part of the valley that an annual Nordic Fest is held each year in July and this is a time of celebration not only of the rich cultural heritage of the area, but also a reunion time for Luther students. The Norwegian American Museum preserves the Norwegian tradition as do many other landmarks and customs at Luther College. Recollections of Scandinavian lore among the students and the faculty, and for that matter the residents of Decorah, are not uncommon and, while no one suggested the possibility of trolls existing somewhere near the Luther College campus, we found this wooded, hillside, glacially bound campus particularly charming nonetheless. Its cultural history is pervasive, its architecture integrated and attractive, and its spiritual symbols everywhere.

Who Are Luther's Students?

Slightly more than 2,100 students are enrolled at Luther College. These undergraduate students come from thirty-eight states and territories and twenty-six foreign countries. One-half of Luther's students are residents of Iowa; 56 percent are women; 3 percent are black; 2 percent are foreign nationals; and only 3 percent are part-time enrollees of the college. Thirty-eight percent of the freshmen were in the top 10 percent of their graduating class; 68 percent were in the top one-fourth; and 96 percent were in the top one-half. Last year, thirty-one of Luther's freshmen were valedictorians of their high school class. During the same year, forty students were elected to Luther's chapter of Phi Beta Kappa. Luther's student athletes have won eighteen NCAA Post Graduate Scholarships, reported as more than any other four-year college in the nation. And, the acceptance rate of Luther graduates into medical schools is almost double the national average. In 1984, 97 percent of Luther's graduates were employed or enrolled in graduate school within a few months after graduation. Luther's recruiting officers boast that all of the forty-two English majors in the class of 1984 obtained jobs or were enrolled in graduate programs. We should add that 60 percent of the students who enroll in Luther College are Lutheran.

The 1985–86 comprehensive fee to attend Luther College was $8,600, including tuition, room and board, and admission to campus activities. An additional $900 (estimated) is needed for books, clothing, entertainment, and other expenses. Consequently, nearly 75 percent of all Luther students receive some form of financial aid from grants, scholarships, loans, or work/study on campus. Regent and presidential scholarships are awarded to applicants demonstrating superior academic achievement. The position taken by the admissions officer is "that no student capable of benefiting from the college should be denied the privilege of attending the college due to limited financial resources." Therefore, the college has developed a comprehensive program of student support. While the cost of a college education at Luther College totals upward of $40,000, many receive support in a variety of forms. Many families are willing to make an extraordinary financial commitment to the education of their children, and students acknowledged and appreciated this sacrifice. The students we met with were readily able to articulate why they came to Luther College, as one education student who had initially come to Luther to be a business major summed up his decision: "Luther is a quality institution in *any* area, not just education, not just business. Most of the students who graduate from Luther find good positions no matter what area they're in."

Just as Luther students did not differentiate the quality of the institution across majors, neither did professors note differences in the quality of students across majors. For example, Dennis Johnson, the admissions officer for the college, observed, "I can't tell you that there's much difference in terms of education students versus other majors." He goes on to describe typical Luther College students. Most students come predominantly from the four-state area of Iowa, Minnesota, Illinois, and Wisconsin. "Only about half of our student body come from Iowa, which makes us more diverse than most of our competitors, which are primarily home-state institutions. It's not uncommon to find some of the 'better' liberal arts colleges in the midwest to be 70 percent home state."

Johnson reviewed for us the heritage of the college and the fact that many students were recruited on the basis of some kind of family connection with the college: "Many of the students are children of alumni. Those large numbers of alumni that graduated in the 1960s now have college-aged children, and they're increasingly convinced that Luther is a good bargain for the money." Johnson continued:

> While we're quite diverse religiously, and socioeconomically as well, we have those Lutheran ties. We don't want to become some kind of fundamentalist bible college, but we do have this Lutheran heritage. The students who come here are very well-rounded. They're competitive academically. They do well and they seem to like this kind of academic atmosphere. Our students tell us again and again that those are the major factors.

We sought confirmation of Johnson's observations from the numerous students with whom we spoke, and we found it. Repeatedly, the students cited their home towns as small, rural communities and told us why they came to Luther. A typical student responded: "Luther's a real family school and my family is devoted to Luther. That's a big part of the reason I came here." Another student shared: "I came here a little bit because my cousins had come here." Still another student observed: "I had a brother who went here." And another student: "It goes back a long way. It goes back to great-grandfathers who went here." Still another student elaborated on the word-of-mouth process of recruitment to Luther taking together the family connections that bring students to Luther and also the religious traditions:

> A big part is commonality as far as our religion. And that's a real tie, much more than a state school; the fact that we're Christians also ties us. Because of this, families feel that it's important not necessarily that the children go to Luther but to that kind of school. . . . I'm Lutheran myself, and that tradition is very strong in my family.

Many students appear to find their way to Luther for family connections and religious affinities, and certainly for Luther's tradition of academic excellence. Given these orientations and the acknowledgement in many instances of parental sacrifice to send them to Luther, it is not surprising that they tend to take their education seriously. As one faculty member observed:

> This college attracts very fine students and we're very proud of the academic ability of the students. The backgrounds they come from help explain why they're willing to work so hard. They have learned to do hard work. The *good* Midwestern kind of work ethic.

Another faculty member shared: "Our students seem to be really hard working. . . . I guess they have to be to spend this kind of money. So, they work hard and they do well." Yet another explanation is offered for the students' selection of and expectation for Luther, which is deeply embedded in a sense of calling or mission, as Ed Epperly, the chairperson of elementary education, underscored for us:

> We have a large number of students who come here with a service orientation. They're looking for ways to serve humanity. They want to be helpful. We have social work majors, we have a nursing major, we have an education major, partly because of the orientation students bring with them. Many of our students—90 percent—come from the Midwest and many of them are rural. Even the ones coming from Minneapolis are, in a sense, rural—their parents often grew up in North Dakota or Minnesota and they bring those rural values of service . . . you've got to do something with your life other than make money. . . . There is, in fact, an element of calling; not as strong as it once was, but it's real. And you see that in many of the students, a lot of whom are still ministers' children and I think that, partly since the relative position of the ministery has slipped, they no longer dream about being ministers the way they once did. But teachers have some of that same element. So I think one of the strengths of the institution is that special commitment the students have.

This sense of calling is also echoed among the students. One of the education majors, talking about her commitment to the education program, observed that criticisms of education classes have to be taken "with a grain of salt," because, " . . . depending on where you are, where you think you want to be going, how well you want to do in something is how well you do. I really like education; that's what I want to do. After all these years, I've finally found my calling." Many of these students are instilled with a sense of mission or service, students who are accustomed to achieving from their own high school experiences, and students who are committed to both the academic and the spiritual life offered by the Luther College experience. This is an experience they often describe in the context of their interaction with faculty members. Thus, we offer a brief profile of some of those faculty members.

What It Means to be a Luther College Faculty Member

There are 131 full-time and thirty-seven part-time faculty members at Luther College. Sixty-eight percent of the faculty hold Ph.D.s or comparable terminal degrees. The ratio of students to faculty is 14-to-1. They come from California and New York, Tennessee and Massachusetts, all the states in the Midwest. They come from Big-Ten institutions, major state institutions, and prestigious private colleges, such as Claremont Graduate School, Cornell, Peabody, Harvard, and Princeton. Faculty members teach approximately seven courses per year, composed of three courses of three or four credit hours each during the regular semesters and a January term. They have also come to Luther College essentially because it is a teaching college. According to Ed Epperly:

> This is not a research institution. No one has ever lost his or her job at Luther because they didn't publish. Many faculty love publishing . . . but they will never really generate a lot of publications in a place like this because the teaching loads are too heavy. So our major duty here is the teaching. How many students do we handle? How effective are we with students? These are the key questions in terms of evaluation and tenure. At Luther, poor performance in the classroom is fatal. There is no way you would be tenured here if you are not acceptable as a teacher. By that, I mean you don't have to be a classroom 'star' most of the time, but if the students consistently complain, if you miss classes, if you didn't deliver quality instruction in some defined, understood sense, you would not be tenured here. If you are recognized as an effective teacher, if the students flock to your courses, you'll not only be tenured, you'll be promoted. It will have a positive effect on your future.

In our conversations with Dr. Thomas Kraabel, vice president and dean of the College, he observed that he saw no hierarchy across departments in terms of scholarship and publication rate. Rather, he is impressed by the sense of community across departments at Luther College:

> We are a community and, for whatever reason, the linkages in our faculty community are there. When we have a faculty meeting as we did yesterday, they are all there. I never went to a faculty meeting at my previous institution. It took me a while to get used to the fact that faculty know each other very well, and your friends are not necessarily people in your own department. They could be professors completely across campus and in different disciplines, because you're neighbors or your daughters are on the high school swim team together or something like that. A lot of faculty have been here for a long time. There are linkages of all kinds, and that means that we treat departments more equally than at other institutions. There may still be some kind of pecking order among departments, but it's hard to put down a faculty member that you work with very closely in the community and who is your neighbor.

The emphasis on teaching and the relatively low faculty/student ratio contribute to the very personal dimensions in the relationships between faculty and students at Luther College. The college as the hub of culture and social context also contributes considerably to this highly interpersonal climate. When asked in what kinds of contexts faculty members interact with students, Roger Anderson observed, "All kinds: Chapel, athletic events, music events. My wife and I used to go to every recital of every student I had had in class. . . . We have students in our home as well." The students also underscored the importance of these personal relationships repeatedly in their dialogue with us. As one student related to us with a good deal of pride:

> There's high quality here on the basis of the student/teacher ratio. I can walk down the street and say hello to Dr. Epperly and he knows I'm a music education major; and yet if I wasn't getting along with my advising professor, I could go to him and he would probably know the situation as well as I would. In a larger school, I don't believe you'd get that. Not that there's any less concern or desire to help the students in a larger school, but the fact remains that there are just too many people out there. . . . I just feel that teaching is so personal and that you have to know an individual so well and through all the years of the program. I think the smaller ratio is better.

One of the students who just returned from teaching in Nottingham, England, said, "Last year I was in a university in England and I was so glad to come back to Luther . . . because we'd walk across the campus and say hello—they don't say hi—and nobody would even respond—I mean ever." Another student shared, "you can get so much help just going down to the office and talking to any of the professors and that's been helpful. They seem concerned about where you're going with your education and they're willing to help you." Yet another student spoke to this personal dimension in terms of her selection of Luther: "I just wanted to get to know the teachers. I had heard of schools where people were in classes with 500 people, and you were just a number and you wait in line forever and then they tell you it's closed. They don't care."

While many of these faculty/student relationships are embedded in what is sometimes referred to as the "cultural island" of the Luther College experience, there are off-campus opportunities available to students as well. There's study abroad in England, an affiliation with the Institute of European Studies and the Danish International School, several Norwegian institutions offer transfer credit, and a year-long academic program at Nottingham, England. Luther is also a member of the Upper Midwest Association for Intercultural Education, which comprises eleven upper-Midwest colleges offering about thirty travel abroad courses during the January term at Luther College. There are, of course, numerous visitors presenting special seminars and programs as well as a semester offered through Luther College and the American

University where students pursue studies for a semester in Washington, D.C., and focus on such topics as national government, foreign policy, economic policy, journalism, urban planning, criminal justice, public administration, and arts and the humanities. There are also special summer institutes and programs offered by the various departments. One recently instigated by the Department of Education was entitled "Effective Education: A Look at the Near Future" wherein Terrel Bell, Carolyn Evertson, and Neil Postman came to Luther College for a week-long symposium on education open to both faculty and students.

Faculty involvement in the life of the campus is emphasized in one of the Luther brochures describing the cultural context:

> Luther's qualified faculty, hard-working students, excellent facilities and diversi-fied academic and cocurricular opportunities would make it a good college by anyone's measure. Yet, the genius of the college is not in these components, but in the way they are put together. Somehow, the college is able to achieve simulta-neous tension and support among its parts. Chemists worry about what happens in the athletic programs. English professors concern themselves with the quality of life in the dormitories. Biologists participate in theatre productions. Mathemati-cians sing the Messiah. It all works a little like a bicycle wheel.

This is the backdrop against which the academic program and the faculty and student relationships play themselves out. It is unavoidable to think about the quality of life at Luther College without attending to the impact of spirituality and music on the Luther College campus. Thus, we briefly turn next to how this influences life on campus.

LUTHER'S SPIRITUAL LIFE AND ITS MUSIC

Religion is central to the life of the campus. First, there is daily morning chapel, which is optional. There are regular and repeated Eucharist services. The bulletin signals some sort of campus ministry every night of the weekend. Already we have reported that more than one-half of Luther's 2,100 students on campus are Lutherans. Another 10 percent of the college's enrollment is Catholic and served by a Catholic chaplain on campus. Other denominations are served by an umbrella campus ministry wherein a group of students explore charismatic manifestations of faith. One student described the re-ligious environment thusly:

> There are tests of faith in any school and not so much tests but awareness that you have to pick . . . you now become more aware. Because of our religion classes, different ideas are promoted. I'm a Missouri Synod Lutheran, which is a branch of the Lutheran Church and it's considered more conservative than the American Lutheran Church. And so you're tested a little bit. Also, the idea of being an individual is promoted here, and I think it's important.

Other students report that their "test of faith" comes as more than a question of how often they attend church away from home. When asked if he attended church during the school year, one student replied, "Not while I'm on campus." To which we probed, "But do you go? Is it something you did when you were in high school with your parents and you still do?" The student responded, "I think that changed for me. When I was in high school, I went all the time. I think my religion classes have made me look at religion and formulate my own ideas instead of just being passive." As students were interviewed about the influences of religion on campus, their responses were often characterized by their decisions about the faithful practice of their religion, rather than any imposed involvement in religious activities from the college.

This individual autonomy about religious activities was also reflected in the observations of faculty about Luther's religious affiliation. When asked if he would consider Luther's religious affiliation as a distinctive feature of the program, Ed Epperly responded:

> No. It doesn't really have any direct influence. About 10 percent of our student body is Catholic and 60 percent Lutheran. There are a smattering of agnostics and everything else. The college is not as provincial as it once was in this respect. I don't attend chapel. I'm a card-carrying Lutheran, but I don't have to be in order to be tenured. It used to be that you had to be. But not anymore. So, we hardly enforce the religion. If a student asks us about it, the college has daily chapel. Certainly, there's a great deal of religious emphasis across campus. You'll see signs of that. But it's a fairly cosmopolitan place—at least compared to what it used to be.

While many students and the faculty appear to assume their Lutheran or other religious affiliation in more personal ways, we also saw many public manifestations of the religious perspectives embraced by Martin Luther. Certainly, for a Christian-oriented college, Christmas is a very special time. For example, in December just prior to the Christmas break, we planned to attend what we believed would be a daily chapel service. We soon learned, however, that this was a special service and, in fact, ended our interview early with a group of faculty members from Arts and Sciences so that they and we could attend this convocation, provocatively entitled "Tomorrow Shall Be My Dancing Day." Soon, both faculty and students (and our interview team) were engaged on our feet, in dance and celebrative gesture, and singing the modern hymns prescribed in the convocation bulletin. On this day, more than 1,000 faculty, staff, and students were involved in this very moving ceremony held in the contemporary Center for Faith and Life. The service lasted about one and one-half hours, and, at the conclusion the organist—seated at the 53-rank, 42-stop, 3-manual, tracker action pipe organ—exploded in full volume with Widor's *Toccata in F Major*, from the Fifth Organ Symphony.

In summary, at this special occasion the majority of the population of the school was present. The performance was led by the voices and dancing of the students. The service had an ecumenical theme. The several choirs, the music, the awesome sounds of the organ, and the celebration of the day made it ever so clear to us, as observers, that this was a Christian campus, that spirituality was not only an important focus but a primary one, and that the students and the faculty were commonly participants in such events.

The Academic Program

Luther College grants the bachelor of arts degree and offers majors in a number of arts and sciences areas with professional emphases in business, nursing, and education, and preprofessional preparation in dentistry, engineering, law, medicine, theology, and several other fields. Luther operates on a 4–1–4 academic calendar with a three-week January term in the middle of two four-month-long semester sessions. Each Luther graduate is required to complete a total of 128 semester hours of credit with a C average or better, with at least seventy-six of these hours completed outside the major discipline. As noted earlier, students accrue twelve hours in Paideia I and II, additional hours in the distribution requirements of the social sciences, natural sciences, and the humanities. Additionally, each senior must write a research paper in his or her major.

With regard to Paideia, the first part of this program is viewed as a prologue to the total educational experience of the Luther College student, providing a foundation for a liberal arts education and for continuous learning. Paideia I is designed to enhance students' ability to read and write and to think clearly, to give students experiences in research methods and use of the library, and to provide them with the ability to better understand their own identities and those of other cultures. Thus, Paideia I looks at Western civilization, African and Asian cultures, and the Western and non-Western influences on the American experience.

After completing Paideia I in the freshmen year, students are required to enroll in Paideia II, where they critically examine prevailing and historical value systems, reflecting particularly on their own values; acquire skills in making informed ethical decisions; gain awareness of the tradition of Christianity; and further extend their reading and communication skills begun in Paideia I. Several students recalled Paideia in terms of a "shared ordeal," as one student recalled:

> I liked it because it's the one thing that all the graduates of Luther have in common. We can all refer to that. I mean, in some ways we joke about it. Yet, people continually refer to it in chapel and in classes—everywhere. It does unify the college in a way. Everybody complained about it at some time. . . . It was tough. It really was.

Repeatedly, the students viewed their progress in Paideia with a sense of pride and a sense of it having organized them for their academic life.

In addition to Paideia, the senior research paper is frequently mentioned by students. Each senior is required to write a paper in his or her major "to give each student an opportunity to participate in independent study, to read relevant literature in the major, and to develop the methods of research appropriate to the discipline." Normally, this paper is completed during the first semester of the senior year. We elaborate later about the kinds of topics education majors pursued in the senior paper, but we wish to underscore here that the senior paper is an important event in the life of the Luther College graduate and is another shared ordeal. As one student observed: "There are two things we *all* have in common at Luther. One is Paideia, which helps us in our writing skills and the other is doing the paper. . . . I wish I had a year to do it."

In summary, the Luther College liberal arts experience is characterized by a distribution of twenty-four hours across the fine arts, the foreign languages, the natural sciences, and the social sciences; three courses in religion and/or philosophy; two courses in physical education; at least thirty hours in the major; and, in many instances, a designated minor field. The January semester offers opportunities for a change of pace in the academic year and a wide range of offerings, including experimental courses and, in the case of education majors, off-campus experiences in the local schools. Fitted into these alternatives, as well, is scheduling that accommodates the kinds of cultural exchange programs and study abroad reported earlier.

With regard to the elementary education program within the academic program of liberal studies at Luther College, one pervasive debate seems to characterize both the tension and the power of the relationship between the arts and sciences and a professional department such as education. This argument is embedded in a general notion of liberal education. Perhaps an entry point to this dialogue is to suggest that the nature of the liberal arts is always a debate among faculty members in any arts and sciences college such as Luther. As Ed Epperly notes,

> We're not sure that we, meaning the faculty, are in agreement on what liberal arts means, anyway. That's a question under periodic review in a place like Luther. We talk about it all the time. What constitutes a liberal arts education? How does a professional program fit into liberal arts? It is just a continuous conversation no matter what day it is. If you have nothing else to say, you can always ask, How goes the liberal arts? and away it goes!

So the notion of a liberally educated student and the appropriate supporting experience is as apparent in the dialogue of Luther College today as it might have been more than 100 years ago at its founding. And as with most liberal arts colleges, the debate over which disciplines and majors may or may not be as important or germane to the liberal education as might others is still contested. Epperly referred to this as a pecking order:

> There is a pecking order in an institution like this. Well, maybe I should say there are multiple pecking orders. For example, the scientists and the physicists tend to look down their noses at the biologists and that kind of thing. And the sciences in general tend to look askance at the humanities—that's too soft for their tastes. The humanities, particularly English, tend to look down their noses at everybody because. . . .

And his voice trailed off. He picked up the dilemma in this way:

> There is some tendency to look askance at professional areas. . . . There aren't very many in a college like Luther. . . . You've got nursing, education, and social work. . . . That's about it. So there is some tendency to look at those people as being somehow different than the rest of the campus. It's not bad in the sense that you're a member of the governance of the college and you're involved in that. But there is still a little bit of that second-class citizenship role.

The tension and embedded nature of the elementary program within the liberal arts program is underscored by Judith Smith,* a former education professor and now a development officer at the college:

> We're a professional training program in the middle of a liberal arts ocean and we have to fight to keep our heads above the water. And in some respects that's a philosophical problem. To me, education, and a major in education, is one of the most liberalizing things there is, because I look at our majors and the range of the courses . . . and they dip their oars in more different kinds of water than any other majors on this campus do. Yet, we fight faculty who believe that we can cope with the problems of a teacher out there and the lack of excellence by cutting education courses to the bare minimum and exposing them to more history and more art and more religion. . . . I guess the best I can tell you is that it is a long, slow process, and I don't think in some respects we've done a good enough job of demanding the dialogue that it would take to hammer that one out.

While the relationship of the liberal arts to professional schools remains somewhat of an issue in a college like Luther, certainly the students seem to acknowledge the importance of a liberal education. As one student remarked:

> Luther is a place to learn how to learn. Because that's basically what we've been here for, is that we can, the rest of our lives, go and find something and want to learn about something. We know how to learn and not get overwhelmed and think, 'Oh, I can never do this.' You learn how to learn. And we get all these bits and pieces thrown at us, and we decide we're interested in developing ourselves,

*Judith Smith's name at the time of this printing had been changed to Judith Smith Nye.

we can do that. . . . So I feel confident that I do have a well-rounded and strong education, and mostly I feel confident in myself and that's certainly a reflection of the college.

Dean Kraabel noted there is this tension students have to

explore the liberal arts broadly and that's one pole, and the other pole is the vocation. . . . So the kind of tension I'm talking about, the polarity between the liberal arts and the professions is a constant pressure . . . the need to prepare the students with a vocation and at the same time have a college faculty strongly in favor of the intellectual development of the student.

The embedded nature of the elementary education program within the context of a liberal arts institution has obvious benefits as well. As Ed Epperly observed, "The department has not, in my judgment, done anything that is particularly unique in teacher education, but I think we have fit in very closely within the overall campus structure. One of the real strengths of a place like this is that there isn't the division between the arts and sciences that perhaps you find in a larger institution." The benefits of this embeddedness include the kind of course assistance that can be gained from the arts and sciences faculty, with a prime example being the department's work with faculty in philosophy and history in the development of appropriate foundations courses for the education major. He acknowledges that the downside of this integration is that sometimes the department has to fight for hours and has to "work the professional education program in around the liberal arts program."

Students also expressed concern about fitting in enough education courses within all the other requirements at the college. "I think one problem I'm fighting here is that because it is a liberal arts college, I have to take all these other classes. I can't take the classes, like the methods classes, when I want to. There are so many other requirements, you can't take these other courses. There really isn't time." Thus, the proper balance of courses remains both a philosophical issue and a practical concern as well. We turn now to a closer look at the Luther College elementary education program.

THE ELEMENTARY EDUCATION PROGRAM

Matriculation

The education program at Luther College is accredited by the National Council for Accreditation of Teacher Education (NCATE) and approved by the Iowa Board of Public Instruction. The education program includes both a secondary major and an elementary education major. The curriculum for the elementary education major (thirty-six to forty semester hours) includes an initial laboratory experience in the schools, typically taken during the January term, typically in a student's sophomore year, and is subsequently sequenced to include courses in educational psychology; instructional strategies; human relations; elementary curriculum including courses in art, music, physical education, reading, and children's literature; courses on exceptional children; a full semester of student teaching; and finally an elementary education major's selection of an area of concentration. This area of concentration can be fulfilled across a range of program emphases ranging from black studies and foreign language; to economics, accounting, or management; to the humanities, including English, history, philosophy, psychology, political science, sociology or anthropology. Each of these concentrations encompasses twenty to twenty-four semester hours.

It is possible, as well, for an elementary education major to obtain an "endorsement" for teaching in nursery school, day-care, or other prekindergarten programs with the completion of an additional nineteen hours of coursework. Another endorsement which elementary majors seek is the "mental disabilities endorsement," wherein a Luther graduate will be qualified to teach children with significant deficits in adaptive behavior and/or subaverage intellectual functions. Consequently, there is a selection of courses to support this endorsement totalling, again, approximately twenty hours.

We look specifically at the composition of the elementary education program as well as the perception of students and faculty engaged in this program. But, given the liberal arts orientation of the college, we examine first the distribution requirements proposed for most elementary education majors. The general education component for elementary education majors, of course, includes the Paideia experience taken in the freshman year and during any semester subsequent to Paideia I. Elementary education students also enroll in two hours of physical education and eight hours of religion and philosophy. As well, students select twenty-four hours of credit from within four categories of the fine arts (four hours), foreign language and/or culture (four hours), the natural sciences (eight hours), and the social sciences (eight hours). Students are advised to select an American history course; an anthropology course; and a specific set of English, speech, and theater courses to support preparation for teaching.

A number of matriculation patterns are found for elementary education majors at Luther College, and graduating within the normal four-year span, while possible, is not always easy. This four-year pattern is facilitated if a student interested in elementary education selects carefully during the sophomore year by enrolling in one of the prerequisites to the elementary program (an introduction to psychology, including social processes, personality, emotional disorders, development, thinking, testing, learning, motivation, perception, psychobiology, and animal behavior) and the enrollment of students in the initial early field exploratory course, Education 20 (ED 20).

According to one student, ED 20 is "just to get an idea of what the classroom is like. We observe and do a little bit of teaching, so then we have a better understanding of what we study in ED 30, when we take that." Perhaps the student's perception of ED 20 is a bit understated, because it is supported by a twenty-page clinical workbook wherein a number of specific instruments are presented to students to use in specific field observations in their field settings. ED 20 has undergone considerable revision in the last several semesters. Florence Lapin and another part-time faculty member, Martha Van Norman, especially have sharpened the focus of this course. Ed Epperly gives us a bit of a history of this initial exploratory experience which every student, both elementary and secondary takes:

> We've changed this completely. The course used to be such that the students were put out and it was a sink or swim situation, depending with whom they were placed. Some teachers gave them a lot of real experience, and they came back either convinced that they didn't want to teach or very enthused about it. Others just tended to stick them in the back of the room and wanted them to stay out of the way. Now we have instituted a much more elaborate observation program.

A review of the course workbook supports Epperly's observations. A range of variables reported in research studies as associated with teaching effectiveness in different contexts are introduced to the student. Then, observation schedules are provided such that students may make specific comment with regard to observations of instructional procedures, direct/active teaching 'guided/ independent practice', instructional strategies (such as transitions), and classroom management (with-it-ness and overlapping, smoothness and momentum, expectations and praise, teacher enthusiasm). The use of narratives as well as observation schedules for gaining perspective on these instructional skills are provided. Student observers are also given specific suggestions regarding how they might best serve in a teacher aide capacity. This experience is typically taken during the January interim session.

If students are moving through the curriculum on an ideal time schedule, they would enroll next in either or both Education 30 (ED 30), "Instructional Strategies," and Education 40 (ED 40), "Introduction to the Exceptional Child." When asked about ED 30, students described the course as "how to run a classroom. The title of it is Teaching Strategies. Today we're talking about classroom management, and it's a good class because she [the instructor] uses a lot of examples from her teaching experience and also lets us tell about our school experiences and the things that we've observed in ED 20." The current instructor for the course, Gayle Liermann,* provides this general description:

> This is somewhat a shotgun approach. I feel I could teach an entire course on almost every aspect of this course. I start out with an historical perspective of education in America, then we talk about learning theories and eventually we get

*Gayle Liermann's name at the time of this printing had been changed to Gayle Luck.

specific in writing objectives, . . . planning. . . . We also review teacher effectiveness research. I provide an overview of some testing and evaluation procedures. We discuss learning centers. Eventually the students have to write a unit
for me, . . . and they move through the various stages as I teach the course. . . . I
try to integrate the writing of the unit into what we're doing, so if they stay with
it, by the time the unit is due, all the components are covered in the course.

This is obviously an omnibus introduction to teaching. As resources, Liermann uses Cooper's second edition of *"Classroom Teaching Skills: A Handbook"* and reserved readings to cover topics described in her report of the
class. This is the primary course wherein students learn to write and present a
unit.

Other courses in the elementary sequence that students take during their
sophomore and junior years include Education 50 (ED 50), "Educational
Psychology: Childhood and Adolescence," wherein students are exposed to
knowledge on human growth and development from infancy through adolescence, and on learning theory and application. Other courses that students
might select during this time include methods courses such as music, physical
education, art, and the teaching of reading and children's literature.

Students are also advised to select during their junior and senior January
terms one of two required courses focusing on human relations: Education 75
(ED 75), "Human Relations in Teaching," which builds to a series of corequi-
sites, including Education 62 (ED 62), "Teaching Reading in Elementary
School"; Education 66, (ED 66), "Elementary Curriculum I"; and Education
68 (ED 68), "Elementary Curriculum II." In this combination of courses referred to by students and faculty alike as the junior *block*, one of the faculty
members, Nanette Eklund, provides a broad fields approach to instruction
through an examination of current practices in teaching mathematics and science, and language arts and social studies in the elementary school, including
laboratory experiences. Judith Smith summarized the program design as
follows:

> It's designed not to have a lot of unnecessary repetition; and yet, there is enough
> opportunity, if you don't get something the first time through, there's enough
> spiraling in the curriculum to go back and pick something up. Lesson planning is
> a classic example. 'Strategies' teaches lesson planning. When Nan starts 'Curric-
> ulum I,' they submit a set of lesson plans. If they're okay, they don't have to do
> any more. If they're not, she reteaches and goes on.

The program is geared to the following general objectives, as articulated
in one of Luther's several accreditation/program approval documents:

- to become academically competent to teach in his or her respective
  field;
- to become a mature, balanced, and socially poised individual;

- to become acquainted with principals and techniques of effective teaching/learning procedures;
- to develop an understanding of the growth and behavior of children and youths;
- to develop insight into the function of the school, the community, and our democratic society;
- to gain an understanding of the social responsibilities of the teaching profession;
- to understand the importance of cooperation between the school, home, church, and the community;
- to develop a professional attitude toward work, pupils, and coworkers;
- to acquire enthusiasm and motivation for service and professional growth;
- to develop a philosophy of education; and,
- to embrace the profession of teaching as a Christian calling.

We asked Professor Epperly to give us an overview of his perceptions of the elementary education program:

> Again, one of the real strengths of a place like this is that there isn't the division between the arts and sciences that perhaps you find in a larger institution. . . . We have to work the professional education in around that. . . . Also, the elementary students have an elementary education major that's a relatively full major. . . . We emphasize the personal closeness of this institution and the ability to have access to the teachers, the fact that the students are working with senior professors, not with graduate students. . . . We emphasize the program as field-centered; in fact, students are put out into the schools at the very beginning of the program. They also go out in the schools in connection with nearly every course in education at least sometime during the course. . . . We try to tell them that if they come here, they'll probably get a job (if they avoid social studies and physical education). . . . Again, we use the quality of the student body as a drawing card. . . . We have some marvelous education majors, bright kids, as good as any student on campus.

This general overview of the elementary education program led us to seek greater specificity with regard to a number of factors attributed to the conduct of the Luther College elementary education program, including a possible dominant conception of teaching inherent therein, the nature of early and continuous field experience, the character of the junior block, and the sense of excellence and pride expressed by the student body and the faculty with regard to the quality of the program.

Conception of Teaching

Any conception of teaching is largely fostered by the individuals who work in the elementary education program. Nine faculty members teach the education

courses at Luther College. Two additional faculty members have had considerable influence on the program over time and been selected for service in the
central administration of the campus; Roger Anderson, who chaired the
education department for twenty years, and Judith Smith, a professor in
Reading, Early Childhood and Human Relations, who is credited as one of the
architects of the current elementary education program. Anderson now serves
as registrar for the college and Smith as development officer. Both receive
accolades for their contributions by their faculty colleagues in the department
and by other university representatives as well. Clearly they have, over time,
made major contributions to the elementary program even though they are no
longer actively involved in the program. Major responsibilities on the current
faculty are assumed by Ed Epperly and Nanette Eklund. Epperly serves as
chairman of the Department and Eklund, as noted earlier, is primarily responsible for the junior block and the placement and supervision of elementary
student teachers. A third active and tenured faculty member in the education
department is Dennis Darling, a professor in music education whose emphasis
is largely in guiding the secondary majors in music, in overseeing music
methods for elementary teachers, and in his very active role in music performances on campus. These three faculty members, in addition to Anderson and
Smith, constitute the five tenured faculty in the education department.

Recently, three faculty members have been added to the department on
term positions: Gayle Liermann, Florence Lapin, and Shirley Steffens. Liermann teaches "Strategies" and children's literature. Lapin's primary responsibility has been to develop a more innovative approach to ED 20, as mentioned, as well as instruction in human relations. Steffens's responsibility is in
special education and education for the gifted. As noted, the program is also
supported by several part-time faculty members. As we talk about conceptions of teaching, we rely most heavily on the perceptions of those actively involved in the current elementary program, although, clearly, Anderson and
Smith have left their mark on the program as well.

These faculty members support the total enrollment of education students
in the program across the sophomore, junior, and senior years or approximately 250 students. Typically, fifty to sixty of these are elementary majors.
The fact that these faculty members teach the classes and supervise the
students in field experiences suggests a very close working relationship, and
the low student/faculty teacher ratio facilitates this.

A prevalent conception of teaching remains the well-educated person, a
powerful vestige of the program designed by Anderson and Smith. Anderson
observes:

> Judy and I, working together designed most of the program. . . . We wanted to do
> the best possible job to prepare the best teachers possible for schools, primarily
> for the Midwest, and we tried to look carefully at how to do this. We like to think
> of ourselves as being very innovative. We were probably the first college to have
> a required extensive prestudent teaching clinical experience. . . . About that same

time, we also started a new venture called LUPACS [Luther College Learning Packets]. Weber State, of course, was one of the leaders in this regard, and we weren't too far behind. . . . I look upon myself as a loyal teacher educator, but I never lost my own vision of the role of the liberal arts in this process. . . . I think as much as anything else a perception on the part of the faculty of this institution is that those of us who were in teacher education were really in liberal arts. We did everything we could to make students academically responsible.

A balance to Anderson's vision of the education program as embedded in the arts and sciences plays itself out in the perceptions of Dr. Smith about the nature of the education program and the process of becoming a teacher at Luther College. Through a series of observations, Smith builds a notion of quality control about why it is people chose to become teachers and what it takes to be a good teacher:

One of the things that strikes me about the program at Luther is its attempt to maintain strict quality control. Because we have such early involvement in the program, students start as freshmen or sophomores with this January term in the school. It is an 8-to-5, five-days-a-week routine. It's quite possible to love children at 9:00 in the morning and by 3:30 you can hardly stand the sight of them.

. . . And so that January term affords us the luxury of seeing someone five consecutive days. . . . You can interview prospective students, . . . and my first question to them is, "Why do you want to teach?" If they respond "I just love children," that isn't going to cut it. There are many ways to love them, many ways to serve them, other than being in the classroom. And so one of the things I think is important is that you get them out early enough to find out whether teaching is what they thought it would be. If it isn't, they have a chance to pick up another major. When Luther costs $9,000 a year and students' first year out they're probably going to make $12,500—we've got to be sure it's the right investment. . . . Many a student has come back to us after ED 20 and said, 'I like 'em but I don't like 'em that much!'. . . . Because our practicum experiences are continuous and they're early in the year, they are going to see how a class begins. They are going to be exposed to the reality of the classroom.

Smith weaves a relationship between the experiential base of the curriculum and the knowledge base, tempered by experiences that help students see that teaching is a difficult endeavor, one which requires both knowledge and the *application* of knowledge. She continues:

My philosophy is going to come right out. . . . I operate under the assumption, and have for a long time, that access to knowledge is one matter and interactive behaviors in the classroom is quite another. The strongest teachers I know, know what teaching behaviors are needed and how to increase their percentages when they work with students and can find the content when they need it. . . . I've taught with many teachers who were inordinately bright but simply didn't know how to package information to children. . . . Basically what you do in a class-room is market information. To the extent that you know the strategies that enable you to market the knowledge to the student, there's going to be some learning. But never, ever be fooled. If you don't run the ship there isn't going to be some learning taking place. You have to be really in charge in the classroom. I do not negotiate my curriculum with the children. I did not negotiate it with college students. I know what it takes to teach a child to read and that's what I'm going to teach when it comes to my standing in front of a classroom. So I'm a strong advocate of methodology and I really believe that if we teach how to access knowledge—if these classes are doing what they're supposed to—they'll know how to *find out* what they don't know.

We see between Anderson and Smith an integration of the knowledge base presented in an arts and sciences curriculum and in the academic disci-plines and an experiential and pedagogical orientation presented in the educa-tion program. Certainly this balance is reflected in Ed Epperly's conception of teaching as well:

We're in a reorganization phase, trying to put more emphasis on methods than we've been able to give in the past. . . . One of the ideas is to try to build some kind of linkage with current research knowledge, in a sense to bring our own faculty up to speed in terms of research literature and current practice. Then we'll try to integrate that into our courses. . . . We're going to try to get them to focus more on what the teacher is doing and what exactly goes on in the instructional process. . . . I'd like to have a methods component that would be . . . research-oriented. A body of research exists on how learning takes place and instruction is organized that is large enough to justify teaching it.

Flo Lapin, responsible for instruction in the entry experience for elemen-tary majors, ED 20, elaborates on this research perspective:

I'm tremendously excited about restructuring the first beginning practicum. We're trying to present a series of instruments outlining instructional procedures and management procedures that have a research base and that are related to good, effective teaching. And this is, of course, the first time that we've done this here. . . . There is a research base that we can bring to the students and tell them what will make them better teachers.

Liermann acknowledges a number of other skills necessary for effective teaching, including communication skills and human relations skills, and she observes, "I begin by asking them what they think an effective teacher is . . . [and] I move from there into what research says about teaching." This com-ment caused us to ask again about the basic elements of effective teaching. Liermann responded:

Knowledge of subject matter, clarity of presentation, organization, being able to identify students who are having difficulties or not getting it . . . modelling, attending to individual differences. We talk about individualized instruction and what that means. . . . I think you have to know kids and know about kids and you'll learn more when you get into the classroom. You have to be willing to be flexible. You have to tolerate a lot of interruptions in the classroom. You have to be willing to work hard. And you have to know how to communicate with people. You have to really understand how children learn and that not all children learn easily.

Still, Liermann distances herself somewhat from research on teaching, as do Eklund and others when they talk about a conception of teaching. She observes that her instructional style does not

bombard undergraduates with research, because it doesn't mean anything to them. The research is important but it doesn't impact them directly because they've never been in the classroom and they don't always understand it. . . . I give them what research shows but not the research. . . . But sometimes questions they raise haven't been measured in research, so it might be a personal issue or experience that I use.

Liermann observes:

A relationship exists between teaching and the way we were taught. I want them to remember what it felt like and what their experiences as children were. The students need to see if they can fit that in with what we're talking about in class and to examine what some options are to this. One person mentions options that others hadn't experienced. I see real value in finding out from your peers what those options would be rather than just the teacher sharing these.

From these comments and from classroom observations, we saw a blend of the utilization of the knowledge base on effective teaching that focused largely on skill orientation to a combination and interweaving of the personal experiences of the various professors.

Both Eklund and Liermann do assign research reviews for their students, and they set aside periods of class where students can come in and talk about the articles they have read. As one student observed, "each professor definitely has his or her own idea about teaching and you get a combination of views." We asked this student how he felt his teacher learned about teaching. He observed, "partly from having taught in schools . . . and partly from watching her child develop. She kept track of all his art work from the very beginning, and she has ideas about that." Of another experienced professor, a student observes, "she has a lot of fresh examples, which is wonderful. And we also read journals, make presentations, and summarize articles, and we look into journal articles to find what research has been going on." Students and faculty alike appear to weave a conception of teaching that is skill-oriented largely focused on classroom management and instructional strategies, knowledge of subjects, and personal attributes of caring and hard work.

Perhaps Dennis Darling's conception of teaching summarizes as well the pervasive notion of providing conditions for wanting to learn and students being able to explore. As we were strolling across campus to observe his music education methods course, with lovely Carillon bells in the background, Darling remarked:

> I was just reading Thomas Aquinas last night where he writes that the most one man can do for another is to lift the window shades of the mind so that the light can shine in. You can't make the others see the light. You cannot fill another's mind with knowledge and facts and have it be really meaningful, you can only provide the opportunities for that individual to see for himself. . . . The teacher must be a mentor, a guide, but he also has to be a role model.

An Emphasis on Experience

The early and sequential nature of the field experience in Luther's program is supported by cooperating teachers. One cooperating teacher observed that she had had students from the Luther College program who were engaged at all levels of field experience:

> This year I've had an experience at each of the levels. One of the things that I really like is that the students are involved from the time that they declare their major. . . . These students start from the time they're sophomores and each year they have a different kind of experience. They start from the observation level and then we just had students from the junior block and then they do some teaching and then they go to small groups and entire classes. So, by the time they do their student teaching they've had experience and they're not quite so inexperienced. And they're more willing to get involved quickly. . . . They are screened, too. Also, the education department evaluates them from the time they declare their major, and periodically they are told how they are doing.

Another teacher commented on the practical experience that students receive at Luther College:

> The faculty make an effort to ensure that students have a wide variety of experiences in their sophomore and junior years and then, when they do their student teaching, they try to incorporate these. And so, they have a fairly good idea of which grade they're most comfortable in. . . .

The cooperating teachers we visited with who assist in the Luther College program underscored the importance of their role. These cooperating teachers reported that courses in supervision are periodically provided for them, that they are consulted about the progress of the students, and that their observations and evaluations are valued. They recite early and continuous contact with students and they note that students are sent to make "courtesy calls" with their selected cooperating teacher before the student teaching experience occurs.

One faculty member observed, "we know the teachers and we do try to match them with our student teachers." This is particularly important as another faculty member stressed:

> The critical person is the classroom teacher because I think they're going to be a role model for the students [recall Dennis Darling's summary comments on teaching]. They're not going to model me even if I'm there every week, and it's not that I don't feel responsible for them, but I think the placement is crucial.

A cooperating teacher confirms this placement procedure as follows,

> I've already met the girl I'm going to have next fall [this being May]. We have information on the students, and usually they stop by at the end of the school year. We make arrangements and they try to be there before school starts so that they can see how you set up and get ready . . . so they don't walk in cold.

These teachers also reinforced for us that students in the junior block were able to experience multiple placements and be more selective about their desired placement for student teaching.

Apparently, relationships between the college and the participating schools are generally good and teachers are an integral part of the elementary program through field experiences. The selection of and communication with cooperating teachers is of primary importance to the faculty in this field-oriented program and, finally, the faculty themselves are involved in the supervision process as well.

Students predictably value the nature of these field experiences as well. One student spoke to the value of "the early exposure we get because we can start in our sophomore year already going out and observing. Also, from there on, once you're in the program, you get experience observing in the schools and helping out." Another student observed, "I went into the schools in January of my freshman year and decided on education. So I think that's one good thing about the education program here. . . . We've been in the schools every year since. Different school systems—I've been in five different school systems since I've been here." Another student opined: "the most significant thing for me is the fact that I've been able to do my student teaching in three different areas. They do kindergarten, fourth grade—actually four if you want to count high school and junior high separately. So I feel that I got a very broad experience and that's great." This blend of field experiences and the academic or didactic experiences of the education students come together as one student reflected on what it meant to be an effective teacher:

Teaching is so much an individual type thing that I don't think we could learn just one way of doing it. We learned a lot of different methods in junior block. We were exposed to a lot of different ways of doing things. We were taught different approaches, different types of resources that we could use . . . that we would draw upon in our student teaching, but then, as we had more experience in classrooms, we started to find our own style of teaching. I don't think that's something we could know. . . . When I first came here, I wanted to teach because I liked children; they are so cute and things like that, you know. After a few of my education classes, I decided that it was a good reason, but it's not good enough. . . . I've seen a more intellectual side of teaching now.

Another student observed: "I think that we get into different approaches and theories and methods of teaching. And then we take those and pick and choose and apply them in our own way according to our personality and what works for us."

The students also reiterated the hands-on, activity-oriented focus on becoming a teacher. One student stated, "one thing that is carried throughout when I'm in the schools is I always think about the 'hands-on' nature of the experience . . . activity-centered things . . . active learning . . . discovery . . . creativity." A hands-on, active-involvement approach characterizes much of the pedagogy apparent in the Luther College elementary education program. As students talked about the nature of the course experience and the field experience they observed a camaraderie develops among them. Students and faculty alike regularly refer to the junior block as a milestone experience, and this experience warrants further description.

The Junior Block

Ed Epperly described the junior block: "All the students, in the spring of their junior year, take children's literature, a reading course, and two elementary curriculum courses. They take that as an interrelated unit of work and it amounts to eleven hours. Then, they all student teach in the fall." By Nan Eklund's own account:

I teach Curriculum I and Curriculum II—everything from soup to nuts with the exception of reading and children's literature. This approach has its good points. It's difficult to keep up . . . the math and science, social studies, the writing. . . . I'm doing it all. But I believe it when I say to these elementary teachers you go out and you teach everything. You're not going to be a spelling specialist. We look at the role quite realistically.

Judith Smith initiated the idea for the junior block. Of this shared ordeal for students she said:

When I came here we had the January term and, of course, student teaching. The junior block was designed to fill the gap between them. I saw the students becoming kind of depressed because it was a long time between that January term and student teaching. And they kept getting all these theories thrown at them and had nothing to attach them to. At the time, I was director of the program and we instituted the junior block, . . . which to me has made quite a significant difference in our ability to see where the fine tuning needs to occur to teach effectively. Also, this is an opportunity for the students to attach that theory to a specific group of children they are working with. . . . Before the junior block, they really didn't know enough to know what they didn't know. When they would come back after junior block, they would say, 'You know, I saw this kid and whenever it was time to read, he would do this and this and this. Why would he do that?' Now the level of questioning from students has changed drastically and I think that the junior block really helps them relate the theories to practice. You can only take a certain amount of content before you have to then find something to hook it to. So now there's a better continuity to our sequence of practicums. And we hope that the cooperating teacher's evaluation becomes more discriminating each time.

Eklund, the primary instructor for the block, elaborated:

I like our junior block very much. We take the entire morning. I don't want it broken up. They're in education classes all morning long and then we send them out into the schools for two weeks and it's just before their student teaching. They are committed . . . they are interested . . . they are doing great, . . . and I think by having them together supporting one another . . . they develop a real sense of community. I do a lot of group work in building the group to start out with because I see that as good teaching.

Obviously, the students do, too, as they talked often and with considerable animation about the junior block.

One student observed of the program in general and of the junior block specifically, "I always thought the program was very demanding, especially the junior block. That's the spring semester of our junior year where we get all of our curriculum classes and that, I thought, was very demanding work and sometimes it made you think, . . . 'Am I really going to make it'?" Other students observed that the junior block "jelled us together." And another student added, "it was very supportive." And finally there was this student's assessment, "I think the one thing that you have here is a certain camaraderie between the education majors. And I really enjoyed seeing everybody grow. That block was as much a learning experience as anything I experienced." From these reflections about the junior block and from the students' sense of shared ordeal, we probed further into the program in terms of rigor or academic challenge.

Academic Challenge

We begin this section with some questions posed of students at a very basic level to ascertain their concept of rigor or academic challenge. We asked if they thought the education department's program was easy. Typical responses were as follows:

> No I don't. . . . It really demands a lot. . . . It's really challenging and . . . it's a different kind of challenge. . . . I did think it was going to be easier when I changed from history to education. I thought it was going to be an easier way originally. But I don't feel that way anymore. Because I understand education better now and what it all encompasses, and I can't say that it's easy at all. I think it's equivalent of being a parent but for many children, and if you think being a parent is easy. . . . I don't think it's going to be easy.

In attempting to sort out differences between elementary and secondary education, one student observed:

> From what I can tell, I've got friends in both secondary and elementary that are majors, the elementary ed majors feel that it is as hard as anything else considering the number of classes and the amount of work that they put into it. They feel they're putting more work into their classes, like their junior block year, . . . and I definitely have to agree.

Another student concurred with some passion:

> Right! As far as the degree of difficulty, I would say I always hear that you go into education because you can't make it anywhere else. I've heard that comment before, and I get very angry. I majored in business, and I had fairly good grades. Toward the end I didn't study much but I would say I study as much, if not more in my education classes than in business.

Typically, these students, as Roger Anderson observes, want to do very well: " . . . quality people have selected themselves into the program and they are interested in what they're doing. . . . They take their education seriously. Teacher education candidates typically have been higher [GPAs] than the average for the college. So we start from a higher base."

Students not only appear willing to work, but they know how to study, as Professor Eklund has observed over time:

> I can send them to the library to do research, put things together, come back, and present it, and they do a good job. I don't have to lead them over there and show them where the journals are. They know how to use the research library. That, to me, is the very good background that they get from going through Paideia. . . .

Students also portrayed the content of their education courses as substantive. One student recalled, "You really have to concentrate on what you're reading because they use a lot of complex terms. It isn't something like, 'Oh, I understand that.' You have to sit down and go over it." Another student spoke to the integrative nature of the elementary education program:

> I value having a liberal arts background because I have seen more clearly how everything integrates with everything else . . . how math can be related to social studies and to music and art, and it just comes alive here because you're doing that all the time. You're always taking subjects that interact with each other. Because your professors spend a lot of time trying to refer to other areas and things like that. I just think that's really valuable to see that integration so clearly. . . . That didn't come together for me until I got here.

The undergraduate experience at Luther College culminates in a final project, the senior research paper, which is required for every student regardless of major. This requirement gives each student an opportunity to participate in sustained independent study, to read relevant literature in the major, and to begin to develop methods of research appropriate to different disciplines. Normally, this paper is completed during the first semester of the senior year, although students register for this course during the semester in which they intend to complete the requirement. Graduation without successful completion of the senior paper is impossible.

The students talked about the senior paper as a culminating experience, and they expressed both pride and relief with comments such as, "I very much enjoyed mine," and "I thought it was a lot of work." When asked to describe these papers, one student indicated, "I did mine on transitional stress in the middle school and what the stress factors were for students. My final chapter was on things that could be implemented in upper elementary classrooms to help alleviate some of this stress."

When asked the length of these papers, one student noted, "Mine was about five chapters." "But we are prepared," as another student volunteered, "We do write a lot of papers. I know just the first year here alone, I wrote between ten and twenty papers." Another student compared Paideia and the senior year, "There are two things we all have in common at Luther, one is Paideia, which helps us in our writing skills, and the other is writing this paper." Another student shared with us that her topic was on right- and left-brain learning and its implications for teaching. This student spoke to the importance of the senior paper, "I think there is so much to get into in our education courses that there isn't room to have this kind of indepth analysis. There is no time."

Consequently, the students view the senior paper as an understandable major hurdle, but also as an opportunity to integrate knowledge, an opportunity to explore intensively a subject, and an opportunity to exhibit the intellectual skills they have honed at Luther College. Other topics of senior papers included "Foreign Language in the Elementary School: Is it Necessary?" and "Utilizing the Language Experience Approach to Teaching Reading in the Elementary Grades," and were thirty to fifty pages in length. The format of the paper is prescribed as well as the nature of bibliographic support. Certainly, as outside observers, we could see the execution of the senior research paper for education majors as a positive influence of the academic environment in this small liberal arts institution.

Luther College's Impact

Our intention in this previous section has been to explicate the nature of the academic program as pursued by an elementary education major. As such, hopefully we have captured the character of the courses required, the nature of the field experiences, some indication of academic rigor in the program, and at least a feel for the conceptual basis of teaching upon which the program is founded. What we have not shared is a broader perspective on the impact a school such as Luther College has on its future teacher candidates. Combining the perspectives of Ed Epperly and Judith Smith, we come out with a notion of the influence of Luther on the education graduate. Smith was asked what the institution does for the character of the students, looking particularly at the parochial as opposed to the liberalizing influence of an institution like Luther on its students. We spoke to the liberating notion of study earlier; Smith provided a more parochial perspective:

> Parents send their children here because of the inculcation of values they hope they'll come out with and, in many cases, these are ones the parents believe in themselves, whether they went to Luther or not. They see a set of values here that, to them, means something, and they're willing to pay for that. I'm not at all convinced that the teachers that we prepare at Luther College will cut it on 49th and Halstead, down in the meat-packing section of Chicago. You've got to value Luther College and what it represents, . . . which to me is a solid, conservative, liberal arts background.
>
> If you look at the statistics regarding our students, and you probably already have, they're basically good students initially. I mean, it's very hard for me to go into Cedar Rapids and convince an average student that he ought to take a look at Luther. And that's unfair because I think some of those students could be very successful here. But they say, and parents will say, 'Well, I'm sorry my son just isn't a good enough student to cut it at Luther'.

Ed Epperly viewed the impact of Luther as modest in some respects, and he corroborated Smith's view about the initial quality of students.

> I don't think we change them fundamentally. The success we have is primarily related to the quality of students that come here. I believe that if you look at

everything—I'm not demeaning what we're doing—I'm not suggesting that we don't have a lot of effects—and maybe the most important thing from a pedagogical standpoint is that they learn technique. I think they learn something about *teaching*, . . . and they're learning more than that. They're knowledgeable, but I don't think we have a great deal of *philosophical* impact on them. And it's partly because they aren't so much different than we are to begin with. We're— everyone's blonde-haired around here—with a few notable exceptions. But they tend to come from Iowa, Minnesota, Wisconsin, Illinois. They tend to be middle- to upper-middle-class. They tend to have those values that are pretty much the faculty's values. And so we reinforce those values. I really think we do. . . . I suppose it's kind of popular to imagine that you'd take this ill-formed clay and shape it into some marvelous product, but I don't think we do that. I don't have that feeling. I think it's more with technique. I read a quotation from a football coach several years ago. They were talking to him about building character, and he said, 'All I can do is teach them to play football'. And that impressed me in a way because I got so sick and tired of the coaches glorifying what they were doing with that elaborate, character-building rhetoric. And I don't feel that way.

Leadership for teacher education for the immediate future is in the hands of this modest chairman of the Department of Education, Ed Epperly. We conclude our portrayal of the elementary program at Luther College with a brief description of this education professor in a liberal arts setting—his philosophy about education and schooling, and his hopes for the future of education at Luther College.

FUTURE DIRECTIONS FOR ELEMENTARY EDUCATION AT LUTHER COLLEGE

Edgar Epperly

Epperly was brought to Luther College in 1969 by Roger Anderson, as were Judith Smith, Nan Eklund, and Dennis Darling. Originally, Epperly was a high school social studies teacher. He received his master's degree at the University of Northern Iowa, taught seven years in Iowa and then, by his own account, "drifted into counseling, like a lot of other people in secondary education." After three years as a junior high school counselor in Des Moines, he went back to school at George Peabody and earned his doctorate in curriculum and supervision.

"In a place like this," says Ed Epperly, " . . . you don't have a speciality. The closest thing I have to a specialty now is Educational Psychology, because that's what I've taught over the years . . . two sections of Ed Psych each semester." By his own recollection, he has taught general methods, social studies methods, the human relations courses, seminars during student teaching, and "like everyone else, . . . I do better in some things than in others. That's what you sacrifice in a school like this. You don't have a speciality in a field. The things we gain are [that] we have a very close relationship with students. . . . You know, after all, everybody's one-on-one in teacher supervision."

Epperly's priorities for the future include acquiring more awareness among faculty members about the extant "knowledge base" on teaching, achieving more diversified field placements, more faculty exchanges to allow department members to engage actively in elementary and secondary teaching periodically, and consideration of majors in the elementary education program. Our portrayal of Luther's elementary education program carries us to a brief explication of some of these ideas for the future, but not without attention to one of Ed Epperly's interests, which speaks most notably to his ability to hold onto an idea and see it through to its fruition.

As indicated earlier, the Luther faculty are active in many directions. Biologists participate in theater; mathematicians sing the *Messiah*; and, in this instance, an educator is novelist and historical researcher—"it all works a little like a bicycle wheel." Early on in our visit to Luther, in the after-hours of our day-long interviews, we chatted with the faculty about their lives in Decorah, their personal interests, and their avocations. It soon became clear that Ed Epperly has a unique and enduring interest which he has pursued avocationally throughout his adult life.

For more than twenty years, Ed Epperly has been hauntingly pursuing the truth about a tragic event that occurred in Iowa many years ago, now referred to as the Villisca Axe Murder. Epperly refers to this as "Iowa Gothic" when he lists this topic as one available through Luther's Speakers Bureau. As it happens, he became particularly intrigued with this heinous mass murder some years ago and has relentlessly traced court records, legal reports and files, and interviewed hundreds of people in the Iowa area where these murders occurred who might recall any of the details of this terrible event. Epperly is writing a book describing the murders. The faculty know that Epperly is pursuing this interest and, obviously, many people in the Decorah community know it as well, because he lends his time to the Speakers Bureau to share his information about this event. We cite this ongoing effort partly to illustrate how Epperly's own liberal education has allowed him to pursue with sustaining interest a tiny slice of history in the Midwest. The pace may be measured, the exact outcome unclear, but his thirst for understanding is unmistakeable. It is a style not inconsistent with the liberal tradition at Luther and a view of learning and teaching.

Future Directions

Throughout our interviews with Ed Epperly were interwoven in the dialogue a number of ideas he hopes to carry forth with his colleagues in the Department of Education. We asked Epperly from where these emphases were generating: Were they provocations which have grown largely out of his own thinking? In typical modest fashion, he responded:

No, it's really not me. It's coming mostly from these reports that are coming out. Obviously, teacher education is under pressure and is going to change, and I would much prefer to change in advance, rather than be dragged into it. These are things that we need to do. I think we need to have a very solid program. I've been a major part of it, but we have been complacent in a sense that it's going really well and why fix something that's not broken, and so on. But I think in the competitive world we're coming to for liberal arts schools, we need to get people coming here because they believe they can get a better program here than elsewhere.

Consequently, one of the most notable of the proposals Ed Epperly has made is to engage the Luther College faculty with research-oriented institutions to achieve a greater awareness and application of research findings appropriate for teacher education. He has developed the idea of a consortium of liberal arts colleges in eastern Iowa, which he proposes will work in collaboration with the University of Iowa's College of Education to improve teacher preparation both for the consortium institutions and for the University of Iowa.

Epperly has other ideas for the consortium as well. For instance, with the NCATE standards demanding that colleges follow their graduates into the field for program evaluation purposes, the consortium schools could join hands in the follow-up effort, wherein Luther would follow up all graduates who are placed in its adjacent communities including Luther College graduates and those of the other consortium colleges and vice versa. In this and other ways, these institutions could cooperate with each other, build stronger teacher education programs, and, most importantly, attend to emerging knowledge and awareness of the research findings on teaching and schooling which are appropriate for curriculum in teacher education.

Similarly, Epperly was fostering more diversified placements of undergraduate students for student teaching, sending students to other geographical regions within range of the other participating institutions in the Exxon-sponsored collaborative and exploring new faculty exchanges with teachers in the schools:

> I'm flirting with a model—and I don't know if I've got nerve enough to do it—where we would exchange—on a two-week segment, for example—where the teachers would come in and take over some aspects of the methods . . . and certain elements of Ed Psych could also be tailored to their expertise, and so on. And I'd go out occasionally and take their social studies classes. . . . In my mind, it's obvious that if we are training teachers, we ought to be doing *some* teaching on a level that we train teachers for and we ought not be relying on what we experienced years ago. . . .

Therefore, Epperly proposes to develop an exchange model wherein, given his own leadership style, he would be the guinea pig for the effort. "If that's going to happen, I'm going to have to do it first. . . . I'm convinced that if you want people to do things, you've got to be able to do it yourself."

Beyond the Exxon-sponsored collaboration and more diversification of the field experiences and exchange of faculty, he also has ideas for elementary majors:

I would like to see an academic major in the elementary program. . . . We currently have an area of concentration which is a five-course sequence in a particular discipline, whichever one the student chooses. Five courses mean either fifteen or twenty hours depending on whether they are three or four hour courses, so we'd only be talking about adding a two course package to that . . . a twenty-four hour package.

When asked about his rationale for moving to the academic major, Epperly made two observations:

The most important reason, in my judgment, is that to some extent it would act as a screening device. We are currently getting some elementary people who feel they cannot do anything else. . . . The other reason it is important is that it would do a lot for the self-concept of the elementary teacher. A lot of others might feel inferior because they do not have a solid, demonstrated major. . . . Many of them are excellent students and they do well in other courses, but they still have not taken a major that stands out in the minds of the general public as being an academic major, and by doing so they would gain self-confidence.

Ed Epperly is considering numerous and, in some respects, far-reaching proposals with the elementary department. How they might be achieved takes us back to Epperly's administrative style and his ability to convince the faculty of the wisdom inherent in these moves.

I don't have any administrative background in terms of developing colleague relationships in the department. I try to give them a great deal of freedom, *but* with responsibility. I try to parcel out the work fairly and show them the basic outline of what we want to accomplish as a *program*. If you have an idea, bring it to me and if I can possibly approve it, I will. I think people work better when given this approach. At other times, I give them the basic direction and let them do it the best way they can. . . . I could goad them and continue to goad them, but I have to live with them and I can't do it by fighting. If I can't persuade them, then we'll probably continue as is. But, I would rather live with just a *little friction* in the machine than I would the friction of saying this *is* the way it's going to be.

We close this vision of the future with an analogy that Epperly used to describe his view of the ideal context for the future of the Luther College education program. He described the way teacher educators regularly try to

relate to the medical model for the fuller professionalization of teacher education programs. Epperly disagreed with this analogy and countered with
another:

> The analogy that's better for education is the extension service—agricultural
> education. And that's exactly what I'm going to propose to Exxon. In some ways,
> our students are analogous to farmers. We are analogous, at Luther, to the
> agricultural extension agent. We have advanced training in the field. It's broader
> than the individual farmer's. It covers more of the field, but we are not generating
> research. We are not even conversant with the literature in a sense. The special-
> ists in research are at the state college, in this case, and in the case of agriculture
> at Iowa State or Minnesota, and they are full-time specialists in the research area.
> They are current in those fields. They are both generating research and, as impor-
> tantly from our standpoint, they are keeping current with research. What I think
> we need to do is set up a mechanism so that those at that level talk to us at this
> level and on a recurring basis. And then we take that up-to-date knowledge that
> we would get periodically that would be translated into advice to our farmer/
> teachers so to speak, and that's exactly what the extension service does. . . . They
> are able to say—like this hybrid corn thing—if you run a class with this type of
> style, you typically get this type of effect. We don't know yet precisely why that
> occurs, but it does. If you plant these hybrid seeds, you get this kind of plant.
> . . . I think there's a tremendous breakdown now in that what's going on in the
> research institutions. It isn't getting down to the field and it will never get down
> to the field if it is not distilled further than in the literature. The people who are in
> the institutions generating the literature, writing the dissertations, ought to distill
> that knowledge better. . . . They ought to come to me and be able to tell me that
> this is what we know and here are the twenty-five really crucial papers on teacher
> effectiveness that you ought to read to know what's going on. You may not know
> as much as if you are a specialist, but you'll know enough to keep your head
> above water. . . . That was the metaphor that I used in justifying the Exxon grant,
> the argument being that you can't be a practitioner and a researcher at a place like
> this—really in terms of doing an adequate job of both. I was casting around for
> some way to better confront the theory/practice dilemma that we always have.
> And I fixed on the county extension services as a model. . . .

So, we leave Luther College in a period of transition. It has a well-
respected, time-tested, elementary education program. It has both veteran and
new faculty members who are interested in pursuing new ground especially
with respect to the knowledge base for teacher education. Ed Epperly has already cast a broad net in this role as chairman of the department. The goals he
identifies are multifaceted and ones he believes to be appropriate for Luther
College at this time. He has an administrative style conducive to achieving
collegiality and collective effort, to moving at a pace that will bring people
along. And he has tenacity, the kind of tenacity that would trace an event in
history until there is no stone left unturned.

He also has ultimate respect for the liberal arts perspective embedded in

Luther College and an intimate knowledge of Luther's history which grew out of the normal school tradition. Thus, our portrayal of Luther suggests a promising state of change, maintaining that which has been enduring about the personal, intellectual, and spiritual life of the Luther College campus and also regenerative in that Luther is exploring its relationships beyond the Decorah city limits and beyond the capacities of its faculty, to the collaborative relationships it might have with other liberal arts and research institutions. These appear to be promising directions for Luther College and, for that matter, any teacher education program embedded in a small, liberal arts college.

2

Beyond the
Normal School Legacy

BALL STATE UNIVERSITY

Context

We are in the tenth-floor office of Dr. Ted Kowalski, dean of Teachers College of Ball State University. Teachers College is the only high rise on campus, and it is dominant not only for this reason but for its central location as well. This office affords a panoramic view of the campus, which is situated in a residential area approximately one mile northwest of Muncie's business center. The almost 1,000-acre campus reflects a harmony of past and present in its architecture. Tudor Gothic is the prevailing architectural style of the many older but stylish ivy-clad buildings which provide a sense of consistency to the campus. The more recent structures reflect a variety of contemporary designs, the most obvious of which is the Teachers College facility.

Dean Kowalski discussed the city: "The view from here presents quite a false picture of Muncie. The wealthiest people in town live right here in proximity to this university; the homes you see from here are hardly representative. If you go to the south end of town you would think that you were in a poor Alabama town. Most of the people who live in the south end of town in fact came here from states like Alabama and Tennessee. They came here to work in the auto industry and now many of them are going back."

Demographic data validate the dean's observation. Muncie is a city of slightly in excess of 70,000, and a recent survey identified it as one of twenty cities in the country which has lost the greatest proportion of its population in the last decade.

For many, Muncie is synonomous with the Middletown studies. This small, midwestern city entered the national consciousness in 1929 when

51

Robert and Helen Lynd, two noted sociologists, came to Muncie to study the basic values and structures of American life. Their code name for Muncie was "Middletown" and their book depicting life in Muncie has become a classic sociological study. The Lynds followed up their original study during the Depression and entitled this examination *Middletown in Transition*. Fifty years later, the University of Virginia conducted yet another follow-up study of Muncie titled *Middletown III*. Vignettes from this study were eventually aired on the PBS television network in 1982 in a critically acclaimed series of six television documentaries on American life. As a result of these studies, Muncie has long been depicted as a "typical American city" because of the strong strain of traditional American values reflecting love of country, strong family ties, and belief in the virtue of hard and honest work.

Muncie originally evolved as a small commercial center when the rail links to the east ushered in a new era of progress in the 1850s. However, it was a later event that set Muncie's future course, as well as that of Ball State's, more fully in motion. In 1886, a large deposit of natural gas was discovered in the vicinity. The prospects of an unlimited supply of low-cost energy prompted a number of industrial leaders to move their operations to Muncie. The five Ball brothers were among those early pioneers and the Ball name has been linked significantly with Muncie ever since. As early as 1906, 5,000 railroad cars of Ball fruit jars were shipped annually from Muncie around the world.

Even today, wherever one goes in Muncie, evidence of the Ball family's generosity is found. Most notable are the Ball Memorial Hospital and, of course, Ball State University. In a recent survey of Muncie residents, the university was overwhelmingly noted as the most favorable aspect of the city. The descendants of the five Ball brothers have continued with their philanthropy to this community in northeast central Indiana and to the university that bears their name.

The university was first founded as a state institution in 1918 when the Ball brothers purchased the campus and buildings of a small normal school unable to sustain itself. They donated custody of this school to the board of trustees of Indiana State Normal School at Terre Haute. The new institution was thus christened the Indiana State Normal School, Eastern Division. As the school evolved from a two-year normal school to a four-year college and eventually to a larger comprehensive university, an understandable inclination has been evidenced for many to mask this normal school origin and teachers college tradition. Typical of this sentiment is a recruitment brochure describing Ball State University today. It begins "born under another name in 1918 the institution became Ball State University in 1965."

As this adolescent institution continues to expand in other directions, Teachers College, its station in the university's sphere of influence, and expectations for the faculty are changing. Protracted faculty discussion has taken place over whether the label *Teachers College* should be dropped.

While considerable respect remains for the faculty and programs of Teachers College, at the same time, a very real need is seen to create an image that the institution has moved substantially to a modern, more diversified university.

Today the university features six colleges: Applied Sciences and Technology, Architecture and Planning, Business, Fine Arts, Science and Humanities, and Teachers College. Doctoral and master's programs are offered, but education graduate degrees still dominate; of the five Ph.D. programs offered, two are in education and an Ed.D. program affords nine areas of emphasis.

Shortly after Ball State Teachers College became Ball State University in 1965, NCATE granted the institution full accreditation for all graduate programs through the doctorate in fields of education. Subsequently, cooperative doctoral programs, which had been conducted at one time with both Indiana University and Purdue University, were discontinued in 1982. Thus, Ball State represents an institutional type across the country whose original emphasis was exclusively in the area of teacher preparation and which, over time, branched out to other disciplines and fields of study.

Dean Kowalski reminded us of this history: "It's no accident that Teachers College is the only high rise building on campus, since teacher education totally dominated this campus at one time. We are now in a transitional period, and, at this point, we are only the third largest college on campus in terms of the number of students enrolled." (These enrollment figures are somewhat deflated and misleading in assessing the scope of effort in Teachers College because a number of secondary majors are not counted as part of the enrollment of Teachers College.) Teachers College graduates peaked in 1972 when approximately 2,000 students received bachelor's degrees. Today, about 500 graduate in teacher education annually. Kowalski recalled with some pride that in 1982 Ball State was reported as the number one producer of education graduates in the country when both graduate and undergraduate numbers were combined.

The EXEL Program

Our specific interest is in a program designed to prepare elementary teachers known as Experimental Elementary Education (EXEL). EXEL was born in the late 1960s and, after numerous modifications, remains today a focus for new ideas. This program evolved from the creative efforts of the elementary program at that time. Professor Kay Stickle, chair of elementary education, was one of the original architects who designed the program and remains a vital force in its continuing evolution today. Stickle is a bundle of energy and any discussion in her office — "the door is always open" — is constantly interrupted by the heavy traffic of students and faculty who seek her. Seemingly able to attend to many tasks at one time she remains a gracious and attentive host in the midst of these interruptions. She traced the genesis of the program to 1968 when Ball State submitted a proposal to the U. S. Office of Education for funding a *model* elementary teacher education program. Ball State was not one of the institutions funded to plan such programs. (No institutions ultimately received implementation funds.) However, the efforts that went into thinking through what a model program might look like nonetheless continued and provided the impetus for the development of EXEL.

Stickle suggested in retrospect that major funding was not necessary:

> The students didn't really need a large grant; they needed good teachers who brought the best out in them. So, we started with our pride, and we put in little things as we could. We took our basic program, and we began to insert various elements into it over time, quarter by quarter. We got experimental approval from the state to go with it and away we went. And we spent the next two to three years designing EXEL.

We inquired whether this climate for experimentation still existed.

> The elementary faculty, ever since I have been here and in fact long before that, has always been a very yeasty group. They are a collection of people who have a history of designing and creating. I never heard anyone challenge the idea that we had to move on. The attitude is rather let's give it a whirl. If you can give me a good rationale, we'll talk it over. Maybe I can add something to it. 'Brain' parties are very common here and they are very informal.

Our discussions with the faculty in the elementary program supported Stickle's contention that an experimental program, by definition, suggests an unfinished agenda. The program is viewed as organic and evolving. Today the EXEL program that has evolved has won more than one distinguished award and the description of the program which is handed out to incoming freshmen reads as follows:

EXEL
An Award Winning Experimental Program in the Professional Preparation of Elementary School Teachers

Since 1970, Ball State University and the Muncie Community Schools have been cooperating in an experimental program for the preparation of elementary school teachers. Students enter the program in *the freshman year* and complete a sequence of professional education experiences that includes two assignments in elementary classrooms each year.

The purpose of the program is twofold: (1) to provide opportunities for students to become acquainted with the responsibilities and challenges of teaching early in their college years as a means of helping them decide whether teaching is really what they want to do, and (2) for those who continue, to provide opportunities for them to integrate theory and practice and personal potential into authentic teaching styles. Each student develops and demonstrates his or her own teaching competencies and values consistent with accepted understandings about children, human relations, communications, aesthetics, society, curriculum, and perceptions of the objectives and structures of the elementary school. Samples of classroom performance are observed, reported, and evaluated throughout the four college years and beyond.

The freshman program continues through two consecutive quarters. During this time (twenty weeks) students spend one two-hour period in selected elementary classrooms in the Muncie area schools and one two-hour period on campus each week. This schedule is continued through two quarters of the sophomore year and integrated with an additional two hours per week in psychology. Students are assigned to different schools that offer contrasting sociocultural settings, and, insofar as is possible, different school and classroom organizations. The central emphasis during this two-year period is on developing skills relating to the way children learn and grow.

The junior year also includes two quarters of work. Students spend four two-hour periods each week in classroom assignments in conjunction with courses in teaching methods. The classrooms become laboratories for developing and practicing teaching methods in all curricular areas and for learning skills and competencies needed for effective classroom organization and management. In the senior year, student teaching assignments are arranged by the Office of Laboratory Experiences.

Additionally, students enrolled in the EXEL program may participate in an overseas program during the autumn quarter of their junior year. This overseas program operates cooperatively with Middlesex Polytechnic in Trent Park, north of London. Opportunities in this program allow for travel and directed study in another cultural setting, as well as for intensive participation in the schools.

It's the Faculty Who Count

While we had to probe to gain some understanding of the program, opinions about the primary people attached to the program, faculty and students, were freely shared and everywhere manifest. References to people invariably began our discussions and were the basic medium by which most concepts were discussed and defined. For example, the history of the way EXEL evolved as shared by several faculty members is a story about themselves and about their relationships with one another and their students. Faculty consistently stated that EXEL was founded by a cadre of faculty bound together by a commitment to provide the best they were capable of for students. This commitment to students is still obvious today and examples permeated our observations as well as our discussions. As we concluded our first visit with Dean Kowalski, for example, he summarized his views of Teachers College as follows:

> We have a lot of good people here, and I really believe that our undergraduate programs have been as successful as they have because of the type of faculty here who have devoted most of their careers to working very closely with our young students. As I travel throughout the state to various school districts, most of the people I talk to from Ball State share with me that the thing that has remained

with them and the thing that they appreciated most were the faculty models which were presented to them . . . an excitement for teaching, a caring for young people. . . .

A question we repeatedly asked faculty members was what they felt was most distinctive about the program. Responses such as the following by education professor Ann Williams were common:

> I know you will think this sounds corny, but it's genuine and sincere . . . the intimate relationships we have with our students. You know, I never did get that sense when I taught at Ohio State. Oh, I would with four or five students, but it's very different here. I have been with these kids now in an intensive way the past eight or nine weeks in the classroom and in the schools as well. I feel a very real kinsmanship with them. . . . I'll feel very badly about leaving them in a couple of weeks, . . . and yet I will keep in contact with them. When I go up and down the hallway, . . . even though I don't have them in class any longer, they will stop and ask how I am, what I think about this or that, . . . or they will tell me about what they did with their students. I really believe that all of us take a very sincere interest in our students.

Students we interviewed concurred with this view of student-faculty relationships almost without exception, as in the following unsolicited testimony:

> When I first came to Ball State with a couple of other friends, I wasn't sure what I was going to do, so I went over to Teachers College and talked with Dr. Stickle. Right on the spot she took us on a personal tour of Teachers College. She took us all around and told us all about the program. And it sounded just right. Even though this is a very large school for me because my school, my high school, had only 4,000 students, and there are almost 20,000 students here . . . that's a big switch . . . it just seemed right away that they get to know you on a personal level. They really do!

A second student extended these remarks: "Dr. Stickle, I agree . . . she is so positive about everything and so willing to help you. You can go up to her and talk to her and the same thing is true of several of my professors. They love this profession and that makes you feel good, too. You say, 'yeah, that's what I want to do'." A third student stated, "Where else can you be where you can make an appointment with the chairperson—as a student—almost any time you want to. You don't have to be in trouble to do it. You just go over there, sit down and talk. I know that she is really busy, but she makes time for you and she makes you feel really good about visiting with her." Still another student enthused: "I'm a senior, and I haven't become hardened at all. The professors here remain the same. They just give, give, give. The faculty here is just great."

Several of the cooperating teachers we met shared similar perceptions: "It's really interesting listening to these student teachers talk about their professors. The communication seems to be just great between these students and their professors. They know one another on a first-name basis."

The Students in Elementary Education

The faculty appear to be genuinely fond of the students in their program and in many ways this appears related to the type of young people who come to Ball State in the hope of becoming teachers. A veteran faculty member, Donavon Lumpkin, characterized these students as follows:

> Predominantly, these students represent central Indiana. They are basically rural and small town, and they're representative of the people and values of this area. They reflect what the studies showed referring to us as Middletown, U.S.A. These students represent a fairly conservative background, modest income levels. . . . They are hardworking, and they want to learn. The majority of them, I believe, are entering college for the first time. That captures it for me.

The dean, in his discussion of undergraduates in the college, concurred with the observations of the faculty: "Most of these students are first-generation college enrollees. They have limited travel and in many ways limited cultural experiences. They are not very worldly, but they are very good kids, and they are hardworking, polite, and courteous (and we need not add likeable)."

Our classroom observations validated the perceptions of the faculty. Class sizes in elementary education courses were typically between fifteen and twenty students. The students tended to be recent high school graduates, with but one or two exceptions, all white, and all female. Their manner of dress was uniform in nature, casual but clean. Standard apparel was denim jeans and sweatshirts or sweaters with an occasional blouse and pants combination (this was December in Indiana). Students often wore their high school letter jackets.

Professor Williams shared why she felt so strongly about these young people:

> there's never a time at graduation during which I don't walk down the aisle and see these parents and the pride on their faces and realize the backgrounds and origins these young people have come from. . . . And the parents, my goodness, they are so proud—they have a child graduated from college. . . . It's a renewal for me every graduation. It gives me such good feelings that I know I can make it through yet another year with these young people, and, even though they are not as cosmopolitan and well-traveled as youngsters at other institutions, they are a joy to work with.

We raised questions about the parochial nature of the student body in terms of the teaching assignments they would assume. In this regard, Ted Kowalski reminded us that a fundamental match exists between the values held by the majority of these students and the values of teachers and parents in the surrounding schools in which most of these young people take positions. (Ball State graduates have a high rate of placement and appear eagerly sought after, especially by regional school administrators.) The dean indicated that he understood the need for a university to broaden horizons, but he reflected: "I'm not so sure how well our students would fare in many of these school systems if they had been exposed to more radical thinking. The fact is that if you take a student who comes from a family with a long history of a certain value system and they're first-generation college students, . . . I mean they aren't rebellious people. They are very cooperative; they tend to do what they are told. Superintendents and principals love them."

A dialogue with Dr. Jean Arrasmith, a member of the arts and science faculty, illustrated the lack of student activism observed by those on the faculty generally. As a leader in the university senate, she thought that a number of students might attend a key Senate meeting the evening previous to our meeting with her when a showdown vote was scheduled on a proposed controversial change from a quarter to a semester system.

> My impression was that there might be a large group of students over there when the Senate convened. In fact, I had contacted the university police to find out whether someone was going to be there or at least be somewhere around there. I had also made arrangements for the senate to meet elsewhere in case we could not accommodate everyone in attendance. As it turned out, we had fewer than fifty students attend. I moved the senators forward and left the back rows open and we didn't even fill those. There simply wasn't any type of organized movement on what I thought would be a major issue for students.

Putting perceptions of social attitudes aside, a common characterization of students by those we interviewed was that they were academically able and, just as importantly, they were willing to work hard. Some went further. For example, Jon Hendrix, a highly respected faculty member, took the position that students at Ball State University generally, including those in elementary education, were academically very competitive:

> I think the general student population at Ball State is equivalent to that in most colleges any place in the United States. By and large, these are good students academically. Eighty percent of them come from this state and 20 percent from out of state, . . . and the 80 percent from in-state are in the upper 10 to 15 percent of their graduating classes. The reason for this is that, in Indiana, we have a very high percentage of students who do not go on to higher education. Those who do are quite able and achievement-oriented, so you automatically get a more select crop of high school graduates and Teachers College attracts some of the best of the students in this state who want to teach because of its reputation.

He was further asked if he viewed any difference generally in the quality of students at Ball State contrasted with those at Indiana University because he has also taught at the latter institution. He responded: "As a matter of fact no, not really." When asked if others might disagree with this observation he indicated with a chuckle, "perhaps someone at Indiana University."

DISTINCTIVENESS OF THE
BALL STATE UNIVERSITY PROGRAM

A Progression of Diverse Field Experiences

The distinctive nature of the Ball State program goes beyond a high level of personal concern manifested for students across the faculty and the willingness of these largely first-generation college students to devote considerable energies toward what they view as a very important vocation. The program as outlined earlier is characterized by its emphasis on early and continuing field experiences. The research literature speaks to the *problems* as well as to the benefits of school experiences for prospective teachers. Thus, we probed to reveal as fully as possible the nature of these experiences in the schools. For starters, students enrolled in the EXEL program at Ball State typically spend twice as much time in a variety of laboratory and field experiences than do students enrolled in the more traditional programs. The time demand alone serves as a screening process in that only those students who are able and willing to devote considerable time to the program are admitted. (The average number of students enrolled at any one time in the EXEL program is approximately 100.)

George Swafford described these experiences as follows:

> We give them lots and lots of school experiences, laboratory experiences, and other types of community experiences beginning in their freshman year. These experiences are designed to become progressively more challenging and sophisticated. During the first quarter in their freshman year just being in a classroom is overwhelming. They are scared to death. And I'm not sure much happens. But, I think, by the second experience, selective screening has definitely set in. Those students know by that time, at least as I see it, whether this is something they want to devote their energies to. We put them out into city schools and in country schools, in team teaching situations, in open schools and in conventional classrooms. They have a variety of experiences with a variety of children. Over time, they can have opportunities to work with rural children and with kids in the inner city.

Students who we interviewed also discussed the incremental effects of these field experiences. In the words of one student:

I have been teaching in one respect or another for four years now, and, by this time, I can just jump right in and start in on everything that is necessary for a successful lesson right off the bat. I don't know if they have this sequence of experiences attached to courses at other universities—I doubt it—but I think it's wonderful that we have it here. I've talked to friends, for example, at Purdue and places like that, and they can't get over the fact that we're out there in our freshman year. Our second quarter on campus and we're out there. It's terrific.

Similar testimony came from another student:

I think it's immensely helpful to have had four years working in schools. You begin in your freshman year working in the lab school with students, you continue on through your sophomore year and by that time you have a chance to work out a lot of the problems or fears that have been built up about teaching in the classroom. I'm only a junior, but my confidence has increased considerably, and now, in each experience, I'm taking on more and more responsibility.

Faculty Teach in School Settings

It is not only the students but the *faculty* who are involved in school experiences. The extent and type of faculty activity in this regard appear to be one of the distinguishing characteristics of the Ball State program. Professor Tom Schroeder observed:

All of us are very much involved in the schools. We go out regularly and get involved with children themselves. It isn't as if any of us haven't taught elementary-aged children in the last twenty years as is the situation in so many institutions. It is not uncommon for me to sit down and work with a child in the classroom. This provides examples which I can use the next morning when I am working with our students here on campus. I can come back in and talk very specifically and very graphically about what happened to me. I believe that this makes a tremendous difference in the way that I am able to interact with the students and in my ability to provide the kinds of examples that I want to provide. So, you see, these field experiences are not only for the college student but also for the faculty and on a continuing basis. And it isn't just lip service. We really are doing it.

Kay Stickle put it this way:

It's rare when there is some type of crisis out there for a student that you aren't aware of firsthand. You are out there yourself. . . . You're working on a specific type of situation, and, when you come back, you can use it at a teachable moment in your own class that night or that afternoon. So you see that the turnaround time for both the students and faculty is a very significant factor in our program. If this isn't theory to practice it is at least firsthand examples of significant concepts.

Addressing the Feed-Forward Program

A problem commonly cited in the literature on teacher education is that preservice students cannot fully appreciate or internalize many principles and concepts they are presented with in the college classroom because they simply do not have an experiential or reality base to assess their relevance or potency. The problem is invariably compounded by the chronological distance from when concepts are discussed in a college classroom, however thoroughly or not, and when the opportunity is presented to observe or apply these concepts. This commonsense link between desired levels of understanding and timely opportunity for applications of these understandings is frequently missing in many preservice efforts. The EXEL program is, however, designed to provide more immediate and direct links between pedagogical content and opportunities to observe or apply this content in a classroom.

A commonly reported benefit of what is referred to as the "block" approach in the EXEL program is the immediacy of being able to relate student experiences in the classroom to sessions conducted on campus. In this block arrangement, EXEL participants are out in the schools in the morning and then come back in the afternoon for their classes. This arrangement allows for a continuing discussion of concepts and methodologies under study in terms of their application by both preservice students and faculty, as well as by teachers in K–12 classrooms. In several of the methods classes we observed, instructors called upon students many times to provide examples from their recent teaching experience to illuminate the topic under discussion. Most of these early teaching experiences appeared to be quite structured and were designed to increase the amount of responsibility the students assumed over time in the program. Thomas Schroeder elaborated on this design:

> I think that what distinguishes what we do best in teacher preparation, and particularly in the block which I teach, is how supervision in these field experiences is handled. Certainly, the students can tell you whether it is heavy handed or not, but I want to tell you that I see *each one* of them *every* week, and I take copious notes on what is going on in these classrooms. I also talk with their students and with their teachers. I observe what they are doing. They're just not out there. We keep a close watch on what they are doing. And of course, we try to follow up in our class as often as possible. So, not only do we get to know each other very well, but we continually tie things that happen in the classroom very nicely to the instruction that takes place in the block.

Curriculum Articulation

This block concept embraces not only the notion of a continuing articulation of activities between the campus and the classroom, but in the EXEL program it speaks to the way in which the curriculum is organized as well in terms of scope and sequence. The sophomore year focuses on more generic kinds of teaching abilities, for example, ways of approaching classroom management and organization are related to coursework in educational psychology. In the autumn quarter of the junior year, study in teaching language arts in the schools is related to the teaching of reading. In the spring quarter, methods in the physical and social sciences are approached in tandem. Thus, another objective in the EXEL program is an emphasis on curricular *integration*— examining common concepts across subject matter when appropriate. Don-avon Lumpkin related to us:

> Our faculty feels very keenly about how we approach curriculum. We aren't into this . . . it's social studies time and then it's math time and then this is reading. Rather, we make an effort when possible to interrelate the language arts with the sciences and literature and math. In the reading block, you will find the reading people emphasizing reading across the content areas . . . using reading skills in the sciences and in the social studies. So, within our program, I think that you will find that there is a great deal of articulation in the curriculum.

Within certain blocks, at least, an effort is made to ensure a desired level of mastery of that content prior to addressing the way that content can be taught and providing opportunity to teach it. Thus, the sequence moves from discussing content and theory to discussing teaching methodologies to providing actual opportunity to teach. Tom Schroeder, a reading instructor in this block, explained,

> In the first class on reading, we teach them what there is to be taught to children who are learning how to read. So, we focus essentially on the skills of reading, the word recognition skills, the study skills, the processes of reading, and then the relationship of the language arts to the experience and background of youngsters and to their stage of oral language development. *Then* we teach them how to teach in those areas. By and large we divide the course into those segments. First, an in-depth approach on what there is to teach and then how to teach it. During that latter period of time, two to three weeks at least are spent on various general as well as specific pedagogical techniques such as lecture and role playing—and then the final weeks are given over to actually working with children. . . .
>
> Normally, we begin by taking them over to Burris, the laboratory school. The students go over and try out specific skills that they have learned in their first reading class. They're hardly overconfident at this time. Then, in the following class, Reading 430, which they are all required to take, they spend the first two or three weeks of the quarter focusing upon diagnosing student needs relative to reading. They develop an informal reading inventory to assess the child's attitudes and skills. Then we go out with them into the schools, and, at this juncture, they work with two children. Ideally, those two children will be quite different in their interests and reading abilities so that we can illustrate to some extent the range of differences a teacher has to deal with in diagnoses and treatment.
>
> So, we begin on a very small scale by having them deal with two children. Next, we go out in the schools and they do a diagnostic workup. Then we bring

them back in to campus for about a week and help them formulate planning for instruction from what they have learned. Then we go back out again two days a week and they teach two hours each day. Throughout this developmental sequence, they get very close supervision. Over time, we build up to more and more complex responsibilities.

A recent graduate of the Ball State EXEL program recalled this developmental approach in these terms:

> One thing that I appreciate about Ball State in terms of its program is that it is a real goal-oriented approach to teaching with specific objectives that have to be met. They know what they want you to accomplish, and you are provided with an opportunity to do this with different people and in different situations. . . . What they are trying to teach I think is that over time these concepts will become grounded deeper and deeper. I believe that this is the one thing I really benefitted from in terms of my preparation at Ball State. Over time, a real clarity develops in terms of knowing what you are about and knowing what you can expect as a result of that.

Cohort Groups

Yet another aspect of this integrative block concept is that of students working closely together *over time* in the EXEL Program. Traditionally, about seventy-five students are admitted to the EXEL program annually, although the number has currently risen to almost 100. These students are, in turn, subdivided into three or four cohort groups of about twenty-five students who proceed through the blocks together. Because the early experiences in schools usually screen out a number of students, by the time that these students are into their sophomore year, the cohort groups have been reduced to approximately twenty students or fewer. This is a group size that allows for considerable interaction with one another and for familiarity to develop over time. Students in a number of instances alluded to the benefits of moving through their program together with the same group of peers. They identified two major benefits: (1) the range of ideas they were able to generate from learning to work closely together, and (2) the support provided to one another as they went through the program together.

Relationships with the Schools

Dr. George Swafford, who at that time was responsible for coordinating the student teaching experiences, indicated that to the extent possible he and his staff tried to match student interests and needs, as they understood these, with the characteristics of the different supervising teachers as they came to know these people. Because many of these supervising teachers have worked continually with Ball State for a number of years, he felt this was possible in many instances.

Generally, good working relationships were apparent not only between students and the faculty, as we indicated at the outset, but also between students and faculty and those teachers with whom they work in the schools. One of the features of the EXEL program which appears to contribute to these harmonious relationships is the fact that faculty are frequently in the schools and occasionally assume teaching responsibilities there. They appear to have credibility not only with their students but with experienced teachers in the schools, as well. Also important to these college/school relationships is that students appear to come prepared to teach in a manner relatively consonant with the experienced teacher's ongoing curriculum. Often they bring a variety of resources to that teacher's classrooms as well. One student described the way they were received by these teachers.

> A lot of the teachers, when we come into the classroom, are really glad that we are there because we bring all these wonderful materials with us. They tell us that they never have an opportunity to use many of the materials like these and that they enjoy using them with us while we are there. I can't even begin to tell you all the materials that are in our materials center.

At this point another student eagerly interrupted:"Yeah, that's right, you name it, we've got it! Models, puppets, anything you want, the materials center has it . . . phonographs, projectors, records, curriculum materials, it's all there."

Ball State Teachers College appears to have excellent material resources from which their students can avail themselves. These facilities include videotaping and playback capabilities for microteaching, a computer laboratory, individual tutoring cubicles, a reading materials center, a language arts laboratory, and the living-learning laboratory used in working with young children.

In our interviews with supervising teachers who work with the EXEL students, these teachers were invariably complimentary about the faculty from Teachers College. In this regard, it should be noted that another relatively distinctive feature of the EXEL program is that specific faculty are assigned full-time responsibility at different times for the supervision of student teachers. The same arrangement applies to student advising as well. In these instances, all, or almost all, of a professor's efforts for a particular quarter are devoted to the supervision of student teachers. As one of the teachers shared with us:

> I have found that professors who supervise teachers from Ball State have been nothing short of excellent. They are extremely receptive to us no matter whether it's a minor problem or a more severe one. They are willing to sit down and dis-

cuss any matter. They're around a lot, and they are willing to adjust. They work *with* you, so that if a student teacher feels weak in a particular area the two of us can join hands and concentrate on that particular problem.

The pride that several teachers felt in their association with the Ball State program and in the contribution which they believe they make was also evident. In an unsolicited testimony, one of the teachers shared the following:

I think that the student teaching experience is one of the most important things that the student will engage in. As you know, you can read a lot of things in books, but it doesn't work out that way in the classroom. It doesn't work out that way when John does this, so you do that. That's wrong! When you do that, John doesn't do this—he does something else. So, from my perspective, if you want to evaluate the time that I give over to spending with a student teacher and the things that I talk about with them you can't put a price tag on it. If you wanted to evaluate this on the basis of the monetary thing, there is no way that it begins to reflect my role. They couldn't afford to pay a teacher to do what we do which is consistent with the value of this activity. Believe me, I think it is very nice they do offer us something, but it is hardly the determining factor as to whether or not you are willing to work with a student teacher.

The Arts and Science Aspect of Teacher Preparation

Perhaps the most unusual aspect of the preparation of elementary teachers at Ball State is the personal cooperation and curricular articulation which has been achieved with the arts and science faculty. This close working relationship between the faculty in elementary education and the arts and sciences can be attributed largely to the fact that this institution was once a teachers' college where the sole mission was the preparation of teachers. Thus, many of the veteran faculty who are still teaching in the arts and sciences taught in that context. Notwithstanding this history, we did not anticipate the degree of integration between coursework in the college and that in arts and sciences nor the approach to teaching manifested by several professors in the content areas in arts and sciences.

The elementary education faculty tended to consider the arts and sciences faculty to be an integral part of their program. Certainly, they often worked together in both formal and ad hoc arrangements. The professional curriculum is in many respects shared. For example, the science methods of *elementary* majors are taught in the biology department, math content and methods are taught in the mathematics department, and social studies methods are taught, among other places, in the history department. Recall, again, that we are not talking about the preparation of secondary teachers but *elementary* teachers. As Kay Stickle emphasized:

The faculty in these arts and sciences departments who teach methods are all licensed teachers. I underscore *teachers*. The people who teach these courses for our elementary students have had to have been licensed elementary teachers themselves. We don't have someone who comes out of biology and drops in to teach science methods. Let me say this again, they are *all* licensed teachers—and they are *all* committed to preparing teachers for the classroom. Also, these faculty remain in touch with the classroom.

Professor Jon Hendrix explained the working relationships across the faculties in this manner:

What we have here is a group of faculty who are concerned about a *whole* program, about looking at an end product as it evolves across discipline lines, across subject matter, and even across departments and colleges to create that effect. What that means for me is that I am free to pick up the phone at any time and say 'hey, Rita,' or 'hey, John, something is going on that I don't like and I think we ought to sit down and talk about this'. We don't have to go through a committee. . . . We are in constant communication. Do you understand what I'm saying?

When asked to explain why this kind of collegiality developed and has been sustained over time, Hendrix responded:

It's largely historical. These types of relationships are built among people and their commitment *to* programs rather than viewing themselves as coming strictly *from* a program as such. We haven't seen vested interests take over here. Thus, it's both a very individual and historically cultivated thing. . . . There is an esprit de corps among the larger faculty that cuts across colleges and breaks down the issue of territoriality that's typically established in most universities. I understand this historically, and I'm not entirely sure what sustains it today. I have often thought about that. I don't want to sound like we're all overly altruistic either because I haven't taught an elementary class in I don't know how long; I did at one time—but, my goodness, it's been a long time. I don't know what really maintains it, but it's there. I *do* know that there is a guardianship of these courses and the integrity of what they are about and who can teach them and what we are trying to do, and that's been there for a long time in terms of the relationship of Teachers College to other departments.

The rigor of courses in arts and sciences curricula, which typically have a content orientation but are adapted to the methods employed in elementary classroom, is an understandable concern. With regard to why the courses have been developed the way they are, Jon Hendrix responded:

If we are talking about secondary majors, I think that those students should take the same coursework as their fellow students in the sciences and the humanities. But in terms of elementary majors, I think you have a different situation there, and I'll tell you why. Elementary education preparation requires a broad-based generalist who has a good command of the interconnection among concepts included in the best of a liberal arts education and at the same time has some basic methodologies by which we can adapt that content and those concepts to teaching students of elementary age. . . . For example, I don't think we should try to place elementary education majors in the same sequence of courses for majors in biology or physics or history. I think that you are doing them a grave injustice. I believe, rather, that you should try to do what we have done here at Ball State— give them content that is still intellectually challenging and exemplifies the discipline but relates as well to how it might be communicated to much younger students . . . I really believe that this is what is most unique about our program. . . . Our special science sections are taught by people who care about elementary teaching majors and who want to see these elementary majors succeed with young children. . . .

These are not watered-down courses, but, rather, they are adapted so that we can take the most essential concepts in the sciences, mathematics, and in literature and relate them to the context in which these teachers will teach. For example, one can take the concept of force in science and force in social studies and force in mathematics. Now that kind of integration is difficult, and it doesn't always occur, but we work at it and when it does, it's powerful. I really believe that is why we have won awards. We deal with important ideas and concepts that cut across our disciplines and beyond that we attempt to relate them to the world in which these young people will be teaching.

This concern for application of basic concepts in core disciplines to the elementary curriculum was obvious in the classes we observed which were taught by the arts and sciences faculty. For example, when we talked with Dr. Alice Robold, who teaches both content and methods courses in the mathematics department, she elaborated as follows on this relationship:

Those of us who teach the methods courses in this department are prepared not only as mathematicians but have been prepared to teach in the elementary school as well. We have an education background and experiences as well as a mathematics background. . . . We are doubly prepared to work with these young people. We plan our required general studies sequence in mathematics this way from the beginning for elementary students. For example, we have four content courses which are sequenced all the way through to culminate in the methods courses. There is both a consistency and a development from one course to another and the curriculum is not fragmented. One person is not teaching one course without an awareness of what's happening in the next one.

In discussing the rigor and intellectual challenge of these courses, Alice Robold spoke with considerable pride:

The mathematics I teach is very carefully prepared. It is *not* second-class mathematics. It is quality mathematics. Now, I admit that I do not deal with mathematics in this course as abstractly as I would for mathematics majors. You can see I attempt to build the abstractions rather than to deal with the content abstractly. I hope you saw that in the lesson you observed today, for example. I began with manipulative materials—we use a lot of manipulative materials. There are two reasons for this. First, we find that it really helps our students to develop essential mathematical concepts better, and, at the same time, it prepares them for what is a necessary approach to teaching given the developmental patterns of the young people they will teach with. For example, in the geometry course that we teach, we will use geoboards to deal with the concepts of area, motion, and coordinate systems. The approach is thus more concrete than I employ with mathematics majors. It's more manipulative and I try to model for these students what I want them to do in the classroom in which they will teach.

The principles of instruction outlined by this professor were, in fact, exemplified in her classroom when we observed her teach. The deductive exercise in which she engaged the students was concerned with identifying the relationship between diameter and circumference. Sixteen students were in the class, seated two to a table, where they worked in pairs. Consistent with the earlier-described general demography of the students, all were female, all were college-aged, and all were white with one exception. Their dress was consistently clean and casual. The interaction between the professor and the students was straightforward.

The bell rang and this small, grey-haired woman with animated bird-like features started immediately, without fanfare, indicating that she was going to talk about circles and the way circles could be used by them to develop important concepts with their own students. She did not indicate to them what the concepts were but, rather, involved them immediately in an exercise which forced them to generalize about the relationship of diameter to circumference, the concept of Pi and the concept of Pi as an irrational number.

The students appeared to be intently involved throughout in this concrete, activity-oriented lesson. Alice Robold used the blackboard frequently to visually develop the primary concepts with which she was involving the students. She knew all the students by name and by the end of the session, we recorded that she had called upon all of them at one time or another and on a first-name basis. The students were invariably polite and responsive. At one point, when two students answered simultaneously, there was a brief exchange between the two students where both insisted briefly but ever so politely that the other student go first in responding to the question which had been raised.

The principals of "active" or "direct" instruction often referred to in the literature on teaching in elementary schools appeared to be exemplified in this lesson. The lesson was fast-paced yet not impersonal. It was well-organized. Students remained on-task. Both formative and summative feedback was given, and the instructor was central in defining both the scope and sequence of the tasks and the pacing and monitoring of activities. Again, this was *not* a methods course in mathematics but, rather, a content course where multiple references showed how content could be adapted to the elementary teaching role which these young people would assume.

In discussing the class afterward with Professor Robold, she elaborated on the way this course differed from a methods course. In the methods course, she indicated, specific laboratory activities are built in and the instructor works firsthand with students in the laboratory school setting. Students design specific lessons much as they do for other classes taught in the elementary sequence and the instructor observes and works with them in the laboratory school setting. In this, one of the general content classes in the four course math sequence, mathematical concepts from her perspective were the first priority, with references to the way they could be adapted to working with youngsters an integrated and secondary focus.

Perceptions of Challenge and Rigor in the EXEL Program

The EXEL program is presented to students at the outset as one that places heavy demands on the students, and the faculty members with whom we visited have high expectations for these students. As Kay Stickle said: "We say to them, it's hard, it takes extra time and energy, for the same credit hours . . . for the same 186 credits that it takes to graduate. . . . So they're the ones that don't take EXEL, . . . and thus there is a nice self-fulfilling prophecy; we're expected to work hard. Many of them are used to hard work—and they do!"

As in other teacher education programs we visited, particular courses were identified which provided an early reality testing in terms of helping students decide whether they wanted to pursue a teaching career. In the EXEL program, approximately 20 percent of the students dropped out during their freshman or sophomore year. Those who remain, at least those with whom we talked, are dedicated to pursuing a teaching career. We also discovered a pattern of certain courses in these different institutions which appear to further sort out the women from the girls. In the EXEL program, these are clearly identified by students as "The Teaching of Reading in Today's Schools," and, "Corrective Reading in the Classroom," courses. Typical reactions by students to these courses before they enter them are apprehension and, for some, a very real fear of failure. During the block sequence, students work hard, putting in long hours outside class. After completing these courses, students appear to have considerable pride in having shared in and passed through this experience.

One student characterized the experience this way:

> Everything you learn in 400 you have to teach to children. So they continually take you out in the schools, you go out and teach children. Twice a week you make up all these lesson plans and you do them in both 400 and 430, . . . but as a

senior you look back at these two hardest courses and think, 'I've learned so much and I know I'll use it'. I'm already using it. I think we know a lot more about how to teach than a lot of teachers who are already out there doing it. And you have to take those classes. Everybody takes them and everybody dreads them. You get through that and it's just like. . . . It makes you feel good that you made it through. That's just a big hurdle. Most people take them together. I took one one quarter and the other the next. And you just get through it. And you really learn a lot. They are probably the hardest courses we had to take in all four years at the university!

A second student echoed these sentiments:

I have the reading course right now, the first one—400—and I know the people in the dorm where I live are glad they don't have to take it. For instance, last week I was up until 2 or 3 in the morning several nights working on plans. Just one lesson it would probably be sixteen or seventeen hours. You just can't realize how time-consuming it is. You just sit down and start working on it and the next thing you know it's midnight and you can't believe it and you haven't done it all. But with all the skills they've taught us I feel very confident writing the lesson and teaching it, but it does take a lot of time.

We also asked students about other students' general perceptions about the difficulty of the elementary major at Ball State. The response was that there were a number of students who viewed it as a "blow-off" major and the following dialogue ensued with a class of senior students with whom we were meeting:

Howey:	A blow-off major—even here at Ball State?
Student One:	It burns me up. Because a lot of times we're studying and they're studying, but a lot of times they just study for the test and then forget about it. We always have something that we have to be doing. Always! And we can sit and work ten hours on a lesson plan, and it may still flop the next day. Well, if you studied ten hours for a test you'd probably do good. And so you have to be content with this.
Zimpher:	How do they get those attitudes?
Student One:	I don't know. Maybe because we're teaching little kids they think you don't have to be smart.
Zimpher:	Well, do other faculty members perpetuate this idea, perhaps in the arts and sciences courses? Where would your roommates at Ball State get this idea do you suppose?
Student Two:	Well, a lot of the assignments that I do like these little circle things I made [laughter!]. I mean they think, well, how hard is that? You know, they think we only cut and paste
Zimpher:	Do they hear you talk about what you do in class? At this point, three other students eagerly jump in.
Student Three:	I think that's right. I come home, and I'm doing something

different every day. And my roommates want to know more. One day I made roller coasters, . . . I made bingo games and the funny thing about it is that I always have stories especially about what happens in school, and they love to listen to me tell them. But you never hear them coming home and sharing stories about what they do. Oh no! They're not having things happen. They have the same day every day. Every day I come home with a different story and talk about all the things that I do. But, on the other hand, they tell me I'm not going to make any money. And I tell them I'm not in it for the money.

Howey: Does anybody want to disagree about the money? [No one in the class of approximately twenty-five elementary education students responds.] No one? . . . Do you know how many years the average person that goes into teaching remains in teaching?

Student Four: Five years [Several students agree.]

Howey: Well, fewer than five, actually. How many of you plan to make teaching a *career*. Raise your hand. [Every hand in a class of twenty-five to thirty shoots up.] [laughter.] All of you have your hands up!

Zimpher: All but one. . . .

Perceptions of EXEL Students

As the above vignette illustrates, these prospective elementary teachers demonstrate considerable enthusiasm about teaching and confidence in their ability (at least this group of seniors who were about to complete their program). They are aware of the way others view elementary teachers and of the conditions attached to teaching given their several placements in schools. When asked directly about teachers' salaries, the following quote from a student captures the sentiment we heard consistently expressed by these young people:

> For me to be able to work the rest of my life, I'm going to have to enjoy what I'm doing. And, yeah, I'd like to have money, but there's more than money. To see some kid that's had problems all year long progress and you know that you've done it—you worked with that kid and you helped him learn, I mean, to me that's a lot more rewarding than pulling in a big paycheck. I've learned that I can be an effective teacher from my classes at Ball State. I've always wanted to be a teacher, and now I'm in the Ball State program and finally I can go out and do the thing I've always wanted to do, and I'm willing to go almost any place as long as I can get a good job.

So beyond enthusiasm and confidence, many of these young people had a sense of special mission. The impression that many students saw teaching as a noble vocation was reinforced by Dean Kowalski as well. He recalled his own career and the way students today appear to embrace the values he did:

I went into teaching because I came from a family background where the aspira-
tion was to go to college and get a degree, and teaching seemed to be a very noble
thing. Now the question is, will my children go into teaching? Probably not. I
haven't discouraged or encouraged them. But they seem uninterested in this
option. What we're now seeing is a return of some of the talented people to
teacher education, and it's part of a larger social context. People are coming back
to teaching because that is what they want to do, and they don't care what anyone
thinks. We haven't had that for a long time, and I'm enthused about this.

We also asked a number of the supervising teachers who worked with
student teachers from the EXEL program in recent years how they generally
perceived the young people going into teaching whom they supervised. The
following comments were typical: good knowledge of content; well-organized, well-prepared, resourceful; having many resources; sound philosophy,
knowing what they are doing; able to deal with children and with parents
(because of their multiple experiences); highly motivated; creative and adaptable; and, able to anticipate problems.

Throughout these discussions, however, a dedication to the task came
through most frequently. As one supervising teacher shared with us: "The last
two student teachers that I've had have been there a week early. Not because
they had to be there. They wanted to be there and find out how the year
begins."

The students identified many of the same abilities as their supervisors
and largely attributed these to their education at Ball State. Two further attributes were commonly shared. They reported that (1) a theme of appreciation
for and understanding of individual differences ran throughout their courses,
and (2) the notion that being well-planned is in many ways tied to the ability
to provide pupils with appropriate hands-on experiences. A senior stated:

I know that if I hadn't had these experiences at Ball State I wouldn't realize how
important hands-on experiences are, . . . how important that we do things really
creatively. A lot of teachers just do things to fill up time. You know, hand the
kids a book and say, 'learn'. If you're one of the kids that learn it that way, then
it's no problem for you. But there are a lot of kids that need those *hands-on*
experiences and they need the *creative* teachers out there. And I think through the
EXEL program, we've learned how important it is that we do things in different
and creative ways so that learning can be fun. And I think Ball State as a whole
promotes that.

THE FUTURE

We discussed the future of Teachers College at some length with those in
formal leadership positions and especially the dean, Ted Kowalski. Dean
Kowalski shared major reservations about advocates, such as those within the
Holmes Group, for postbaccalaureate programs. His view was rather that we

need to provide experiences early on at the undergraduate level in order to select out those who really do not want to teach. He sees little need for expanded programs:

> Let's look at why teachers fail. Most people ignore this. Why do most teachers end up being failures? Is it because they can't read or write? I don't think so. It may be in certain parts of the country, but it's not true in Indiana, it's not true in Minnesota, it's not true in Ohio, it's not true in Michigan, and it's not true in Illinois. It could be true in Arkansas, it could be true in Louisiana, I don't know. But a major reason that teachers fail in our state is that they can't get along with people.

Kowalski expanded on his concerns about directions advocated by the Holmes Group:

> I'm a very open critic of the Holmes Group. I believe that, for a variety of reasons, teacher education ought to remain an undergraduate experience. Some of these reasons are political. For instance, until we start paying teachers a more decent salary, I'm not enthusiastic about asking them to do more to get into a profession that many aren't interested in entering now.
>
> I also believe there's elitism involved in the Holmes Group, and this is the wrong time for education to move in an elitist direction. Who's going to prepare the teachers to teach in Gary or on the South Side of Chicago? Somebody is going to have to get their knuckles dirty and do that. When I recruited teachers as a superintendent, there was a tremendous difference, for example, between teachers who went to a small private institution and those who went to Ball State. I knew that if I hired a teacher from the private school, there were certain advantages and certain disadvantages. And, of course, we provided in-service for teachers; we will send teachers off to graduate school—so they can learn how to teach reading better than they were taught initially. But you see, our people can go into Gary and succeed right away and stay there because they had a strong teacher education program. I think the socioeconomic background of the people that come into the profession is critical in terms of where students seek work and can be successful. The vast majority of teaching jobs are going to be in blue-collar areas and particularly in areas where there are high minority populations. And so, we're trying to recruit people who can make it in these places, and I believe our best hope is to give them a bachelor's degree and the ability to teach well at the outset. Somebody's got to do that. See, I'm convinced because I think I was a pretty good teacher after four years of college. I believe I was effective. And I believe I became a better teacher when the State of Indiana made me go *back* to school and get a master's degree. I felt this was a relevant experience for me after I had some teaching experience. I don't know about anybody else but I think this a good pattern. A lot of people are effective teachers after four years of college.

The dean continued his advocacy for undergraduate teacher preparation by once more pointing out that it is more than general aptitude or even a

quality teacher education program, at whatever level, that is needed to succeed as a teacher:

> If you have SAT scores of 850, you can't get into De Pauw. You're not going to
> get into Purdue, and you're probably not going to get into IU. But you can get in
> here. Albeit, it will be on probation. But you can get in here. So, we're func-
> tioning somewhat at a disadvantage at Ball State. Maybe I'm wrong, but I pre-
> sume that you generally get better-prepared students at the Big-Ten institutions
> than here. Now the question comes that focuses specifically on teacher education.
> You might get better students in the University of Minnesota than at St. Cloud
> State University, but the question is, do you get better teacher education students
> than St. Cloud does? That's a different matter. That's where I think the profes-
> sional school concept is important. Roy Weaver, associate dean in Teachers Col-
> lege, and I are doing a study right now on outstanding teachers, and we're very
> interested in finding out certain things about those people. We're asking ques-
> tions such as, 'What kind of student were you in college?' 'What kind of student
> were you in high school?' 'What kind of activities did you participate in?' 'What
> are your general interests?' 'How much do you read?' 'What do you do outside of
> teaching?' My guess is, and I go back to my days as a school superintendent, that
> the best teachers I had were not necessarily the straight 'A', students but those
> who *love* to teach. It is in their blood for whatever reason. They like to be around
> people. They like to be with students, and that's where our strength lies in this
> institution. When someone wants to be a teacher and they're really sold on that
> idea, they pick Ball State in Indiana.

The way then to attract the students who *really* want to teach and who
know this early on, from Kowalski's perspective, is to continue to promote
Teachers College as a quality program for teacher preparation. He concedes
that Ball State will probably never have a national reputation as a research
institution because such reputations are developed at the graduate level and in
quality doctoral programs. His view is that Ball State must move very select-
ively and cautiously at the graduate level and at the doctoral level, especially
given their resources, their history, and what they do best.

A more purposeful and openly acknowledged pattern of differentiated
staffing for the faculty in Teachers College will probably occur if they can
acquire more autonomy as a professional school. The dean believes that
certain professors can be rewarded for graduate training and research as befits
university norms while other faculty can focus more specifically on undergraduate teaching and clinical supervision without being penalized by *all-
university* norms which place a priority on research.

Dean Kowalski believes he can accomplish more at an institution such as
Ball State with regard to teacher preparation than most schools or colleges of
education in large research-intensive universities will be able to. He has little
doubt that Ball State can be on the cutting edge of innovation in teacher preparation. He elaborated on the conditions needed to enable this:

First, we believe that we've got to operate and be funded more like a professional school than an undergraduate school to survive and that in doing this we have got to do something about the role of the clinical professor. That's one of our highest priorities. It may seem like a strange idea because at this same time we're also emphasizing the research and publications more. [Howey interjects to clarify whether this is the basic differentiated role-expectation arrangement he foresees.] That's right. That's exactly what we want. One of the things I've said repeatedly that I believe is a problem in schools and colleges of education is that we have a complete reversal of roles from other professional schools. The clinical professors in education have the lowest status instead of the highest. And so we're looking at ways to reverse that condition.

On a second matter, I happen to be a person who believes strongly in the value of research but integrated when possible into our undergraduate curricula, and we haven't done a lot of that. Consequently, we're sinking many of our resources into this area. This will be applied research, and it will focus more on the undergraduate experience in teacher education, . . . in the best of our programs such as EXEL. We're interested in identifying the best way that we can prepare teachers in a four-year program.

If I were president of this institution, I would sit down and look at our chances for success and determine where they are the greatest. Teacher education should be right at the top of the list. We would continue with what we do well. We would provide quality instruction and *personal* attention. I firmly believe that when students leave here they ought to leave with some kind of *portfolio,* which is a collection of lessons or strategies, different models of teaching that deal with different individuals and groups, so that, wherever you are, you have a foundation for practice instead of scratching it out for a year on your own or working occasionally with a mentor teacher. You've got some liberty and some freedom initially because you've been given a range of options for teaching over the four years of undergraduate study.

Also, we are looking seriously at using a telecommunications model to expose students to more and better field experiences via television. We plan to pilot this approach first in an experimental group. For example, instead of spending five, one-hour sessions out in a public school, we can spend four of those hours watching different teaching models in one day in a clinical setting, where you can better analyze what you see and critique it and even do research on it. Clinically, what we're trying to do is to prove to students that this is a unique institution; that there are some benefits and there are some drawbacks.

We try to be above board with our students about coming here. One of the benefits is that they will get to know their professors here better than at a large institution. Yet, we're not small, we're 17,000 plus students. Second, we do certain things in education here that other institutions do not. I've mentioned several of these already—continuous field experiences; an expanded laboratory component; an articulated, developmental curriculum; good working relationships with our schools. . . . Also, from a curricular standpoint, our students in elementary education will get more instruction in reading methodology, and I think they get more than at any other institution in the state. Now they'll also get more instruction in language arts and the other basics. We believe that all of this is translated into the fact that these people will have better opportunities in the job market. They will, as beginning teachers, be prepared. Ball State prepares teachers who can go and successfully get the job done whether the school is blue-collar or white-collar.

3

New Vision and
Vestiges of CBTE*

This is a time of change for the University of Toledo, and we were on campus in the throes of that change. The primary agenda of the dean's staff and many of the faculty members with whom we spoke was the curricular revision efforts that they were engaged in for most of academic year 1985–86.

HISTORICAL PERSPECTIVE:
A WINDOW OF OPPORTUNITY

Some say that the Holmes Group constitutes *the* window of opportunity in the 1980s for many in teacher preparation to make bold initiatives to improve this important endeavor. Such widespread interest in and support for teacher education occurs only rarely, perhaps every twenty years or so. Another window of opportunity presented itself in the late 1960s and early 1970s. The College of Education at the University of Toledo was in the forefront of changes for teacher preparation charted at that time, and the program of teacher preparation that we came to study evolved then and remains in part today. Perhaps the most significant actor in the development of that program, even though he is no longer involved, is the former dean of the College of Education at the University of Toledo, Dr. George "Ed" Dickson. Thus, we begin our descriptive portrayal of the Toledo program by going back in time with Dean Dickson.

Dickson recalled when he first came to the University of Toledo:

*Competency-based Teacher Education

77

I inherited a faculty that were fairly advanced in their careers. So, the first thing
we had to do was to attract more good people. And I didn't have any way to go
out and hire any names. There wasn't that kind of money. The only way I could
do it was to hire beginners. I did a lot of traveling in this country meeting people,
. . . identifying faculty who people thought were real 'comers', and I was able to
hire some of those from all over the country. You begin to put together some
interesting people. Now, you don't expect to keep them. Some of them left. I did
not get more than three years out of some of them and they were gone, but a lot of
them stayed.

Clearly, Dean Dickson viewed the deanship at Toledo as a opportunity for
leadership. He reminded us later, "I think good deans ought to be people who
are looking for opportunities to develop educational ideas and programs. And
there are always possibilities that you can find good ideas and you can engage
in development work."

Dean Dickson reflected on an opportunity the university had to become
involved in a major, federally funded project concentrating on elementary
teacher education: the Comprehensive Elementary Teacher Education Models
(CETEM). As soon as Dean Dickson arrived at the University of Toledo, he
began to build relationships with funding agents through regular trips to
Washington, D.C. On one of these trips he heard about funds that were to be
released shortly which would focus on the development of models for preparing elementary teachers. His ability to get his institution and others in the
state organized to respond to this opportunity came, he feels, because he was
one of the first aware of these funds and he had a slight head start on the other
institutions. He had time to think about the kind of proposal the University of
Toledo and the state might offer in designing innovative teacher education
programs. He needed an angle, too, and at that time the notion of systems
theory was becoming very popular. He said, "I wasn't a systems person and I
didn't know a lot about it, but when that movement came on the scene and the
opportunity was there to use federal money to do something significant, we
did it. You take your chances and see what happens." We asked if that was a
window of opportunity. "Oh, yes. And I think . . . when those come along
and make themselves available, that's where I think the educational leaders
take over. Others weren't astute enough or adventuresome enough to take a
chance to see what happens."

The University of Toledo competency-based teacher education (CBTE)
program really began when feasibility studies were requested from institutions
to develop specifications for these elementary teacher education program
models. Dean Dickson's notion of the deanship was that he should get involved in research and development. Dickson opined: "I think for deans to get
involved in research is unusual." As a result of this perspective, he saw the
advantages of this project and used it as an opportunity to involve a large

number of his faculty members in "on-site program development and research."

As well, he saw the wisdom of ultimately involving people in this project who would most likely be involved in the implementation of the project. Unfortunately, the federal government did not subsequently fund the implementation of the CETEM program. Nevertheless, by 1970, the University of Toledo began to implement the program as explicated in the specifications they had presented to the federal sponsoring agent. Through the use of computer analysis and the systems approach, their feasibility study had generated more than thirty-two versions of what the elementary education program could be, and they pared the specifications so that they were able to implement a program within local constraints of time and money. This was the beginning of the competency-based teacher education program at the University of Toledo. By 1975, the dean and several other persons at the institution began to develop a comprehensive evaluation system to test the efficacy of the CBTE program.

Dean Dickson believed some strides had been made in measuring the competence of students in the CBTE program and thought it could best be measured in the student teaching phase and in the first year of teaching. Problems remain, however, and this issue of measuring competence is still very much on the minds of both the current dean, Phil Rusche, and the associate dean, Ed Nussel. Nussel observes, "One thing we were never able to do, and I've asked the question over and over again, . . . what is acceptable practice within a module, . . . within a course? . . . Total competency, partial competency? . . . What criterion level within the module? What is the minimal criterion measure that would be acceptable for that?" When Dean Rusche was asked what the essential or critical feature of CBTE was, he responded, "What are the minimal competencies? I think that's where CBTE went awry. I'm not sure that the energy it takes to try to measure everything is worth it, but minimal competencies and the demonstration of minimal competencies, to me is the important thing." Thus, defining competency and the assessment of the efficacy of a CBTE program remain current concerns of the existing faculty and a problem which continues to haunt the dean emeritus.

Ed Dickson's recollection of where the CBTE program came from, how it was implemented, and where it needed to go under his leadership clearly appears to have been an earlier window of opportunity. The federal funds made available to study the feasibility of alternative comprehensive teacher education models was the opportunity that ultimately thrust the University of Toledo into national teacher education prominence. It was a development period that has lasted almost twenty years, not in terms of the actual length of the program but in terms of the span of time wherein the dean began to build a faculty and the faculty began to build a program. Although we address at some length the changes that await this program currently, it is useful first to look more closely at the specifications of the model which evolved in the early 1970s and as it was subsequently implemented as the University of Toledo CBTE program.

THE CURRENT CBTE PROGRAM

A Developmental Perspective

The CBTE program at the University of Toledo has been operational for thirteen years. This program has gone through systematic development and implementation which, as we indicated, began as a project of the Bureau of Research from the U. S. Office of Education in October 1967. At that time, ten goals were adopted which guided the development of the teacher education program at the University of Toledo. These goals were adopted from a statement on quality education from the Pennsylvania State Board of Education and read as follows:

1. Each teacher should be prepared to employ teacher behaviors which will help every child acquire the greatest possible understanding of himself and an appreciation of his worthiness as a member of society.
2. Each teacher should be prepared to employ teacher behaviors which will help every child acquire understanding and appreciation of persons belonging to social, cultural, and ethnic groups different from his own.
3. Each teacher should be prepared to employ teacher behaviors which will help every child acquire to the fullest extent possible for him mastery of the basic skills in the use of words and numbers.
4. Each teacher should be prepared to employ teacher behaviors which will help every child acquire a positive attitude toward school and toward the learning process.
5. Each teacher should be prepared to employ teacher behaviors which will help every child acquire the habits and attitudes associated with responsible citizenship.
6. Each teacher should be prepared to employ teacher behaviors which will help every child acquire good health habits and an understanding of the conditions necessary for the maintenance of physical and emotional well-being.
7. Each teacher should be prepared to employ teacher behaviors which will help every child acquire opportunity and encouragement to be creative in one or more fields of endeavor.
8. Each teacher should be prepared to employ teacher behaviors which will help every child understand the opportunities open to him for preparing himself for a productive life and should enable him to take advantage of these opportunities.
9. Each teacher should be prepared to employ teacher behaviors which will

help every child understand and appreciate as much as he can of human achievement in the natural sciences, the social sciences, the humanities, and the arts.

10. Each teacher should be prepared to employ teacher behaviors which help every child to prepare for a world of rapid change and unforeseeable demands in which continuing education throughout his adult life should be a normal expectation.

Later program developers organized these goals to accommodate five "contexts." This also assisted the developers in translating these general goals into more specific behavioral objectives. These five contexts were: (1) organization, (2) education technology, (3) contemporary learning-teaching processes, (4) societal factors, and (5) research. Faculty ultimately generated more than 2,000 objectives and then specifications were developed to accommodate these behavioral objectives. Through a complex systems approach to program design and through a simulated computer process, planners in the consortium were able to design particular elements of preparation programs and develop alternate models for teacher education according to the various environments where teacher education would be conducted in Ohio. A five-year cost estimate for the implementation of CBTE models at the University of Toledo resulted in a proposed five-year budget of $5,932,000. Neither the funds for implementation nor the grand design itself were forthcoming. As Dickson indicated, the faculty went ahead nontheless in major innovative ways.

A salient feature of the CBTE model developed by the University of Toledo was the integration of the multiunit school concept:

> The concept is a simple one; as simple as respecting the professional competence of teachers. It assumes that teachers believe that there is a more effective way of meeting the needs and interests of today's children than putting one teacher and thirty children in a self-contained classroom. It assumes that regardless of the curriculum resources or structure, it is the teacher who makes the difference. If the teacher is enthusiastic about the subject, if the teacher has personnel to individualize instruction, if the teacher is part of the decision-making process, instruction will be improved. (Nussel, et al., 1971)

Espoused advantages of the multiunit organization are that it provides for planning and curriculum building through flexible use of time. It also exposes the child to a variety of adult models including unit leaders, teachers, teaching assistants, and teacher aides. Finally, such an organization facilitates the development of evaluation models allowing for feedback to teachers to let them know about their own progress and the progress of their pupils. Embedded in this approach to schooling is the obvious consideration that staff development must include teaching teachers to work cooperatively and effectively within a differentiated staff. Roles of various members of the teaching unit are prescribed and collaboration, and cooperative working relations form the cornerstone of a multiunit school.

Not only was the multiunit school organization significant in the field-based aspects of the CBTE program at the university, it also had a considerable impact on the way in which faculty were organized for service in the college. Professor Joan Inglis recalled that simultaneous with the development of the CBTE model at Toledo, the local schools in the city were also moving toward individually guided education (IGE) as an instructional approach in the multiunit school. According to Professor Inglis, "we became the first university outside of Wisconsin to start IGE. And with the funding from Herb Klausmeier's R & D Center at Wisconsin, we had unit leader, principal, and teacher workshops as well as curriculum development workshops." Initially, Toledo had four IGE schools in which it arranged for field experiences to complement the CBTE on-campus experiences. Soon, concepts in the multiunit school, such as teaming, were reflected among the faculty. Through the evolution of a multiunit school Metropolitan League for Teacher Education, faculty members and school people worked together to design school programs and teacher education programs that had considerable accountability. Funds were made available and considerable in-service was provided for both teachers and faculty in approximating the multiunit school notion.

This mirroring of the multiunit school concept by the University of Toledo faculty is reflected in Inglis's observations:

> In our college, we regrouped and took on the interdisciplinary team concept to integrate methods, educational psychology and sociology, and educational technology. Team leaders provided organizational leadership for our college teams. The IGE schools identified unit leaders for each teaching unit. The unit leaders represented the teachers in the units at the regular meetings of the IIC [Instructional Improvement Committee]. The school principal chaired these meetings. The college version of the IIC was the CIIC [College Instructional Improvement Committee] comprised of team leaders and administrators. The CIIC was chaired by the dean. The college facilitators met with the IIC in the schools, and teachers met with the CIIC on campus. Later, the CIIC was dropped or perhaps evolved into Team Council—team leaders' chairs, and division directors. The council elected its own chair. Team Council remained the curriculum coordinating body for many years. At any rate, we were doing many of the same things that the schools were doing. So if teachers complained about how hard it was to work together in teams, we knew exactly what they were talking about.

Professor Inglis sums up those times as "the most fun I ever had in my life."

An Overview of the CBTE Program

The CBTE program at Toledo was operating a fully developed CBTE program by 1973. This program was a single, comprehensive effort to bring about educational changes in the way elementary and secondary teachers were prepared as well as educational changes in the schools where these teachers were most likely to teach. In addition to the notion of a working partnership with the schools, the faculty determined that the program must be field-based (related to the real world of teaching in classrooms), and would specify the knowledge, skills, attitudes, and values (referred to as competencies) teachers needed to be effective. The faculty intended that there would be alternative means and varying lengths of time for reaching such competencies, usually within the format of an educational module.

Educational modules, as defined by the University of Toledo faculty, reflect a system for delivering instruction to achieve a specified learning outcome or objective. Modules consist of objectives, in specified behavioral terms, wherein students are administered a pretest, given instructional activities, and then administered a posttest. Modules are embedded in courses such that one course may consist of a number of individual modules.

Specifically, the CBTE program in elementary education at the University of Toledo is organized into six instructional blocks: Education 100, "Career Decisions," and Education 201, "Inquiry into Education," at the lower division; Education 320, 324, 328, and 340, "Teaching and Learning I, II, III, and IV," respectively, at the upper division level; Education 392, "Student Teaching." Each of these courses has field components that are executed as follows: During Education 100 and 201, students serve as aides during their field experience. Assignments are determined through a mutually agreed upon written contract between the student and cooperating teachers in the field and are further explicated in a field handbook. The interrelationships established in the operation of Education 320, 324, 328, 340, and 392 are basic to the entire elementary program. Each of these "blocks," taught by an interdisciplinary faculty team, has an appropriate number of schools included in the block. Each of the schools has a faculty facilitator assigned to each building. The facilitator's role includes supervision of both block students and student teachers placed in that school. In order to further explicate the nature of this course sequence, each of these courses is briefly described.

Education 100, "Introduction to Life and Career Planning," focuses upon real life decisionmaking related to three major areas of a person's life: education, work, and leisure. Students develop and use skills in self assessment, career exploration, and life planning. An important emphasis of this course is the exploration of career and educational opportunities and alternatives in educational and helping professions. Students attend class for three hours per week each quarter and participate in field placements for three hours per week for seven weeks.

Education 201, "Inquiry Into Education," is designed to follow Education 100 and must be taken prior to the professional sequence courses. It is designed to provide further information about the experiences in elementary and secondary schools. Through seven modules the students explore and participate in both university and school exercises stressing actual performance and assessment. The areas of competence developed in this course include assessment of self-concept, teaching strategies, classroom climate, curriculum, school climate, teaching roles and planning, and learning theory.

The professional sequence begins with Education 320, "Elementary Teaching-Learning I," which focuses on math. Each student must prepare to teach a mathematics unit for a group of elementary school children. The first six weeks of the course are spent learning the principles of teaching mathematics, lesson planning, and an introduction to the multiunit school system. During the final four weeks, the students are in the schools teaching children.

The second block in elementary education is Education 324, "Elementary Teaching-Learning II," wherein concepts of cognitive development and learning behaviors are incorporated into the general content of language arts. This course also includes the use of media and materials. The modules included in this course are handwriting skills, teaching reading from theory to practice, individual needs, motivation, effective teaching strategies, educational psychology, recording observed behavior, contemporary teaching-learning processes, and the cognitive development of children.

Education 328, "Elementary Teaching-Learning III," is designed to help students refine skills in developing unit plans as well as evaluation plans and procedures, with particular emphasis on elementary science instruction. Specific skill development in inquiry, questioning, classroom management, and problem solving are major modules.

Education 340, "Elementary Teaching-Learning IV," is a synthesis of skills and concepts and extensive supervised field experience in social studies. Students are provided with information on social studies methods of instruction and curriculum resources and learn about values clarification methodology, simulation and games, community resources, and the advantages of cultural diversity. Special education is also integrated into this course.

The elementary education program is grounded in a sequence that reflects the university's commitment to general education, providing a firm liberal education foundation upon which to develop the more specialized content, process, and skills of a professional training program. As well, the school expects that students in their general education program will acquire the language skills necessary for a mature mastery of writing, reading, and English. It further asks that students explore the three broad areas, "in which man orders his knowledge and experiences," including the humanities, the social sciences and the natural sciences, and mathematics.

Upon completion of the general studies program, the student enters into courses which represent areas of specialization. Each elementary candidate must select between twenty and twenty-eight hours of coursework beyond the general education requirements in one of the following five fields of elementary instruction: (1) early childhood education, (2) language arts, (3) mathematics, (4) science, or (5) social studies. One hundred ninety-two quarter hours are required for graduation and an elementary education teaching certificate. The general studies component totals approximately 109 hours; the professional education sequence sixty-four hours; and the area of specialization, twenty to twenty-eight hours, leaving the student only two to ten hours of electives, only if certain courses fulfill more than one requirement.

Conceptions of Teaching in the CBTE Program

The conception of an effective teacher embedded in the CBTE program can be viewed from multiple perspectives. We will begin with the students' perceptions. We asked students: Who models good teaching for you? What are the sources of your inspiration? How would you describe the teacher you are becoming? Responses varied but were generally compatible. Students remarked that those who modelled good teaching for them are the teachers with whom they work and also some of their professors. For example, one student noted that he remembered his elementary school teachers the most, ". . . teachers that made learning fun. I don't want it to be boring for the kids. I don't want them to stop learning; I want to make teaching a little more exciting so that it's a challenge for them and they really enjoy it." Another student mentioned a professor who was viewed as very enthusiastic and who had a lot of experience. This professor, the student noted, "is always learning more. He writes books. He encourages us to learn more, too. This professor points out resources and makes you actually want to do it. So you do it." The emphasis was on professors who were seen as challenging, enthusiastic, and creative. We asked students about the diverse perspectives the professors brought to the block courses. One student, commenting about the differences between two of her professors, recalled: "I think both perspectives are important and if you can incorporate both of them in one teacher it would be wild! . . . You try to adapt the teaching styles you see." It was not uncommon for students to suggest their notion of teaching would evolve. To wit,

> It will be easier once you're out there and teaching the particular subject, because you can get into a routine of covering what you have to cover, you can do it at your own speed, and you can adapt it to how the students are learning. If they're picking it up, you can move along faster or if they're having problems with it you just slow down and give individual help.

When asked if they could articulate a theory acquired in this program, one student responded, "We learned about Piaget. You know, the stages." When asked what one does with Piaget, another student responded, "It's just the idea. When you're in a classroom, you can be aware of it by not giving the children too difficult work to do because they're not ready for it." We asked the students if they were encouraged to be reflective about their teaching. A student responded, "Oh, yes, they encourage that in science class, and then we come back and talk about theories and what we saw violated or what was good or bad." When asked if they thought the CBTE planning process was what they'd do as a teacher, one student responded:

The CBTE program teaches us to overplan. You're always prepared. Since I have
been out in the field, I have felt I was really prepared. I mean I haven't gone in
there and said, 'What am I going to do today?' Yet, you see some of the teachers
you've had, and you compare their lesson plans to our lesson plans, and it's like
night and day.

Another student concurred, "no objectives, no goals"; and yet another student
added, "You don't ever see the curriculum guide either." However, on the
topic of planning, another student remarked: "I don't think there is any
conflict with that. You accept that they've been doing it longer and they've
gone through everything that we have and they're at that point that they don't
need to write this all down. Most of the teachers you get are very helpful with
your work."

We also explored with various faculty members which philosophy of
teaching and schooling undergirded the CBTE program. Dr. Robert Wilhoyte
is a professor in philosophy of education who has spent a great deal of time in
recent years in schools reflecting on general instruction and teaching and
learning. Wilhoyte's conception of teaching flows from these observations:
"I tell my students that we have to make distinctions between skills and
concepts, and I think elementary education in general reduces content to
skills." He attributes some of this reductionism to publishers and the production of teachers' manuals where skill acquisition is approached as if we were
"putting together a toy at Christmas." Professor Wilhoyte expressed considerable skepticism about the way students learn to teach: "Perhaps they learn in
spite of us. . . . We don't prepare them to be good teachers. They get there on
their own. If we address only the experiential dimension, then we turn out
people who are . . . streetwise." In contrast, he noted, if one assumed that the
modules only emphasize content, then "we would turn out teachers with book
learning and no common sense. We've got to synthesize those two, . . .
operationalize content, deal with real experiences of the learner and focus on
concepts. I think the CBTE program addresses that from the back door." This
professor advocates a conceptual and reflective approach to teaching.

As noted by several of the students, the faculty have contrasting styles
and orientations to teaching. A good illustration of this was an interview we
held with two professors, who seemed to approach the notion of competency
from diametrically opposite positions. One professor was a staunch advocate
of the explicated behavioral objective. In contrast, the other professor tended
not to refer to behavioral objectives in any of the concepts he taught in his
courses. A third faculty member joined us during the interview, and, at the
end, he observed,

Your last interview ought to offer you living proof that alternative philosophies
can exist hand-in-glove within the CBTE structure. They have been on the same
team, and it doesn't make any difference how you approach the subject with

either one of them, they haven't moved off this track since they've been in the program—either one of them. And I thought at one time that one of these professors might move a little bit toward a more behavioral approach and he never has. And, yet, he functions quite successfully. What a nice contrast for the students to see.

These two concepts of teaching can be contrasted by brief vignettes from our conversation with the two faculty members. The first professor observed about teaching:

One of the secrets of teaching reading and literature is that in the middle of the lesson something occurs that nobody ever thought of and, on the spur of the moment, you do it. It's not in your lesson plan and you don't evaluate it, but it's the teachable moment. Something happens. For example, I was teaching a class of elementary children and we were talking about William Armstrong's *Sounder*. At the very end of the book, I just happened to say, 'I'm so glad that there's a sequel to this book because this is very sad'. (Sounder dies, the father dies, and to me it ends with hopelessness.) And this little boy said, 'Oh no, that's not sad'. And I said, 'What's happy about it?' And he read the last two lines which say something like, "forever and ever the moon would shine down on the forest where the great coon dog Sounder travelled." That's full of hope, which had never occurred to me, and so we started talking about the way the author built up this hope to lead into the next book. . . . Well, I never planned to talk about that . . . those things you can't write down. To state that every child will do this or will do that with a certain degree of accuracy is impossible because we're talking about feelings and emotions. Something always comes up. I don't think you can always predict these events.

The second professor replied:

I'm not necessarily opposed to functionalism or seizing upon the teachable moment. However, I think that when we state in measurable terms what pupils are going to get, what we're saying is since this is the *minimum*, this is *the* money back guarantee. Now beyond that, there's a lot you get that you don't know about ahead of time and that's great. But as a teacher, I want to be comfortable that at least you're going to get this. You've got a target. If you hit the bullseye, that's great; but at least you've got a target.

Given the original emphasis on team teaching in the CBTE program, teaching is also promoted as a collaborative endeavor. As one professor stated,

Our vision was of a person who had the ability to work in a team teaching situation with other people in a school and be a part of the ongoing delivery system in the school. . . . At times, the individual could take leadership for instruction and, at other times, they would be in a support role for that instructional program.

They would have diagnostic skills and the ability to assess in a manner consistent with the school's objectives, the needs of students. And, they would also enter the profession—that first job—with a streetwise experience that came from having worked with kids in the classroom, real classrooms for four solid years. We had that in mind in this program.

Another professor discussed teaching from this perspective: "It's tied to learning theory, . . . although we rarely talk about learning theory, it's what we really are involved in after all, isn't it, . . . some view of learning that guides how we teach."

We asked whether the teacher effectiveness literature was incorporated in the program. One professor made this observation:

> Well, here's honesty. I know that as we're going through this reorganization of the program, that is a part of what we're saying, that we must better incorporate some of the new research, such as the research on teacher effectiveness. In certain courses, it is used now, so I know it exists, but it's not organized programmatically.

As we analyzed the actual modules, a great deal of skill orientation was obvious, much of which is compatible with the teacher effectiveness literature. A strong experiential base is derived both from the experiences with cooperating teachers and with the demonstration or modelling of the professors who spend a good deal of time in schools. In an attempt to put theory and research in perspective, one professor opined: "We can give them all the theories that exist, but a lot of it [teaching] is personal chemistry, confidence, and how you interact with different individuals. I can walk in and have difficulty with a student and you can walk in and the student will be an angel."

In summary, our attempt to capture various conceptions of teaching yielded some patterns. Explicit in the CBTE program at the University of Toledo is considerable emphasis on the specification of knowledge, skills, attitudes, and values, which are currently explicated in series of modules connected with each course or block experience. The behavioral orientation is pervasive. Faculty continually refer to it; students are very aware of it. Still, students, professors, and classroom teachers with whom we spoke also talked about teaching that is largely personal in nature, somewhat theory-based but mostly experiential and reflected differently depending on which professor is teaching the course or module. In the final analysis, students are aware of what they are expected to know and do. As one student summarized:

> They give you concepts they want you to grasp by the end of the class or quarter. The program has given me competence and confidence to teach in an elementary classroom. So, whether I have all the competencies, I may be lacking in one or more, but I think overall we understand the material we're going to teach, classroom management, behavioral management, test writing, and being able to

handle the situations that arise. The way you do that is being very well-trained and adaptable.

THE DISTINCTIVENESS OF THE
UNIVERSITY OF TOLEDO'S CBTE PROGRAM

In each institution we visited, we sought to describe the distinctive character-istics of the elementary education program. We have called on the multiple perspectives of faculty, students, members of departments across campus, and teachers in the field. Our inquiry at the University of Toledo was no exception. And, because we arrived at Toledo and found the teacher educa-tion program essentially in a state of change, we attempted to identify distinc-tiveness by pursuing with the faculty those aspects of the program that they would most likely want to preserve. The associate dean for undergraduate programs, Professor Jim Johnson, had a number of ideas in this regard. Of the distinctiveness of the CBTE program Johnson stated:

> We're committed to a *module-based format*. We like the notion of modules that are public to the students, so that they see in advance performance objectives and some indication of the kinds of classroom activities they need to achieve these and the form of evaluation. I think that's enduring. We're also committed to *teaming* in those areas where we think it's the best way to go. So, we're not going to move teaming out of the program, but we're going to use it more selectively. We're committed to *faculty visibility in the field* in supervisory activities as distin-guished from sending out only clinical professors. We are committed to *coopera-tive relationships* with the public and parochial schools. We have excellent relationships with them. It amazes me the amount of cooperation we get with very little remuneration on our part. We want to keep those bonds strong and make sure they endure. Finally, we are committed to *preventing such department autonomy* that they lose sight of the total *program*.

These attributes were reinforced by the associate dean for graduate studies, Ed Nussel:

> Jim Johnson summarized it very well. One thing that's enduring are the *certain general or generic skills* that all students need in the elementary or secondary program—the faculty agree on that. *The structure* will also be the same. That's very important because the structure came about in a very sound way in terms of the way the curriculum was developed. The most important persisting arrange-ment in the program is the field-based part of the program. This program would not succeed if we didn't have the cooperation from the schools.

Later in our descriptive profile of the University of Toledo, we describe other enduring characteristics of the program that have more to do with the delivery of the program than with the actual curriculum characteristics described in the above interviews. Particularly, these attributes are faculty field supervision in the program, the interdisciplinary nature of the program, and the nature of team teaching. We return to these features, but here we review some of the enduring curricular features mentioned in the interviews above and reflected as well in the faculty and students' descriptions of what occurs in the program.

The Developmental Sequence

On paper, the CBTE program has a definite sequence. It begins with an introductory career decisionmaking course, moves through general pedagogical concerns, and proceeds through methods of teaching the various disciplines. The manifestation of the program allows students to move through the program in a block format, wherein four hours of every morning are devoted to a particular disciplinary block including time during that four-hour block to work in the schools. We found in interview after interview attestations to the developmental sequence. One student described it as follows.

> I like the way they gradually build up to the amount of work. Before beginning in a math block, you work up to designing a unit, and I think that helped me a lot. That's one thing I liked about it. It wasn't that, all at once, you have to write a unit. I was prepared for it. You don't actually have to write a whole unit by yourself until you're in the social studies class. In the math class, you write lesson plans. In language arts, you do write a unit but it's not as complicated. In science, you team teach with a partner and that's good because you have someone to help with the load and you combine ideas. And then in social studies, you write a unit by yourself and teach it by yourself. By that time you're supposed to know what you're doing.

Complementary to the notion that the students' sense of security is built up over time is the way their skills are developed. Professor Darryl Yorke describes the growth of those students from technician to artist.

> As they move along, we'll say to them, 'Suppose your objective is to recite the letters of the alphabet A to Z in sequence. What kind of condition statement are you going to have to accomplish that? What kind of degree statement are you going to have to assess that?' Either you can do it or you can't. In some cases, a degree may be presumed. And then we start to lean on them and say, 'Now, put it through your own heads—test this out. You were technicians before. We want you to become a little more like scientists now'. When Herb Sandberg [another professor] deals with them, then, they become artists.

Yorke spoke of this developmental sequence of increased responsibility over time. He has seen these students grow, develop, and emerge as more self-confident, capable teachers:

Even the students say, 'I was scared to death. Now it doesn't even bother me.' I'm sort of like a drill sergeant saying, 'Hey, you've got to get this in shape'. Now they've got it in shape and they get all pumped up and they say, 'I'm ready to go out there'. And the first thing I know, they're going to dig in their heels because you can't plan something on paper that's going to work that well when you put live bodies in it. Somebody needs to be there and give them a push, . . . if I'm not there, they're going to say, 'hey, you were the son-of-a-gun who got me to plan this thing . . . now I want you out here to watch me succeed, too'. Well, the affect is incredible. I go right off the chart at the end of the quarter. They love the guy they hated at the beginning of the quarter.

The notion of the developmental sequence is corroborated by the sense in which the students experience cohort groupings and a sense of shared ordeal as they move through their blocks. We address this program attribute next.

Cohort Groups

In each institution visited, we sought from the students a sense in which they measure or assess the nature of their time together, the extent to which they are enabled or facilitated when they were in cohort groups and what it means to experience the teacher education program in some shared capacity. As we asked about the sequential and developmental nature of the program, students seemed to be saying yet another thing about the program. Some of the comments were, "It's just easier for you, I think, to go through this together." "Yeah, it's nice to stay with the same group." Another student noted, "It's also the same people and if you have problems or need some ideas, you can call a friend that's in the same block and it's easier for you to get something done." These views are corroborated by faculty members Hughes Moir who dreams a bit in an interview about the way he would like to see a four-course cycle and then student teaching in the continuing development of this program. He would like to see the students participate in the development of their instructional skills throughout five consecutive quarters. He observed, "We came to recognize that we needed some sort of ongoing relationship with students. That's how we began it. And indeed, during the first two years, I worked with only two groups of students. We handled hundreds of students in teams of people from elementary education, social foundations, and educational psychology."

Consequently, from the beginning, the faculty intended to build some kind of cohort group experience. The attempt to develop cohort groups, however, is compounded by the fact that most of the students do not live on campus and a lot have jobs, some working full-time—forty hours a week. One faculty member said, "We do have a lot of mobility in students. They really don't feel much affiliation with the university as a way of life." Thus, creating some kind of life space and socialization is difficult. Socialization is inhibited as well by the lack of building space for students to gather in small and informal groups. Even so, student reports of the way they work together and the time they spend on shared projects in the blocks suggest that some semblance of a cohort concept is embedded in the developmental sequence.

Competency Modules

We have already directed some attention to the notion of modules of instruction embedded within the course structure. As many as nine to fifteen modules may exist in a given course, each one typically organized around a specific skill area. One student says, "the modules are like a guide, like a skeleton of the course, and they present the materials that you're going to learn in the course." Each module must be completed by a certain date. Modules not only make it clear to students what is expected of them, but also serve as a way of keeping some consistency in the curriculum. As Nussel noted:

> Our experience with traditional teacher education suggests that the course may be very different if one professor teaches or if another does. And yet it's the same course. There's no consistency. Even with a common syllabus, it gets distorted by whoever teaches the course. The nice thing about this program is that all the students get the same modules, and they may have some variation built in with who ever happens to be on the team at the time, but there is a consistent thread no matter who staffs those teams. Over time, some of the modules have changed very little, others have changed a lot, and still others have disappeared.

These modules range anywhere from twenty to 100 pages. They are characterized by behaviorally stated objects, assignments for the students, and means of assessing these. The modules are packaged in plastic covers and three-hole punched, so that when students purchase them from the bookstore, the assumption is that these modules will go into the student's notebook. We asked students about their ability to retain modules and find materials when they needed them, and no particular difficulty was expressed.

Mastery Learning

Hughes Moir recalled that, from the beginning,

> the essence of the program that we have now is built in part on a model—a learning model that was behaviorally oriented and was organized around IGE programming. There was an attempt to do pre- and posttesting and mastery learning. I should add that some people were zealous about this and other people had not the foggiest idea about it, and then there were other people in between at the beginning.

While the mastery concept has been embedded in the program from the beginning, it has also been somewhat troublesome in the minds of the program architects. Jim Johnson reflected, "Mastery learning is certainly important to us, I suppose, but it remains a concept with which a number of us are not quite happy. To a certain degree the concept of mastery learning has moved to a questionable list in the new program." Mastery learning is predicated on the idea that given enough time, enough options, and good instructions, students will achieve minimum competence. The practical problem Johnson notes is the use of the incomplete (I) grade, which is carried into the next quarter when students don't complete modules. If too many modules are incomplete, the student cannot advance into the next block. This is exemplified in the following informal, but nevertheless important rule:

> If a student received an incomplete in a particular course, if it were not a teaching performance criterion but if it were some reading or a curriculum requirement— something like that—and he or she could complete it over Christmas, we would probably let that person go on unless it were into student teaching. If there were major things, however, we would say, 'Hey, you've got to come back next quarter when these modules are taught again'.

Johnson, then, saw the problems with the mastery notion not in terms of assessing mastery reliably but in terms of problems of time and logistics, especially when students must recycle lessons two or three times.

> One begins to wonder if some faculty aren't, in fact, putting words in the student's mouth and trying to get him to understand the concept in order to avoid additional recycling. We're also concerned with grading, in terms of whether a person who takes three times to it get it right and then eventually comes to the desired criterion performance level should get the same grade as the person who got it right the first time. And, what are our obligations in terms of communicating that to the public schools? If you don't perform well the first time, is the highest *grade* you can get in the module a B? Should the highest grade attainable be reduced with each recycle? I'm committed to having students recycle, but the recycling to an A in every module I don't know about, and there are a lot of individuals on the faculty who have some problems with that.

Thus, while mastery is still embedded in the program, its future is problematic largely, we suspect, because it continues to be extremely difficult to operationalize in a traditional university organization of courses and quarters.

Sense of Rigor

As we journeyed across institutions, we probed students and faculty to assess the nature of academic rigor reflected in the teacher education program. Often we asked how difficult a particular education course was compared to other courses in the university. We asked how taxing the assignments were, the readings, and the expectations of the professors. At the University of Toledo, the stage for each discussion was set by vice president for Academic Affairs,

William Free, who opined, "perception is that grades are easier to get in education than they are in some other fields. The toughest standards are still in engineering. They're also the best students." Vice President Free extends his comments to say that CBTE is often a misunderstood program from the perspective of this mastery concept. "The concerns for quality are raised in terms of the real thing in the program—that the student works at that competency until he or she gets proficient in it. And that's probably a good thing, too. What philosophically is a problem, though, is that there is some point at which you must establish accomplishment within a certain amount of time."

One student particularly countered the Provost's perspective about the rigor attached to engineering: "My brother's in engineering and he says, 'Oh, you have the easiest courses'. Yet, I'm doing homework constantly, and he never does homework. So maybe it's just the time we put into it. It's not that it's so much harder." And another student added, "It *is* time consuming." There are differences in terms of the quality of the coursework, as one student observed: "It is a lot of busy work." This is countered by another student who said, "It's not busy work if it's important. You have to do the research if you want to learn what to do." Yet another student who attempted to reconcile these positions remarked:

> If you don't have a lot of knowledge about a topic, you can't teach it. If you go in there thinking you know about the topic, it's always in the back of your mind that somebody's going to ask you something you don't know. You want to appear to know—to make them believe you know. Some preparation is busy work, but I think it gives me a lot of satisfaction going in there prepared, knowing that I know everything I'm going to teach them.

Still another student observed that "you get out of it what you put into it. There are some days when I can think that it is busy work, but there is more to it than actually meets the eye." Another student corroborated this: "You can get as complex about it as you want. You don't have to take the skin off the topic, but you can get more out of it if you want more out of it. You can go beyond the minimums in modules."

A student advisor capsulized what is needed for a CBTE program to be understood by students:

> There are some negatives that some of them struggle with. There are a lot of skills, a lot of objectives, and a lot of work to do—a lot of paper work—in the field, on campus, in different places on campus, and at times they struggle with keeping all of the loose ends together. And some of them are more organized, and they're better able to handle it. Others tend to procrastinate, to not be well-organized and are going to have difficulty with the competency-based program. Some students will say that the academic part of it is not as demanding as the process that they actually go through. I think it's probably a misconception because a lot of times they are learning a great deal, but they don't see it as a

chapter or if they had read a book in a traditional course. They don't realize that the objective they're dealing with is a very complex knowledge type of objective. They just may not see it that way. It's a shift for them to move into the objectives and the modules, and they don't see it quite the same way as they do a science course.

The faculty was continually struggling with the need to better articulate to the students the new and different meanings of a CBTE program as it differs from a traditional program. This is yet another indicator of the difficulty of sustaining a very unusual curricular format in a traditional university setting.

The Relationship of the Arts and Sciences to the CBTE Program

We asked at this and other campuses about the perceived importance of the arts and sciences or general studies program. In general, the students reported that most of the courses they took in general studies were because they were required and in many instances, the courses were not functional or useful for the kinds of knowledge or concepts they needed to present in a classroom. They seemed to accept with some reservation the necessity of completing a general studies requirement and the idea that it would somehow lead toward a more liberally educated person. Some students described what happened in these courses as, "a little deep." In some instances, particularly a few courses mentioned in the natural sciences, the curriculum was simply not appropriate, they felt, for education majors. On the other hand, not all students were as vocational: "I think you should be a well-rounded person. You have to know what's going in the world, and you can always apply that curriculum. I think if you're not reading, you're just not going to be prepared."

Understandably, Vice President Free supports the importance of the general studies curriculum. "It's another reason why you need to have role models in the teaching cadre in the College of Education that show the students that it's not enough simply to be someone who relates well to students. You must have some higher notion or higher vision." Furthermore, Free observes that a quality general studies education is linked to the quality of our faculty. He says, "That's the attribute of a prestigious institution and by implication it is these people in the general studies with whom our students in all professions should come in contact."

Keeping in mind the developmental sequence of the program, the development of cohort groups, the modular concept, and the concept of mastery learning, the sense of rigor embedded in the program and the relationship to the arts and sciences, we will now look at the nature of the field experience component in the curriculum and the delivery of those field experiences, and other structural aspects of the program.

The Field Component of the CBTE Program

Clearly, the field component of the CBTE program constitutes a distinctive feature of the college's program. Joan Inglis was, in many ways, the architect of the field component for the CBTE program, and we rely heavily on her reflections to characterize the nature of field experiences in the program. Field experiences are part of each of the professional education courses, from Education 100, the career decision course, through the methods blocks, and, of course, in student teaching. From the beginning, according to Inglis, the faculty intended to devise a substantive field component.

We asked Inglis what her contribution was to the development of the CBTE program. She replied, "My task was to develop the field program." She recalled the fact that as the faculty were developing the CBTE program, the city of Toledo was beginning to integrate the concept of the multiunit school or IGE in some of its own buildings.

> As we were developing the model program, it was [Ed] Dickson's creative genius that started it and then he turned it over to faculty development. I can remember we were working on all kinds of specifications and courses and cost analyses and that kind of thing . . . then we used Klausmeier to tell us about his ideal elementary school. And we became the first university outside of Wisconsin to work intensively with IGE.

In the process of developing the model program, four schools were opened with the IGE concept. Particularly, Professor Inglis recalled one school where she was sent with thirteen student teachers and one research assistant to work on the development of the IGE concept: "It was an all-black school and we were all white people and we had a time. But at the close of the year, we had an IGE school." It was at this time that Dean Dickson appointed Inglis to develop the undergraduate field experience and become a major administrative officer of the college. During the course of her tenure, all aspects of field experience were ultimately pulled under her jurisdiction, from early field experiences, continuing field experiences in the methods courses, to student teaching. She reflected:

> We turned it around, and we developed our own college program modelled after IGE. We were convinced, and I say we, but really Ed Dickson saw it, and a bunch of us agreed that if we were doing the same thing as the schools, we could communicate better with them. And so they were brought into all of our development. The teachers in those four schools were members of our retreats—the program development stage. Then, together, we started a multiunit school metropolitan league for teacher education.

The intention of this was that the University of Toledo could draw on IGE schools as its field resource in several ways. One way was that understanding the organization of the multiunit school could create not only a model for instruction on campus, but a way of thinking about teaching for the students. It included an emphasis on team teaching that would be modelled by the professors and executed by the students. It offered, as well, a way of decisionmaking in curriculum development that was collaborative, and a sense of the nature of goals in the schools and the intricate relationship between these and the expectations of the teachers in them. Joan Inglis recalls that she and faculty colleague Tom Gibney "marched over to our closest school, and I don't remember how many students we had in that block, but we put them all in that one school for the field component, and we basically spent our lives out there." So the CBTE concept was facilitated not only by placement in IGE schools but also by saturating one particular building rather than having students spread over different schools in the area.

Another concept supported by this match of the IGE multiunit school with the CBTE program was that teachers who ultimately served as cooperating teachers were reflecting the same philosophy and knowledge of the program as were the faculty. There was great exchange and interaction between the faculty and the teachers, all of which supported the development of the student. In summary, it appears that the CBTE program historically worked well when there was a compatible conceptualization in the schools which served the program. According to Inglis:

> There was a period of time in the elementary program when the elementary faculty were absolutely living in those classrooms and giving teachers all kinds of support. And at one time, the teachers had major control over student evaluations. They were expected to go through the student teaching modules and complete numerous checklists designed to record student growth. It was the same way in each of the teaching blocks. Then, as faculty members began to stay in the same schools, they developed this tremendous rapport with teachers and students and they sort of took over a lot of that responsibility.

Over time, problems evolved in the field component because of the waning interest in IGE in the schools, difficulties in staffing the schools with faculty, and the time-consuming nature of the field experiences. But, historically, it was the multiunit concept mirrored both on campus and in the field that, in many ways, was the glue that tied together the field and on-campus components of the CBTE program. How the field component aspects of the program were managed is informative and we turn now to that topic.

The Notion of Field Facilitators

The field experience component Dr. Inglis described was constituted on the notion that faculty members would be assigned as facilitators in school sites. They would not forsake their teaching responsibilities but would, in fact, take on a particular school and adopt it as their own. Several professors have been identified with certain schools for long periods of time. Professor Wilhoyte, for instance, has now been at one diocesan school for nine years and is so established there that instead of calling the principal to see if students can be placed in that building, Professor Inglis talks directly to Professor Wilhoyte. As Darryl Yorke recalled, the continuity of the CBTE program at the University of Toledo was largely based on providing pedagogical knowledge in on-campus settings and then travelling with the students to the field to attest to the execution of that knowledge. That, Professor Yorke acknowledges, is the "magic" of the field component.

The University of Toledo was one of the first institutions in Ohio to adopt the notion of early and continuous field experiences. The university created an early experience in the "career exploration mode" in the early 1970s. The faculty continued the notion of field experience throughout the general pedogogical courses and the special methods courses, such that three years before Ohio required these increased field experiences for teacher education, the university was requiring more than 600 hours of field experiences, including the student teaching experience. In this respect, the University of Toledo was the model for the field experience aspects of the state standards. Two other program dimensions characterized structure and organization of the CBTE model: team teaching and interdisciplinary education.

Team Teaching and Interdisciplinary Curriculum

The notions of team teaching and interdisciplinary education are inextricably linked. Certain courses are blocked together and professors from various disciplines design and teach those courses together. As Jim Johnson recalled:

> We put together the program years ago, and we made a commitment to inter-disciplinary team teaching. We thought it was a good idea. We still believe it's a good idea. I've taught for thirteen years on the Secondary Education 340 team, which is somewhat equivalent to the Elementary 340 team. It's a twelve-quarter hour course, which is equivalent to three courses. Math, science, English, and social studies majors are all assigned to that course, and both general and content specific methods are addressed. The general methods include instructional strategies, but methods needed in social studies and math or science are also taught there, along with some attention to reading in the content areas. We also used to integrate educational psychology and special education and some attention to media, all of which we've since moved into another course. It's been a big blend. In that particular course, you've got to have, as we initially conceived it, a minimum of five professors to span the content.

The way these blocks are staffed now is somewhat less than the five professors described by Johnson, but multiple professors are still in charge of instruction and the students are distributed over several schools for the field component. It is, from all perspectives, a monumental staffing concern to place professors in these methods courses and also to ensure that professors are in the schools, to observe the students during the block experience.

Faculty reported many positive features of the team teaching and interdisciplinary concept. Not only were they able to integrate various curricular and discipline interests, they were able to share with each other by virtue of observing and being involved in one another's teaching. The exchanges we reported earlier from two professors who see themselves on opposite sides of "the behavioral objective issue" is an example of the dialogue provoked when professors are teamed in these block experiences. This kind of diversity was the original intention of the team teaching notion.

Change in the Stable Setting

In summary, in 1973 the University of Toledo implemented a comprehensive elementary program, the CBTE program, subsequently adopted by the secondary disciplines as well. The model, at that time, manifested many of the aspects that were associated nationally with CBTE. The program was explicated in the form of objectives manifested in modules. The modules were linked in courses which became heavily field-based blocks. A mastery-level approach to instruction was employed. The conception of schooling undergirding the program reflected the multiunit concept embraced in the schools which were used for field placements. The organization of the faculty and the process of curriculum development mirrored the IGE concept. Faculty were organized for course instruction through interdisciplinary teams and also served as field facilitators.

When such a major and comprehensive curriculum development effort occurs, it often becomes locked in place. Hughes Moir commented, "We needed to put several things in place and some things got implemented to the point where they weren't perfect, but it was decided that they would be fixed and we would do no more tinkering with them. There is a need for that at some point. But at the same time it violated the notion that the program had grown."

We want to address this tension in this particular section of our description of the program's history. The point being, can a program so elaborate in its design and difficult to implement be constantly changing? Ed Nussel recalled: "This is a program that was built on change and sometimes the change has been well thought out and sometimes it hasn't." He went on to reflect on the way this program achieved some stability over all these years but also how it has been receptive to necessary changes:

> We are our own critics. In fact, in some respects we're almost masochistic in the way that the program changes over time. The only thing that really runs up a red flag with me is when somebody makes the remark that the program needs to be

changed, as if we never changed the doggone thing. And anybody who says that about this program just doesn't know anything about the program. It has changed a number of times, in terms of the sequence of the courses and programmatic changes within the courses. Modules are dropped out and new modules are put in; not always as systematically as we would like, but often as a result of some task force recommendation. We get feedback from students; we get feedback from the field; we get feedback from each other; and sometimes the changes are imposed by external agencies. For example, NCATE says that multiculturalism is to be a part of the *entire* program . . . the same thing is true with special education.

In Nussel's mind, change has occurred rather continually in the program. Now, however, the faculty is into what Nussel refers to as "fairly significant revisions." According to Johnson:

The faculty are not interested in destroying the program and going back to square one, but this is a significant revision. At one time a couple of years ago, I thought maybe that it would mean a whole new program. But when it came down to really doing it, the faculty reaffirmed its satisfaction with the general operation of this program, the way it's set up and the philosophy behind it.

During our visits to the University of Toledo, the faculty were and continue to be engaged in this significant revision process. We were interested in the questions being raised in this major revision about the students, the institution, and the setting wherein the program exists. The changes proposed should be helpful to all teacher educators considering new program development.

THE SUSTAINING NATURE OF THE CBTE PROGRAM

The University of Toledo has benefitted for many years from close ties with the Toledo community. Toledo, the nation's fortieth largest city and the fourth largest in Ohio, is the trading center for fourteen counties of northwestern Ohio and southeastern Michigan. Lake Erie and nearby waterways provide excellent facilities for fishing, boating, water skiing, ice skating, and other water activities. Toledo is known as "the glass capital of the world" and the home of the world-famous Jeep vehicles. The city is one of the nation's principle railroad centers and houses the headquarters of six of the 500 largests U. S. industries and businesses: Sheller-Globe Corporation, Dana Corporation, Champion Spark Plug Company, Libbey-Owens-Ford Company, Owens-Corning Fiberglass Corporation, and the Owens-Illinois Company.

Major attractions in Toledo include the internationally famous Toledo Museum of Art, well-known for its collections of glass, paintings, sculpture, and decorative art. It is host to world acclaimed musicians during regular performances of the Toledo Symphony Orchestra and the Toledo Opera Association. The Toledo Zoo is toured by more than 350,000 vistors annually. Toledo is, in every sense of the word, an urban community. Because the University of Toledo was a city university before it became a state university, it reflects a curriculum that is responsive to students in the Toledo area. Vice President Free described Toledo in this way:

> Toledo is a blue-collar city, and this university has its roots in the blue-collar ethic. Traditionally, it's been an urban university whose mission has been to bring in the middle class—people who were first-generation college students. And, so, there is some of the blue-collar attitude. Students go into the major that pays the most. We have a 100 percent placement rate in pharmacy, and the average salary last spring was $29,000. Well, you can imagine they're pounding down the doors to get into pharmacy.

Historically, 90 percent of the University of Toledo's students came from the Toledo area. Of this year's freshman class, 55 percent came from Toledo. The university is moving rapidly to achieve a balanced ratio of in-city to out-of-the city students, which suggests that perhaps someday the university will become more residential than it currently is. According to Vice President Free, the university's clientele look on college largely from a vocational perspective.

In addition to this vocational perspective, there is the question of the social perspective of the students. Even though Toledo is an urban area, one gets the sense that students are largely middle-class, not lower-middle-class, and more suburban or small-town in orientation. As one student recalled, "I came from the country, from a real small school, and I always felt when I started that I wanted to go back and teach in a small school where there were no blacks in my school. But now that I've been here I would like to teach, not inner city, but a public city school. That has changed for me." In terms of financial support, nearly 85 percent of the students are now receiving some kind of financial aid. As one counselor reported, "we have a lot of students who come in that middle class where they have to work. And many families have several children in school simultaneously. We also have a lot of parents in school. We have average student age of twenty-six, not eighteen or twenty-two, so we have a lot of adults attending school." The counselors documented the number of students who are returning, already with a bachelor's degree, but who want teaching certification. This number constitutes more than 20 percent of the college's applicants; 25 percent of the College of Education students are residential.

A portrait of the typical student served by the CBTE program suggests the following: The students are typically nonresidential and hold full- or part-time jobs while attending school. The University of Toledo program is in a densely populated area, thereby allowing for placements in geographic regions approximate to Toledo, such that commonly students do not have to leave the area to acquire teaching positions. The CBTE program creates modified cohort groups so that even though students are not in a residential experience, they can build relationships with other students during the block program.

Students do not appear to come to the University of Toledo's College of Education because of its CBTE program. It is, rather, that students attend the university because it is convenient, it is financially affordable, and the job prospects for Toledo graduates are good.

Nonetheless, the College of Education has brought a great deal of acclaim to the University of Toledo and has received many accolades for its CBTE program, including the AACTE Certificate of Recognition (1974), the Ohio State Department of Education identification of Toledo as the first college evaluated under its new teacher education standards with 100 percent compliance (1981), and this commendation by the NCATE in 1982: "Of the nearly 100 institutions whose programs in professional education were evaluated by NCATE in 1981–82, this report was clearly the most positive."

In addition, the college has a research arm through the Center for Educational Research and Services whose goal is to assist school districts by researching a particular local problem for a school district, conducting on-site in-service, providing educational consultants, conducting evaluations, and developing joint proposals with university and school involvement. The college also sustains an Educational Improvement Center, which provides diagnostic and tutorial services in reading and mathematics for the metropolitan community. The Ada B. Stevens Early Childhood Education Demonstration and Research Center provides a model preschool curriculum for community preschoolers and is a locus of clinical and research activities and Carver Teacher Education Center serves as a laboratory for undergraduate students in the CBTE program.

It is obvious from the commendations the college has received and from the familiarity exhibited by the provost and other faculty members whom we interviewed that the CBTE program is viewed favorably, perhaps because it has a nationally recognized program that has attracted interest from all over the country; our visit being one example.

At this point, then, we direct our attention to prevalent concerns expressed by faculty members focusing largely on three areas of concern: the nature of the field component, the nature of team teaching, and the interdisciplinary approach used in the blocks. We found these three distinguishing characteristics of the university's CBTE program most enduring, most meaningful in the minds of the faculty, and yet most problematic in terms of sustaining that program. James Johnson, an associate dean, is responsible for coordinating planned changes. He is well aware of this tension: "I'm very concerned about being able to change the program to meet faculty desires. What I'm concerned about is that I retain a program that has a distinctive identity with the components that have given it a recognizable national identity." While Johnson and other members of the faculty are interested in sustaining the program, they must address the economic inefficiences and the commitment of time necessary to maintain the extensive field component of the program against pressures to increase the research capacity of the college, while also creating opportunities for several new faculty to be creative architects in the program.

Beginning with the interdisciplinary team teaching concept, according to Johnson, "the price to obtain that was very high. And the faculty are very clear. That's not a price they want to pay right now. If you remove too much of this teaming, then you pull back and you've got a program that looks pretty much like anybody else's. The problem is that, over the years, team teaching has turned into 'turn' teaching; whereas faculty used to teach together, now one person comes in and teaches and then another person." The associate dean speculated that ultimately, over time, there will be more turn teaching, and that although experiences would be blocked, they would be taught sequentially in a single disciplinary fashion. According to Johnson, "interdisciplinary team teaching is gone in the block, but you will find it in two places." He was referring to the revision of two of the entry-level courses wherein the curricular content will be revised, but with an effort to retain some of the best features of team teaching because multiple disciplines are involved here. Thus, the best of faculty working with graduate students will offer a strong core, interdisciplinary introduction to the program.

As to faculty serving in facilitator roles in field experiences, Johnson projected: "We want our faculty in the school, but we don't want them there five days a week running around like they were clinical professors. . . ." What's envisioned is a team of perhaps two faculty members and two or three graduate students in specified schools where the faculty members would be there less frequently and on call to deal with major problems. Currently, faculty members as facilitators have eight to ten students. The basic plan is that faculty who teach the course (for instance, a math education course) would have a vested interest in ensuring that the field experiences are well-articulated and well-managed, but most observations would be handled by graduate teaching associates attached to the course. Graduate students would be prepared for their supervision responsibility in an ongoing supervision seminar.

With regard to the notions of competencies, modules, and mastery learning, we asked what the future might hold for these. The faculty has engaged in a review of the competencies desired of students in the program. As faculty evaluate students, Johnson suggested that a core list of not more than twenty competencies is a goal in this revision process. When asked whether these would continue to be called competencies, Johnson responded, "We're not going to get rid of this focus. The dean is committed to this. We're going to revisit the question of which competencies and why." In terms of the future of modules, Johnson speculated,

I don't think that we'll retain the term *module*, but there will very probably be the explicitness in what we want our students to achieve. Maybe they will call it a *syllabus*, but that's immaterial. The difference between a module and a unit is a semantic distinction as far as I'm concerned. If I have a syllabus that is competency-based and broken up into units, that's fine. Whatever we do is going to be standardized, and there will be no resistance on the part of the faculty in this regard, because we will have faculty members coming in and out of the program and we must have a monitoring system to assess the competencies. We can't have the same freedom of changing a syllabus whenever we feel like it, as we do with other programs. We're going to have to devise a standard curriculum framework that is reminiscent of the modular format, whether we choose to use the term *module* or not.

We reviewed with the dean and his staff the various aspects of the CBTE program, some of which will be sustained and some of which will probably be eliminated in an effort to make the program more effective and efficient. Clearly, the impetus for the current change effort at Toledo has been precipitated by faculty interest. A high-quality program is the first priority. As Johnson noted, "If the faculty believe the program is no longer effective, then we need to do something different. While Dean Rusche and the faculty continue to be concerned with the distinctive nature of the program, Johnson observed that, "if the faculty members are satisfied that they have delivered a quality product to the marketplace and those students find success in their jobs, then they are less concerned about citations for a 'model' program."

More important, and uppermost in the minds of program developers at the University of Toledo, is the need to sustain those people who were the original architects of this program while integrating the interests of new faculty who have recently come to the University of Toledo. As Ed Nussel observed, "The old guard is pretty thinned out. And that makes it interesting because the program has persisted even though many of those people have moved on. I suspect that the program would have changed more slowly had they stayed, but as I said there's always been this change disposition built in." Jim Johnson reflected, as well, on the changing nature of the faculty:

> Some of the old guard are still here, but we have some new people now and if a program is going to be vital, they must have ownership in the program and they've got to like it and they've got to implement it in their own ways. Yet, we don't want a whole variety of imprints that make the program lose its integrity. This is partly a therapeutic activity for faculty and we want to build ownership.

The current change at the University of Toledo is significant, yet many of the program tenets remain. The program is distinguished by a very resource-intensive, field-based, competency-based orientation. This is a time of change for the University of Toledo because its faculty is changing — its goals are changing as scholarly inquiry is becoming more and more central to the mission of the institution. As Dean Rusche noted, "The changes being made in the teacher education program at Toledo will not destroy the concept of competency-based teacher education, but adjustments to the program and its mode of delivery will create efficiencies that should better allow faculty at this university to continue to fill the multiple roles of researcher, teacher, and community educator."

The College of Education at the University of Toledo has a rich and sustaining tradition of innovation, and we can only speculate that the impetus for changing the competency-based program will allow for the continuing development of a no less committed faculty to the preparation of future teachers, in keeping with the most positive attributes of the competency-based teacher education movement.

4

Hard Work and a Commitment to Teaching

THE UNIVERSITY OF WISCONSIN-EAU CLAIRE

Most of us, however distant past it might be, can recall with considerable clarity, parental advice. A pervasive theme for both of us growing up when we did in Protestant, middle-class, Midwestern families focused on the value of hard work. "You get what you earn." "Hard work never killed anyone." This value was manifest daily; parents toiled long hours and, early on, expected similar behavior from their children. Thus, we were not unfamiliar with a work ethos. Those who extol the fruits of hard and honest labor are hardly uncommon today. Rarely, however, have we observed this so centrally and explicitly stated in an academic setting at whatever level as in the elementary teacher education faculty at the University of Wisconsin-Eau Claire campus. "Hard" work is the major theme in our portrayal of this program.

THE WORK ETHIC THEME

The chairperson of the elementary education program, Ben Thompson, recalled expectations set forth for new recruits to his program. Not without passion and almost parental pride he began:

> I tell them if you come here, you're going to work. These are all people who have recently been in college and in Ph.D. programs and typically in a large university where their major professors have two hours of classes a week, and I tell them they have to be here at 7:30 or 8:00 every morning, and they're not leaving until 4:30 or 5:00. You're going to be flooded with students all day long. If you're not supervising, you're going to have students in your office, so you're not going to be able to do any extended preparation during the day. You're not going to be

able to check any papers during this time. If you think you're going to do research, you're going to have to do that on Saturdays and Sundays. I tell them that this is the kind of institution we are. Don't come here if you think you're going to have the kind of life you've seen in a large university, because you may not even have time to eat dinner some days. And I tell them that's what we *want*. And if you don't *want* this kind of job don't come. And we have some people laugh at us, of course, but maybe we're really lucky because eventually we get good people: Glennellen Pace, Sherrie Macaul, Ken Schmidt—these people are all doing it.

Indeed, these people appear to be doing *it* although not without problems. Thompson informs us, for example, there is considerable aggravation among faculty at an out-state campus in a state system such as UW-Eau Claire because of the lower salaries compared with the faculty of the main campus in Madison. (The UW-Eau Claire is a master's-level institution with a teaching as opposed to a research and teaching priority.) He discusses a recent legislative proposal to provide faculty members at institutions such as UW-Eau Claire with catch-up salary increments and how these are needed in order to address what could be a fundamental morale problem at institutions like his own.

Despite what some faculty perceive as a lack of recognition for their efforts, formal leadership in the School of Education expects a lot from them and appears to get it. We asked Rodney Johnson, then dean of the School of Education, if he could describe the ethos in the School of Education and the Elementary Education Program, particularly, from the perspective of students enrolled. Typically reflective in our discussions, he responded quickly on this occasion: "Well, I think these students would say that it's based on hard work. I think they see that this faculty works very hard and that, in turn, the faculty expects them to work hard."

In a subsequent discussion, the dean shared the following assessment of his faculty:

We always have a concern that our faculty attend to the teaching task as well as possible because we all know that they are models for the students who are going out to work in classrooms. I think you will see that people on our faculty, while maybe not 'fashionable,' are neat and clean. They are well-dressed. You don't see any grubbies or dirty jeans and so on. That's the way we want to direct our teachers to the schools. We want them to have some pride, and also we want them to plan and work hard at teaching. There's that phrase *hard work* again!

There are some who attribute this work ethic as indigenous to this relatively rural, Midwestern location. Ronald Satz, dean of the School of Graduate Studies, described the typical student at UW-Eau Claire as follows:

Well, there's a real work ethic here. Many of our undergraduate students are first-generation college students. Many of them are coming here at great financial sacrifice into the future. They're either on loans or a combination of loans, work study funds, and scholarships. They take school very seriously. They work hard. They also have fun . . . they play hard too. They do both, of course, but they do work hard. I think that's probably truer here than at other places I've been . . . in Illinois, Maryland, and Tennessee. . . . . Certainly it's truer of any of the places I've been in my career.

When we asked the faculty to describe the program or characterize campus life, we did not bring the work ethic into the conversation; it was repeatedly volunteered.

The then vice chancellor at UW-Eau Claire, Dr. Norman Doorenbos, was quite familiar with the elementary program. We had the opportunity to visit with him at length and he talked knowledgeably about several aspects of the program. It was also apparent that he regularly viewed various types of data employed in assessing the program and its graduates. He took pride in the reputation achieved by the School of Education and particularly the program that prepared elementary teachers:

> We consider ourselves, . . . in a long-standing manner, . . . the top program for preparing teachers in the state, and we have no intention of relinquishing it to anybody—including Madison. What accounts for that top status? What is the distinctiveness of the elementary program? I think the thing finally that's distinctive is the fact that we work very hard at it.

A conversation with Sherrie Macaul, a new faculty member in the elementary program also underscores the work ethic that seems to pervade the program at UW-Eau Claire. (The interviewer, Sharon Strom, was a doctoral student who served as part of the research team.)

Strom: How would you describe the collegiality which exists among the faculty?

Macaul: They're very busy, and it's difficult to spend a lot of time interacting with one another. Yet, as a new faculty member, I've been invited to people's homes.

Strom: Do you feel like an outsider?

Macaul: They spend all their time working, so that's also a problem. As a faculty, we just get so busy observing students and teaching classes. I find a lot of times when I go to visit other faculty they're with students talking about classes or advising. People are very nice and we do get together for coffee once in a while, but we are just so busy it's hard to find enough time to do this.

Strom: Is that how you would describe your first year—busy?

Macaul: Yes. [Laughter.]

Strom: Certainly, we've observed what a hard-working, dedicated faculty this is.

Macaul: Even when they are bogged down; you just can read it in their features and you know they've had a long day, yet they don't burn out. That's amazing to me.

Given this type of climate, it was not surprising that students we interviewed echoed this disposition for hard work as critical to achieving success as a teacher. A common question we raised with the students we interviewed was, What are the attributes of an affective teacher? The following are typical responses from students at UW-Eau Claire:

Student 1:   The key to effective teaching is being patient and being tolerant; realizing that you are working with young children. Also, a teacher has to be well-organized and willing to be available. She has to work hard.

Student 2:   I think that a successful teacher is an effective disciplinarian and a hard worker. Also he has to be really a good planner and an organizer. I used to be a procrastinator, and there was no way I could get through this program behaving that way. I mean, once you get out into the block forget it. If you procrastinate, you're out.

Student 3:   A teacher definitely has to be organized. Things have to be planned. If you plan, then you can be more flexible. This is very important and a key thing. You have to be able to adapt to different levels and to different types of students; you have to be able to go up or down while you're teaching and try to make them understand, . . . and all of this takes hard work.

We also asked students what they believed might be the single thing that would set their program apart from other programs on campus. A characteristic response to this question was:

I think the primary thing would be commitment. You have to be very committed in order to spend the amount of time required. You *do* put in a lot of time. I live with students from all majors of the college—chemistry to business—and no one has to work any harder than we do. It takes a lot of work to get through this program.

Bob Shaw is the associate dean of students at UW-Eau Claire. He is also a member of the City Council. In summarizing this pervasive work theme, Dean Shaw described the people of UW-Eau Claire as follows: "The quality of our workforce is just simply excellent. And while there is a strong democratic labor tradition, it should take nothing away from the fact that when folks go to work around here they give a fair day's work." He then provided us with a description of the community where the college is located and the history of the university and the School of Education within it.

THE ENVIRONS

The city of Eau Claire has a population of about 55,000 citizens, and it is the largest city in northwestern Wisconsin. Its Chamber of Commerce identifies it as the fastest-growing city in the state. Nonetheless, Eau Claire manifests a small-town quality, dotted with quiet, elm-lined streets and lovely neighborhood parks, baseball diamonds, and, during the cold Wisconsin winter while we were there, a panoply of ice rinks. The city is ninety-five miles east of Minneapolis and St. Paul and 240 miles northwest of Milwaukee, the two largest metropolitan areas in proximity of Eau Claire.

Eau Claire rests at the confluence of the Chippewa and Eau Claire Rivers, and it is not difficult to understand why the community developed. The French fur traders first sought their fortune along the banks of these two rivers and gave Eau Claire its name after the "clear water" they found there. By the mid-1800s, lumbermen had discovered the many benefits of this area as well, especially the ability to transport the majestic white pine logs down from the vast forests just to the north of Eau Claire. At one time, up to nineteen sawmills stood along the banks where Eau Claire is now located, thereby dubbing Eau Claire the "Sawdust City."

The banks of this same Chippewa River now support what in many respects is the centerpiece of the community—the university. Commonly referred to as the most beautiful college campus in Wisconsin, the university spans both banks of the Chippewa River. The campus, which embraces more than 300 acres and comprises approximately 25 major buildings, is separated by the river and by Putnam Park, a natural forest used by students for both recreational and research purposes. Situated on the lower campus area are several academic buildings, the administrative offices, two residence halls, a student center, an arena, a theater, and a library. A foot bridge across the scenic Chippewa connects the Fine Arts Center and the Allied Health and Clinical Services Center to the main campus. The School of Education is in an unpretentious, although not unattractive, brick building attached to a former laboratory school on the lower campus. Its modest outward appearance belies the beehive of activity within.

The enrollment at UW-Eau Claire approximates 11,000 students who are served by a faculty and staff in excess of 675. In 1987, the School of Education had more than 700 students admitted to professional programs, with 270 enrolled in the elementary education program. UW-Eau Claire is basically an undergraduate institution, but it does offer a limited number of master's degree programs, including a Master of Arts in Teaching (MAT), a Master of Science in Education (MSE), a Master of Science in Teaching (MST), and a Master of Education—Professional Development (MEPD). Additionally, master's degrees are offered in business administration and nursing. General Master of Arts and Master of Science degrees are also available.

UW-Eau Claire was founded in 1916 as a teachers' college as was the situation with so many institutions for postsecondary education at that time. It has evolved over the seventy intervening years to a comprehensive university and is now the third largest campus in the thirteen-campus University of Wisconsin system. The UW-Eau Claire campus serves a largely regional and resident student body and draws a substantial number of students from Minnesota whose eastern border is only sixty miles away. It currently provides residence for more than 3,600 students in nine on-campus residence halls. Except for married students, students living with parents and guardians, or veterans of the military, all freshman and sophomores are required to live in university-operated residence halls when accommodations are available.

Common Folk: Caring and Conservative

Respect and *integrity* were words often used when describing the university and its programs. Susan Evenson, an experienced classroom teacher, was employed on a temporary basis to assist with the elementary program. A graduate of the university, she described UW-Eau Claire as an institution with tremendous integrity. When asked to elaborate, she responded,

> Each department has its strong points, and the education you receive here is very good. You can apply what you learn here to whatever phase of life you enter after you graduate. It has integrity across departments. I think the faculty members really care about you. The students know that teachers take their work seriously. I've lived here for eleven years and have had contact with this university for all those eleven years. This is very much a place where people *care about* and *understand* what they do. And they know their field. We have a fine business school, . . . a nursing school, and . . . our school of music is renown in the Midwest for their jazz—there's just a lot of good things happening here.

This general perception of the institution as providing high-quality instruction and at the same time emanating a sense of caring, was also shared by Vice Chancellor Norman Doorenbos, a noted scholar who has taught at major research-intensive institutions, in the following conversation:

Doorenbos:	I had a number of offers, but this was the one that I accepted. It was the quality of the institution and the faculty that attracted me. It was the type of institution with which I would like to be associated. One of the characteristics of this university is that it's a caring place— caring for students, caring among the faculty and staff, and so on. It's a very strong part of the institution.
Howey:	How would you compare it to the other institutions with which you've been associated?
Doorenhos:	More favorably than any others I've been in. But because of that and some other factors, this also presents a problem for a vice chancellor. Most faculty came here as their first professional appointment and stayed, so we have had little inflow of new ideas. We have many faculty members who have been here fifteen, twenty, twenty-five years, even more than thirty years. So, in a sense, we're highly inbred; not in the sense that we have Eau Claire graduates on staff, but in the sense that we have individuals who have

been nowhere else in their professional career. Their only experience is the Eau Claire experience. The faculty and staff are comfortable with the ways things have been done at this university. In a
sense it's quite a conservative institution. It takes a long time to interest them in a new idea or a new way of doing things. They can be
threatened by it. And so things move slowly.

This sense of stability, comfort, and a concomitant generally conservative posture which the vice chancellor noted was manifested in other discussions and observations. In fact, there was considerable pride in taking a
conservative posture toward education by several persons we talked with as
the following dialogue illustrates:

Evenson: The university tends to be rather conservative. The community is very
          conservative.
Howey: The university tends to be conservative?
Evenson: Yes.
Howey: Is your elementary program here conservative?
Evenson: I think so.
Howey: In what way?
Evenson: It provides the basics. I don't feel comfortable in being way out here
          in left field teaching something that I'm not so sure works.

Bob Barganz, a faculty member for a number of years, provided the
following reasons why he decided to pursue his career teaching at UW-Eau
Claire:

I'm from Madison originally. I went to school for a while on the East Coast and I
taught in Maine, but I guess I like the Midwest. There's a certain egalitarianism
about the Midwest that I like, that I didn't find on the East Coast, so it's comfortable being in Eau Claire.
     Institutionally, I think I'm doing the kinds of things I went to get my doctor-
ate for. I think it is important that people are committed to good teaching. I was
when I first started teaching. I taught for the Job Corp Center, and I was really
upset with what happened to poor people and disadvantaged kids. I was working
with young women, eighteen to twenty-two years old, who were illiterate; I came
out of a background where I went the Chaucer and English literature route, and I
was just aghast. Also, I had a number of supervisors when I was learning to
teach, and I thought they were incompetent. They were just terrible, and they
didn't know what they were doing with such neophytes. They were pompous, and
I decided that if I was going to have an impact on what happened in classrooms, it
would be through teacher education. Consequently, I have been more interested
in teacher education than staying in a research and development center and working on materials.

Ben Thompson, chairman of the Elementary Education Department,
elaborated on what he believed the faculty felt about the program:

I think what they'll tell you, what they've told me—and what really surprised them when they came here—is that we all work together; we help one another. We don't have such an ego that we won't share our tricks-of-the-trade and our syllabi and our materials. I think we're all happy together. We're typical people —just normal people getting along—doing the job.

Certainly, this ethos reflected the perspective of the recently retired dean, Rod Johnson, who discussed his philosophy about teacher education with us. At one point, we shared an article the university newspaper had published about him, and we asked whether it had accurately characterized him. He said:

The article referred to me as steady, conservative—not trendy—and that's right. I hang on to what's good. I look at what's going by and pick up some good things along the way, but I don't jump at new ideas. I want to know the consequences before I make a decision. That tells you a lot about me, and it will probably tell you a lot about the way I think our enterprise should operate.

Dean Johnson seemed to understand the community and the schools within it. Discussions with local educators about students from UW-Eau Claire coincided with Johnson's views. For them, one of the appealing qualities of the education students, in addition to their apparent confidence and ability to manage a classroom initially, was their conservative attitude about education. One principal underscored that Eau Claire was a conservative community, which was a major reason why parents like to raise their children there. When asked whether he thought there were professors on the faculty or student teachers from UW-Eau Claire whom he would characterize as radical, he indicated that one reason the community hires students from UW-Eau Claire is because they are *not* radical.

The Elementary Education Program

The elementary education program in the School of Education at UW-Eau Claire begins in the first or second semester of the junior year. The first course that all students take is Elementary Education 203, which focuses on general principles and methodologies. In this course, students have the opportunity to design, for the first time, an instructional lesson and to utilize it in a micro-teaching session. The course also incorporates approximately twenty hours of classroom observation and participation and is typically preceded by one of two electives that provide students with an opportunity to assess their career choice of elementary teaching. Elementary Education 150 provides an overview of current trends and developments in elementary education concurrent with the opportunity for observing or tutoring elementary-age students. Elementary Education 134 again emphasizes the tutoring aspects of teaching and presents opportunities for working one-on-one and with small groups of students.

The major emphasis in the elementary program, however, is the semester-long block during the senior year. Students attend courses on campus from 8:00 a.m. until 12:00 p.m. and then follow through with related experiences in local schools for the remaining one-half day during four of the seven weeks. During this block, students teach in teams of two where they jointly plan for instruction, take turns teaching or teach with shared responsibilities, and have multiple opportunities to observe one another.

During this time, students devote all of their time and studies to the elementary program taking three methods courses concurrently with a general principles course. They then spend two weeks in schools during the morning and return to campus for seven weeks of concentrated study followed by two intensive weeks in the schools. This block semester is illustrated diagrammatically below:

THE BLOCK SEMESTER

Nine Weeks	*Nine Weeks*
Seven Weeks' Class	Seven Weeks' Class
General Principles 204	General Principles 204
Reading Methods 310	Reading Methods 310
Science Methods 308	Language Arts Methods 307
Math Methods 306	Social Studies Methods 309
Two Weeks' Practicum	Two Weeks' Practicum

Following the intensive block semester, students take courses in educational media, including computer applications. They also pursue in-depth work in the teaching of reading, especially in the area of diagnosis and remediation. The primary emphasis following the block semester, however, is student teaching, during which time students spend entire days in the classrooms. Related coursework is offered in late afternoon and evening.

RELATIONSHIP WITH THE SCHOOL OF
ARTS AND SCIENCES

The arts and sciences faculty at UW-Eau Claire, from all accounts, has an excellent reputation within the University of Wisconsin system. We inquired as to why this was the case and Rod Johnson provided an historical perspective:

> When the teachers' colleges were first started in Wisconsin, each had a specialization—Platteville, mining; Whitewater, business education; LaCrosse, physical education; River Falls, agriculture; and Stout, industrial arts and home economics. By 1916, when they started another teachers college here at Eau Claire, no

specializations remained, so liberal arts became the emphasis over time. Since that time, the liberal arts aspect of this institution has been emphasized. In our elementary program, for example, we require an academic minor taken in arts and sciences. Throughout our professional sequence, many of the supporting courses are offered by our colleagues in arts and sciences. All of the educational psychology courses, for example, are offered in the psychology department and there's coursework in English, mathematics, art, and music that supports the preparation of elementary teachers. In fact, the entire general education component of the elementary education major is offered in Arts and Sciences. The only coursework that is offered in elementary education or in any of the education departments on this campus is that which doesn't have a place in the liberal arts; the strictly professional content.

Doorenbos viewed the close association between the School of Education and the School of Arts and Sciences as extremely important. To wit,

When I look at an institution, I'm very interested in who the university is serving and what their needs are. And I think very important here is what we can provide in the way of graduates who are going to teach our youngsters. Certainly, one of the strengths of this institution is the close relationship between the School of Education and the School of Arts and Sciences in the preparation of teachers. And almost every department in the School of Arts and Sciences and at least one department in the School of Business are intimately involved in preparing teachers. I consider this *all-university* teacher preparation an important part of the mission of this kind of institution. Other people might look to business, but in terms of the long-range impact on the state and the communities—and we're primarily a state institution—I think the preparation of teachers is the mission of this institution.

We discussed further the importance of the arts and sciences with the dean of the School of Education. When asked whether he could conceive of a situation at UW-Eau Claire where an expanded knowledge base in pedagogy would add credits to the professional sequence and, in turn, whether an augmentation of the professional program would diminish the degree of involvement of education students in the arts and sciences, he responded, "I've been telling faculty in education for years that we would have troubles if we did that. So, if we are short on education credits, it's probably my fault. The answer to that is no. In fact, there are days when I sound more like an arts and sciences dean than an education dean."

We also had the opportunity to visit with Arts and Sciences' faculty members who were involved with the education programs and specifically with the elementary education program. One of the most centrally involved faculties in the education of teachers is the Psychology Department. Dr. Barbara Lozar, chairperson, indicated that she was part of an excellent faculty and that her department was able to offer a rich curriculum. We asked what areas of psychology students might be able to pursue from her twenty-two-person department. She responded:

> We offer just about everything you can think of. We have the traditional psychological studies; that is, experimental psychology, abnormal psycho-pathology, general educational psychology, counseling, industrial/organizational psychology, school psychology, and special education orientations, so the course array that we offer is a long one. The only emphasis we don't have that I can think of is parapsychology. For a student who wants to explore these various areas with a course or two and complement this with independent study, they could pursue almost any concentration.

When asked how many of those orientations were brought to bear in courses offered for education students, Lozar said that more than one-half of the faculty would be involved in education in some way.

The School of Education faculty were also favorable in their assessment of the Arts and Sciences curricula. Juanita Sorenson, Director of the program for the Gifted and Talented Children and who has been on the faculty for more than twenty years, spoke from firsthand knowledge about several departments. She enthusiastically described the School of Arts and Sciences:

> It's very strong and it's what gives this institution its reputation. The science departments, art, English, all the departments are good; History is overstaffed and everybody dislikes that, but it's not the department's fault. They are staffed by good, strong people. Again, I think that's what gives this school its reputation.

Another veteran faculty member in the School of Education, Professor Elmer Winters, spoke of the extent and quality of involvement between those in the School of Arts and Sciences and those in the School of Education:

> There's a great deal of interaction. I serve on almost every one of our master's degree programs that results in either an MST or an MA in history. I either advise or critique the historiography papers. We require all of our secondary education majors to have a full major in one of the academic areas in addition to twenty-four credits in at least two related fields.

The institution, then, has a rich history of commitment to the Arts and Sciences, whose faculty appear to work well with the various professional schools, including education. Of course, some attrition has occurred. When the transition from a teacher preparation institution to a more comprehensive university occurred, changes also occurred in the orientation of faculty throughout the university. While many of these were positive, they nonetheless may have contributed in some ways to less of an understanding of or an appreciation for and commitment to work with education students.

Dean Johnson reflected on this evolution:

Often, I think about the way this institution is maturing or developing. Twenty or twenty-five years ago, this was a state teachers' college. Everybody on campus was enrolled in a teacher education program. Students had no other reason for coming here. Gradually, the university began to offer other programs and it became a state university. Then, the university was organized into schools and so on.

Many of the people who are still on this campus teaching today were employed when this was a teacher education institution. Over the years, I have appreciated that those people understood our teacher education efforts rather thoroughly; when they taught math, they were interested in how that student was going to take math out to elementary and secondary students. I now sometimes wonder what problems will befall us when that whole generation of faculty has been replaced and we hire people whose only elementary and secondary school experiences are during their own educations. Most of the longer-standing faculty were high school teachers first.

RELATIONSHIPS WITH THE FIELD

When asked what he believed was most distinctive about the elementary program beyond the dedication of his faculty Dean Johnson said:

The answer to that is the supervised field components. We make every effort to expect that most of the faculty work out in the schools in some way—either in the block program or the student teaching program or in an internship program. They keep up with what's current in the elementary schools. When we assign students to schools, the faculty go out and keep track of what's happening as well. They don't have to be there every day, but they've got to know what their students are doing. The faculty take the advising and supervision responsibility very seriously—so seriously, that every hour of their week is filled with what they're doing either on campus or off campus.

From our observations and interviews, close communication occurred between those in schools who typically work with the students from UW-Eau Claire and the elementary education faculty. Ben Thompson outlined the care with which cooperating teachers were selected. All cooperating teachers take two courses in supervision and, in addition to providing general knowledge and skills in supervision of student teachers, considerable orientation to the elementary education program is provided as well.

Chairman Thompson talked about the detail and specificity that went into student teacher assignments to classrooms. He indicated that considerable care was taken so that both the student and the experienced teacher with whom the student teacher was working were very clear in terms of what was expected of them:

The students have specific assignments to do. In their first laboratory assignment, they may or may not be visited by one of our faculty members. It depends on how much time the faculty member has and whether the students are having problems. But it's not just a matter of placing them and forgetting them. The cooperating teacher does not merely deal with the students as they can. No! When we get to our block again, besides the learning acquired in our methods courses, these students have this classroom experience—and I think this is unique about our program. It's not that other institutions don't do this, but I don't know how *well* they do it. I'm not prepared to say. We won't put students out there unless we can supervise them. They have a clear objective to meet in these early field experiences. The cooperating teachers know what that is, and the cooperating teacher is on a first-name basis with us and will help us if and when we need help.

The students verified for us that the teachers and principals in schools were usually fully apprised of what was expected of them. Students reported they clearly knew what was expected of them and the level of performance they would have to demonstrate in order to succeed. The following student's comment illustrated this: "I had an excellent experience in the school. My teacher was just excellent. She *knew* our program. She *knew* what she was doing."

FACULTY COMMITMENT TO STUDENTS

What is perhaps most distinctive about the elementary education program is not the block configuration which places considerable emphasis on studying courses in an interrelated way, but rather the time and attention which is given to students and the effort to ensure that faculty were involved in the laboratory and clinical aspects of the program as well as providing quality instruction in the college classroom.

On the basis of our limited observations in classrooms, the faculty appear to be well-prepared for their classes. We were able to observe a number of the faculty teaching and were impressed by the variety of teaching styles made available to students. It was not unusual for example, to see within the space of a one-hour class a lecture, some visual presentation, a structured written assignment, and a variety of small group activities, such as a group problem-solving exercise.

The elementary faculty we interviewed expressed considerable pride in the fact that they are teachers, as Ben Thompson illustrated:

Today, teacher educators criticize their teacher preparation programs. You don't hear doctors criticizing medical programs. So if we don't have pride in what we do and where we've been, how in the world can we expect anyone else to do that? On this campus, we have a lot of pride. For example, last summer our graduate dean had a meeting with about fourteen faculty members from Arts and Sciences. I'm rather outspoken, and I asked what they thought about the education faculty and if they were as good as faculty in other fields? When some reservations were expressed, I got on my bandstand; I told them that I received my Ph.D. from the

University of Wisconsin-Madison. I had a few education courses, but more than forty credits in biology; I taught chemistry for nineteen years in a prestigious Chicago high school; and that this kind of preparation and experience is true of most of our faculty. They have excellent credentials. They are excellent *teachers*.

Thompson also elaborated on this pervasive commitment to students on the part of the faculty:

The unique part about our faculty—and this program—is that they care about our students, we 'mother-hen' them right through. We start when they are *freshmen*, and we advise them through their senior year. It's really necessary because we don't have a fixed program; that is, a student cannot open a page in the catalog and determine what to take first semester and what to take second semester and so on. We have so many minors . . .

Thompson was hardly alone in his expression of a considerable commitment to students. Professor Elmer Winters, for example, shared a similar conviction:

After nearly twenty years in our program, I don't think that we do anything that other institutions don't do. I think we do the same kind of things done in other institutions—we're rigorous—but I don't think that much more demanding. What I'm saying that does make a difference here is that I think we as a *faculty* single out each and every individual student in that program and get to know those students. I know that Dr. Pautz and I have a conference with *every* student who goes through this program. They write papers for us. They come in and discuss those papers with us. We feel we know who they are and what they think. And we think we can challenge them better as a result of that.

Another education faculty member, Professor Don Burk, shared the observation that students were *first* at Eau Claire. The faculty commitment was not to research and service, nor even to colleagues as such, but to the *students*. With some passion he explained his orientation as follows:

We're not investing in a program—we're investing in the students in a very personal way. I don't think there's a single student that goes through our program who doesn't have a friend on the faculty. I'm not saying that some wouldn't have two or three friends on the faculty, but they all choose somebody with whom they can talk when they are upset, somebody with whom they can share the things they do, and somebody from whom they can ask for advice. I have students in special education—who are in a different major—who come to me when they have a problem. And they come to me as a *person* not as a professor—certainly not as one of their major professors—simply because we get along well. We can interact in that way. Everybody is the same way and there are people who come to them. Part of that is Eau Claire, but a larger part is the elementary education program. I think it is what we feel we have to be to our students in order to treat them as whole people and good teachers. We have a great commitment to the people who we've chosen to come here to teach, and we think, simply, that anything less than the best is inadequate.

LEVEL OF EFFORT EXPECTED AND
QUALITY OF PROGRAM

Ben Thompson, the chairman of the elementary education program, discussed at some length the high expectations he held for students in the elementary program. He indicated that it was not unusual for students who had completed (read, survived), the junior block to celebrate this event in a variety of ways. Block parties were common and students frequently silk-screened shirts indicating that they had survived the block. He shared with us student feedback which clearly illustrated that they believed that they were *overworked* in the block—that too much had been expected of them in terms of the credit which they had earned for this experience. The ultimate feedback for him and his colleagues, however, was the testimony of students after they had been out teaching for some time. Each year recent graduates of the program came back in to talk to the current cohort of elementary education students. He described their change in attitude at this time:

> In this block semester, we work them very hard. All of a sudden, they find that they can't go out in the evenings. They don't have much free time for anything anymore. They have to learn how to be organized. They learn how to organize their time as they never have before. But then when they become student teachers or first-year teachers and we have them come back and talk to our classes, they affirm that what is assigned in the block is very little when compared to what is expected of student teachers. When the first-year teachers come back to address the student teachers in our seminars, the first-year teachers start telling them about seventy-hour weeks. Then they realize that the block experience was for their benefit.

The methods courses are not the only block courses perceived as demanding, however. For example, Elmer Winters, who teaches in the "Foundations of Education," talked of the demands he places on his students:

> Winters: The three-credit sequence we have is rigorous and intellectually demanding. The students work—and we don't take a great deal of pride in the fact that we happen to have the lowest grade point average in our department in the whole School of Education—so we do make them work very hard.
>
> Strom: Do you have a lot of out-of-class assignments?
>
> Winters: In every one of these themes, they write essays, and we check the *writing* as well. Throughout, we use it as a means of screening those who need additional help. At least one take-home essay test is as-

signed over *every theme*—for example, the philosophy test—which is a written review of a book with philosophical issues, although it doesn't have to be contemporary. I'll go back to Dewey and assign them books to read; they have to analyze his ideas and philosophies. I start from the premise in all of these classes—I'm sure Dr. Pautz does the same thing—that what we *believe* makes a difference in what we *do.* We try to show them how what we believe influences practice. We make them read books expressing different points of view. I encourage them to read books that express different points of view than those they already hold. We begin our sections with a pretest, which is an instrument that we developed. They study at least three major philosophical positions. We ask what they believe now, and then we use that as a basis for analyzing positions they take throughout their work.

One indication of the quality of a curriculum is the review process to which new courses and new programs are subjected. At Eau Claire, courses are ultimately approved at the all-university level. When we discussed the review process and the rigor of the cirriculum with the dean of the school, he observed:

I think the curriculum is solid in that sense and it's been solid as long as I've been here. The commitment this university has to teacher education is a *total university commitment.* It's not just the School of Education, it's not the elementary education department. When elementary education proposes something, it has to go through all the steps to the faculty senate. It takes a long time to do that. Also, we are involved in a consortium of the four universities in this area—Eau Claire, Stout, LaCrosse, and River Falls—what we call the West Central Wisconsin Consortium (WCWC). One of its functions is program approval. Consequently, program development not only goes through this institution but through that consortium, regionally, before it goes to the Board of Regents. The process is sometimes overly long, and, of course, sometimes there are turf battles. On the other hand, time forces you to do a better job in putting programs forth. You'd better be ready before you start. You need a good rationale, and it needs to be documented in writing.

Students shared the faculty's perception regarding the demands the program placed upon them. When we reviewed written student assessments of the courses they had been involved in, more than 90 percent indicated that they were intellectually challenged by the course. On a ten-point scale, students generally rated the overall program quality between eight and nine, with an occasional ten.

We also asked students in the program what they thought other students' perceptions were about elementary education majors. The responses we received were typical of those from students of the other campuses we visited. For example, one student shared the outlook of a young man she had dated:

I dated an engineer during my freshman year. We discussed what I planned to major in, and I told him I was debating between music and elementary education, leaning more toward music. He laughed and said he thought music was an incredibly easy major. Then I said well, I was also thinking about Elementary Education. He laughed again, even harder. And you know, I started in music—I had theory in music—that is hard. I didn't know why he was laughing. And Elementary Education is just as hard, if not harder!

We asked if she was still dating this man, and her response was an emphatic "No."

Students were not unanimous in their assessment of the intellectual rigor of the program. For some, it was viewed as more time-consuming than academically challenging:

Student 1:   When you're going through the program, you ask yourself why you have to do all these papers, but I think the idea is to instill discipline so that when you begin student teaching, you have an idea of the work involved, of how much you have to put into this, and of how dedicated you have to be to what you're doing. Some of the assignments are busy work maybe, but it really makes you discipline yourself.

Student 2:   As they say around here, the education program is a 'cut-and-paste' program, but I think we're in the library as much or more than other majors here.

Zimpher: Who says that you cut-and-paste?

Student 2:   Business majors, for example.

Zimpher: There's a pecking order?

Student 3:   Oh, yes, Education . . . we're the baby classes.

Howey: Did you spend a lot of time in the library?

Students: Yes, yes [general agreement].

Strom: Doing what? Looking for materials?

Student   Looking for things to use in class; looking for ideas; looking for books to bring in; looking for tests—lots of reasons.

Student 4:   Last quarter, I made more trips to the library than I did in all four years combined.

Student 1:   But the block experience, intellectually was not very hard. Most of the work I did was busy work, looking things up . . . it wasn't very intellectual.

Student 2:   It depends on the instructor. Some will challenge you—push you to your limits; others are more lax.

Again, the majority of students with whom we talked believed that they had been challenged intellectually and that they had worked hard; that they had a combination of intellectual and more practical activities and that ultimately they were prepared to teach. We asked these students about their readiness for assuming a teaching position and the following brief dialogue captures their prevalent belief:

Student: I think I'm being prepared. My brother graduated from business and
            it was like, am I going to be able to do this? I don't know anything
            about it. But when you get through this program, you have been in
            the classroom many times in the last four years.
Howey: You're ready to go, aren't you?
Student: I am *ready* to go. I could start tomorrow.
Howey: Do all of you feel that way? [Speaking to a class of students.]
            [Rapid nodding of heads and general nonverbal agreement.]
Zimpher: You do look confident and excited.
Student: And we're not even done yet.

FACULTY

UW-Eau Claire is a teaching institution and, as indicated, the commitment to
teach, grounded in the experience of teaching in K–12 schools, is a major
consideration when faculty are hired. We discussed this commitment to teaching with the various faculty members in the elementary education program,
including those who had graduated from research-intensive institutions and
who had the skills to conduct scholarly inquiry. Glennellen Pace was one of
those faculty members. We asked whether she were interested in pursuing her
career in such an institution. She replied:

> I don't know. I would like to be able to do research in classrooms. I enjoy doing
> that. However, I *love* teaching. I get a great deal of satisfaction from working
> with students—from getting them to look at things in a way they never did
> before. I like challenging them to think in new ways, upsetting their balance so to
> speak. I don't ever want to be in a position where I'm not teaching, so I wouldn't
> want to get myself into a situation where research and publications become the
> driving force.

We were interested in the way teaching was viewed and approached in
the elementary education program. We asked Ben Thompson what was most
distinctive about the *content* of the elementary education program and his
response was similar to that of other faculty and students:

> What's distinctive about the content of the elementary education program? Well,
> I guess it's the "nitty-gritty." We've had coursework lately focusing on the
> [Madeline] Hunter model and there's nothing there that we haven't used and
> expected from our students for a long time. We're very nitty-gritty about what we
> do here. The lesson plans we ask for practically go down the line with what
> Hunter has been saying. These guidelines have been around for longer than I
> have, and the things that we teach in our courses are very down-to-earth.
>   Almost all of our people have had direct experience in the elementary class-
> room and they know what the students need. For instance, when we hire a new
> Ph.D. we always say they need to have elementary background to teach here so

that we don't have to remind them that they spent three or four years getting a Ph.D. in reading, for example, and shouldn't try to teach these young students all that in one three-hour class. Students must be able to student teach so that's what the professors have to help them do first; *then* students have to be inspired to continue after that . . . to want to become a better teacher of reading. And they aren't going to be able to do that now, even if you try to make them a Ph.D. in a three-credit course. So keep it relevant.

These aren't lectures that are done from a book. They're lectures that are done from *experience*. Most of our faculty use textbooks very casually. Several courses don't even have any texts. But we have a lot of materials. A lot of activities for students to do in class.

Thompson's perceptions were reinforced by the dean. When we asked Rod Johnson about the strengths of his faculty, he indicated that his faculty were very knowledgeable in terms of current classroom practice. He indicated with some pride that, unlike many faculty in institutions of higher education elsewhere, most of the faculty could step right into a classroom in the public schools and be rated as outstanding teachers.

This posture that a basic foundation be provided to beginning teachers was not limited to the methods courses. For example, Professor Winters in "Foundations of Education," who earlier shared his concern about students being exposed to multiple philosophies, also expressed his goal that the teaching profession be comprised of people with the fundamental skills needed for effective instruction. He expressed this as follows:

Faculty in other departments might argue that we have been too permissive— teaching progressive thought. I disagree. I've never seen myself as a progressivist, although I teach Dewey and my doctoral dissertation was on Harold Rugg. Also, I'm more politically involved than many. But I think it's essential that students in the program are confronted with the ideas that they're going to find in every teachers' lounge in every community in this state . . . and that they have some sensitivity to that. I don't see myself as a wild-eyed liberal educator, but we're talking first about a person who's decent and who establishes reciprocal relationships with the students.

When asked what else makes up an effective teacher he replied:

Well, the very basics, of course, teaching skills, personality, communication skills, and knowledge. I would hate to see an elementary teacher out there who lacked a good general education. I view teachers as community leaders. As a parent, I view teachers as people who have been educated as a model for the community; if they can't spell or they can't communicate effectively, they go down in my estimation. As an example, in my classes I use a *Time* magazine story about picketing teachers in Houston, Texas, who were carrying misspelled picket signs. What do you do for a profession presenting an image like that? I cringe when I see that, which is one of the reasons we give written assignments.

FACULTY AND THE CURRENT KNOWLEDGE BASE

Certainly, the preception of some in the arts and sciences with whom we talked is that the elementary education curriculum is driven primarily by the practical experience of the faculty and by the curriculum of teachers who are currently teaching in K–12 classrooms. Several persons raised questions about the extent to which the curriculum reflected a theoretical and empirical base. Given the emphasis on a curriculum that assisted students in coping with the realities of daily teaching, such perceptions were understandable. However, we were made aware of a variety of ways in which the elementary faculty at this institution were able to keep abreast in terms of new knowledge and recent research. For example, Bob Barganz discussed the way he kept current in the field of reading where considerable scholarly inquiry occurs:

> I have a comprehensive subscription to all of the IRA journals and publications. I attend conventions. Five years ago, five or six institutions in the state established a graduate-level consortium; in the summer, we hold a seminar conducted by top-notch researchers. They write and present a paper summarizing the research in an area. We plan two follow-up studies of specific research. We've been able to do this because our institutions work together, although it's mostly working as individuals across the state. The organization is a small, informal one for teacher educators in Reading.

We asked Glennellen Pace how she integrated research into her teaching:

> I show application when I can. Where research raises important questions—not necessarily answers, but questions—I include research in conjunction with particular strategies and assumptions; for example, curriculum materials, commercial materials, may or may not be supported by research and that they may at least be questionable. Also, I use research in conjunction with classroom observations and feedback on actual teaching.

FACULTY COLLABORATION AND CURRICULUM INTEGRATION

One of the characteristics of a relatively small faculty and a program scheme which has courses taught in close connection with one another is the opportunity for articulation across the curriculum. Faculty in the elementary education program have opportunities to observe one another teach and, on occasion, to team teach. Professors share the same facilities for teaching and the working relationship between various faculty members is apparently close and informal enough that no one appeared to be bothered by having another faculty member in the room. Professor Juanita Sorenson provided us with one example of curriculum articulation or cross-disciplinary teaching that occurred:

Sorenson: We have block meetings about where to teach certain concepts. Cutting across subject areas can really be a lot of fun. For example, Glennellen Pace and I did a session on integrating science and writing, and we had people really excited about it. The response was terrific. We had a ball going around to illustrate basic science concepts and we couldn't get them to give up the ball to start writing! Our faculty over the years has worked together in this way. That's where the content comes in and the qualifications . . . *faculty have to know their content.*

Howey: Do you think there's enough of an empirical base undergirding most of the subjects taught in the elementary program that it makes a difference in terms of the faculty that you recruit, whether they are committed to scholarly inquiry themselves?

Sorenson: I think fundamentally it's *how* you teach it. I was just watching Ben [Thompson] teach this morning. And I think the way you teach science is important . . . your knowledge background enters into that. First, you can't teach science if you don't know it; second, what is the proper way to introduce students to these content areas? That's where content and experience enter.

Zimpher: Do you teach them? Do you watch each other teach a lot?

Sorenson: Not a lot. We do see each other teach. Ben and I use the same room.

Students were also able to identify aspects of their coursework that were approached integratively. They were able to provide numerous examples for us of the way science instructors were able to bring in mathematics concepts or language concepts or the way reading cut across content areas. They acknowledged that an interrelated, holistic approach to elementary curriculum was modelled for them. One of the students justified the approach this way:

The faculty are integrative, and that's important because when you're going through the day as an elementary teacher you don't always have time for this and then this and then something else. You can incorporate a little bit of one subject into another when you don't have time to teach everything formally. Your day is just too full to teach every subject individually.

Finally, one of the cooperating teachers we interviewed underscored how much she valued this integrative or holistic approach to instruction in elementary teachers and saw this in the best student teachers from UW-Eau Claire. She valued a teacher who could take concepts across subjects and who understood when a teachable moment occurred. She believed the elementary curriculum at UW-Eau Claire produced this type of teacher and she described them as follows:

Every occasion is a teachable moment for them. For example, if we're all outside for physical education, and the student teacher asks about the velocity of the softball. All of a sudden, we're doing math! Even with the junior block students, you can often tell those who will struggle forever and those who will see content more fluidly.

STUDENTS

During our discussion with Vice Chancellor Doorenbos, we asked about his assessment of the student body at UW-Eau Claire vis-a-vis the other institutions at which he had taught. He opined that students in the School of Education were not that different from the other students on campus:

> We have an interesting student body and one which is somewhat different from the students at the "Big 10" institutions. In excess of 50 percent of the students on this campus come from communities with populations of fewer than 10,000. They grew up either in small towns or on farms. Typically, they've lived in one family. They are first-generation college students; their parents have not been to college. Often, they're the first ones in their peer group to attend college. They've not travelled. I've met many students who have not been outside of Wisconsin—or, if they have been, it's only to the Twin Cities [St. Paul and Minneapolis]. That's as far as they've travelled. They know no minorities. In fact, many have never met a minority. Consequently, one of our goals is to acquaint them with minorities while they're here.

Our discussions with faculty members reinforced the parochial background that many students brought with them to this campus. Faculty felt students were very concerned about being effective teachers and that they were concerned about and committed to helping others. These young people's view of teaching, however, and certainly their view of the world was in many respects contrained at this stage of their lives. Professor Bob Barganz described the student population as very apolitical; in some ways, very similar to the 1950s.

We inquired further about the extent to which he believed the young people coming to the program had a sense of social consciousness beyond a general altruism connected with wanting to teach and the extent to which they were aware of cross-cutting problems in society:

> There isn't much altruism, so I have to stress that heavily once in a while to make progress. For example, I emphasize that most reading literature doesn't address the disadvantaged adequately. That is, generally when they talk about reading problems, they're talking about dyslexia and other reading difficulties but, in fact, most students who receive reading assistance are in Chapter I programs because they're impoverished. I underscore that point heavily.

We further discussed the level of understanding and general respect for diversity by these prospective teachers with Janet Reinhardtsen, who is the faculty member primarily responsible for the curriculum concerned with students with special needs. She, too, was concerned about the limited social perspective that students tended to bring to her course. She indicated that many of the elementary education majors who came into her class initially demonstrated considerable apprehension in working with children who were different in some way. Thus, she indicated that she structured her course so that students had opportunities for and support in experiencing diversity, and built in issues and debates that were designed both to broaden perspectives and to increase a respect for human diversity and for students who were handicapped in various ways.

In our discussion with the students, it soon became evident that the great majority of the young people with whom we visited came from small communities of fewer than 1,000 people. When we talked to students in groups, we found that they liked to compete with one another in terms of how small small is when they talked about their hometowns. The following exchange with a student illustrates this point:

Student: Coming from such a small town, I didn't want to go to a large school like Madison. They have more people on one dorm floor there than in my whole town! I thought I could never handle Madison, Eau Claire is just the right size. I know I needed experience meeting people who are from different backgrounds. Everyone from my town is Polish—100 percent Polish.

Howey: And Catholic?

Student: And Catholic. Everyone in my whole town is Catholic. We have one church and four bars and after church half of them go to the bars. But everyone has the same lifestyle, everyone knows everyone else's business. They know when I come home for a weekend. I have learned that people are different than this.

The student demography, especially in the elementary education program, is quite uniform. More than 90 percent of the students are female. All of them are white and, with a few exceptions, all of them are recent high school graduates. Their appearance was clean cut. When the students were on campus they generally wore sweaters or sweatshirts and jeans or skirts; when the students went out to student teach, however, they generally dressed quite fashionably in dresses and high heels.

We probed through our interviews with students about campus experiences that broadened their horizons or allowed them to make acquaintances with people different from themselves in the larger student body. The total university population included a limited number of minorities. There were, interestingly, more students from foreign countries than from minority populations in this country. Thus, the opportunity to interact with people who were different was, at times, interpreted in terms of students from other countries. The following exchange illustrates this:

Student: I think Eau Claire is a really nice size. At least for me it was.
Strom: Do you meet people from different cultures here?
Student: Oh yes, I've met so many foreign students. One of my best friends was
           a foreign exchange student from Sweden. We still write to each other. I
           was just fascinated by the foreign students. I had never met a foreigner
           before, and I liked talking about the different places he had been and
           trips I might be able to take some day.

We asked students whether they thought UW-Eau Claire could be characterized as a conservative university. The following dialogue was typical:

Student One: Oh, I think it's conservative.
Student Two: Yes.
Student Three: People go to Madison, but they come back here. . . .
Student Four: [to Student 1] What do you mean conservative?
Student One: Well, calm. Not so fast-paced. Pretty mainstream, you know
                . . . they tell people that when you go down there [Madison] you
                are going to see things that you'd never ever seen here. Like
                there's a girl here on campus from England who has purple hair
                in back—its dyed . . . and people say, well you see that all the
                time in Madison.
Student Two: Well it stands straight up and the ends are dyed purple. For
                someone from a small town that was really—wow! And they
                say you get a lot of that at Madison.
Howey: Did your question get answered? Are you satisfied with how she
                defined conservative?
Student Four: Uh huh.
Zimpher: Could we assume that you are conservative—that you like the
                same qualities . . . not so fast-paced and mainstream—does it
                make a statement about you?
Student One: I don't think it's bad to be conservative—to be a little re-
                strained.
Student Four: I don't ridicule anyone who looks different and I'm open to
                other views but. . . .
Zimpher: Is there something deeper than that? Because you are all women,
                do you experience in a conservative environment anything
                that's bothersome? If it's just getting used to different ways of
                dressing, that's no problem. Is there something at another level
                that bothers you?
Student Three: No, I think we're encouraged to be professional and to be
                ourselves, in our careers and in other aspects of our lives.
Howey: If somebody said that she wanted to go into elementary educa-
                tion but was concerned about the low pay, what would you tell
                her?
Student One: I'd tell her that's not why she's going into teaching. It should be
                because she enjoys children. So that's okay.
Howey: Is there ever a need to be militant as teachers—to demand more
                money, better conditions, fewer students?

Student One: I don't know.

Student Two: It would be nice.

Student Three: In my high school we had some small classes—fourteen students. And yet, when I did my student teaching, we had twenty-six students in the class. It's hard, but you do have some advantages that you don't have otherwise.

Howey: Has anyone shared the statistic with you that well in excess of 80 percent of elementary teachers are women, yet only a small percent of elementary principals are women? How do you feel about that?

Student Two: Maybe women do not want the position of principal. I cannot see myself being a principal. I'd rather be in the classroom teaching.

Student Two: I would, too.

Student Three: It could have something to do with that. Maybe men are not encouraged to go into elementary ed. We have two males in our class, and I think there are two, three, four maybe in the other sections. They might just not be encouraged. But the ones that are there that I know are great with kids.

Zimpher: Do you think they'll become principals?

Student Two: No, no.

Student One: I think a lot of it has to do with the money in the field, too. Education is not a high paying job, and a lot of men are worried about security and supporting a family and as a woman, if I can make enough for me to live on, I'll be happy. The money situation scares a lot of men. They pay the same for their educations regardless of the majors. They can make a lot more money if they major in business.

Zimpher: Do you talk about these issues other than when researchers come to talk with you?

Student Two: No.

Student Three: No.

Student One: My roommate and I talk about what we'll do after graduation and the fact that I don't plan to be the primary bread-winner in the family.

Student Four: It's realistic. You have to think about it. If I was planning to raise a family on my own with an elementary teacher's salary, I couldn't do it. But, I don't plan on being the primary bread-winner either. As a single person, I could make enough money to live. I don't need a lot of fancy clothes or this and that. Maybe a little junk car, OK?
                 [Laughter]

We asked these students whether they would consider moving out of the area or out-of-state to take a teaching position. Most said they would prefer to teach in a community similar to Eau-Claire or, in many instances, similar to the community from which they came. Several students wanted to teach in rural areas. Conversely, many of the students enrolled in the elementary program had grown up in suburban Milwaukee, which is a large recruiting area for the program. These students enjoyed living in Milwaukee and would not consider it an undesirable place to begin teaching. As one student indicated, "I would like to go back home to Milwaukee [not the city of Milwaukee but a suburb thereof] and teach in the schools there for a while so I can live at home and save money. That's what I'm looking for right now."

SUMMARY

The elementary education program at UW-Eau Claire has several desirable features. The program unit is relatively small and appears to have good communication among faculty in terms of articulating basic concepts and desired skills which are expected of students. Excellent cooperation is evidenced between faculty in the elementary education program and those in the arts and sciences. Good working relationships appear to extend into work with those in the schools as well. The teachers and administrators with whom we met indicated that they understood and agreed with the program's basic goals, and appeared to have a high regard for the program.

Faculty appear to keep current with regard to their fields. Their instruction methods were diverse, and they provided frequent laboratory and school experiences for their students. Considerable demands were placed on students. Students completing the program believed they were challenged, that they had worked hard, and that they were ready to teach.

It is not the program as such, and we speak here of the program as those experiences beginning in the arts and sciences and extending through student teaching, which appeared most to characterize teacher preparation at UW-Eau Claire. It is, rather, the faculty's devotion to their students as Ben Thompson summarized in his view of the success achieved over the years:

I know that I'm repeating myself, but I believe that our basic success is due to the quality of the faculty members we have. As I told you, they have a *fierce* professional loyalty. They are so strongly professional that they could not do less than an excellent job for their students. They don't have any of the self-aggrandizement that you find at times in research institutions. They're not concerned about the time they have free for other pursuits. They're committed first and foremost to teaching our students . . . to be the *best* teachers they can. Consequently, many of them are here at 7:00 a.m. and often on Saturdays and Sundays. Our students don't even bother to make appointments. They expect us to be here. They just walk in. For every one hour in the classroom, we probably spend three more hours assisting students, making plans for teaching, and solving myriad problems. And they come back with problems they've had and we help find a solution for that. So, our students get what they won't get at many other institutions. They get faculty members who are dedicated to them.

Given this orientation, it is not surprising that students who graduate from the elementary education program are commonly characterized by a similar commitment to teaching. Hard work, as we said at the outset, seems to pervade the institution—both its faculty and its students. In this regard, we conclude with an observation of the education students by one of the supervising teachers:

> The students often choose to go the extra mile. For example, a student teacher might feel weak in discipline and asks me to suggest some books or offer advice. They are neophytes, and they will just assimilate many of your successful programs. But these people go that *extra mile* to succeed. They bring in an enthusiasm, and, because of their university affiliation, they are able to get a lot of ideas. They are very organized . . . and *workers*. And they don't wait for you to lead them. My last student teacher *anticipated*. There were days when I thought, 'Why am I here?' She would anticipate things that had to be done before I had asked her to do them. She was good at self-evaluating, too. She would teach a lesson to one group and before I had even had a chance to make suggestions to improve the lesson, she had already changed it for the second group. These students continually work hard to succeed.

5

Coming into the Age of Technology

INDIANA UNIVERSITY

Major, state-supported universities, especially those with a land-grant charter, often form a system of higher education institutions designed to serve populations in different areas of the state. While these coordinated campus relationships vary among states, in many respects the coordinate campus arrangement in Indiana is unique. When we interviewed Howard Mehlinger, Dean of the School of Education at Indiana University, he began by addressing the distinctive nature of the Indiana University cooperative endeavor:

> You're here in Bloomington, but the school of Education is more than Bloomington. The Bloomington and Indianapolis Schools of Education are operated as if they were one school . . . as if they were in the same building. So there is another education faculty—about thirty members—based in Indianapolis. We have a *core campus* or *merged school*. This arrangement began in 1974; and so I have an office in Indianapolis as well as Bloomington. The associate dean for Academic Affairs, who has an office here, is in Indianapolis today. And the Indianapolis campus associate dean spends a day or two each week in Bloomington and so it's back and forth, and insofar as we can we try to integrate the two programs as much as possible. This approach makes this institution different from most others.

When we inquired as to why he referred to an *associate dean* rather than *dean* at the Indianapolis campus, he elaborated on this merged school concept:

> There is only one dean for the School of Education for Indiana University; thus, I have identical responsibilities at the Bloomington and Indianapolis campuses. I

135

have budgetary responsibility, and I have promotion and tenure responsibility. There are two budgets, however; one for each campus. When we go through our annual review of faculty, both campuses have the same standards, and the faculty are all members of the same department.

Understandably, some myth is connected with this merged concept. Even though they are treated philosophically the same and abstractly as if they all lived in one town and all were in the same building, most of the faculty who teach in Indianapolis teach only in Indianapolis and most of the faculty in Bloomington mainly teach here, but there is some cross teaching. Even more complex is the fact that we have six other campuses scattered around the state—Gary, South Bend, Fort Wayne, Kokomo, Richmond, and New Albany. I'm also the dean of those campuses.

Mehlinger is seated in a wooden rocking chair in his office. He thought-fully fields questions, and pauses in the conversation are punctuated by the gentle movement of his chair. We raised a number of issues, including the question of faculty governance. Dean Mehlinger explained the governance structure for this coordinate campus as follows:

What we have, at least at the moment, in terms of faculty governance, is a Policy Council. This is similar to an elected faculty senate, as found at other universi-ties. The Policy Council is an elected council from both the Bloomington and Indianapolis faculty, and that's one place where they're treated as if they're one combined body. This council meets every third week. I chair it, but it's a faculty council and they are the governing body of the core campus of the School of Education. They are the ones who set the standards, the curriculum, the entrance requirements, the graduation requirements—all the issues and policies that fac-ulty deliberate.

There's also the Education Council, which consists of faculty elected from *all* of the campuses and they meet four times each year. The Education Council must approve any changes in a common program, which is one that is offered on all the campuses.

There are unique as well as common programs, and the main campus at Bloomington is understandably in the best position to offer a number of unique programs. In fact, a primary reason we selected Indiana University as a research site was its extensive history with alternative approaches to teacher preparation. At the time of our visit, emphasis appeared to be placed on a common curriculum across the seven campuses. Mehlinger informed us that a primary reason for this is that throughout the Indiana University system students have virtually free movement. Students could begin work in Fort Wayne and after two or three years decide to attend classes in Bloomington. These students are not considered transfer students but Indiana University students, regardless of where they began their studies. To be certain, the curriculum is similar in these common programs but hardly identical given the fact that they are taught by different faculty members. To wit,

As you know, faculty members teach courses with the same title, even the same syllabus, but they can teach quite differently. The same thing is true here. In theory, there is no qualitative difference; in practice, there is. These qualitative differences, however, are not always related to the size of the institution. In my judgment, in the case of particular faculty members, you will find better teaching on the smaller campuses.

We also visited with Michael Cohen, the director of Undergraduate Studies in Indianapolis in order to gain further understanding of this coordinated approach from the perspective of a key education faculty member at a campus other than Bloomington. We asked Cohen about faculty movement among campuses, specifically whether faculty from Indianapolis taught on the main campus in Bloomington on occasion as well:

> Some of our faculty in student personnel and school administration go to Bloomington. I held a graduate seminar down there a couple years ago. We have more faculty from there coming here and my perception is that we're getting the better faculty. We're not getting people sent up here that can't make it at Bloomington.

Cohen was enthusiastic about a number of cooperative endeavors which he had engaged in with faculty from Bloomington:

> There are some very positive aspects of this arrangement. We recently submitted a grant jointly developed with faculty at the Bloomington campus. It was funnelled through the Bloomington campus. The associate dean for Research, whose office is in Bloomington, drove halfway here, and we met him in the parking lot of a restaurant. We signed and transferred papers. He went back to Bloomington, and we came back to Indianapolis. We got the grant.

Cohen apparently took considerable pride in being a member not only of this merged faculty arrangement, but in being attached specifically to the Indianapolis faculty. He talked at length about his colleagues and the way, in many respects, they compared favorably with their counterparts in the School of Education at Bloomington. The Indianapolis faculty was portrayed as a faculty with considerable autonomy but one which benefitted from cross-campus cooperation and development as illustrated in Cohen's following antecdote.

> I'm teaching only one science class each semester now, which is one of the first classes the elementary students take. Also, I personally think that it's important to have a quality science course in your background. This course was developed mostly on the Bloomington campus, but it's been adopted throughout the system. Because it is the students' first science course, we were able to get the School of Arts and Science to accept the course as credit for their basic education requirement. It's not really a science methods course; it's science content. (This is one of

the areas where we do an excellent job because the students also take a three-hour science methods course.) But *this* three-hour course meets five hours a week, during which time they typically have two lengthy lab activities that were developed in the elementary science projects in the 1960s. By the time they take a science methods class, they have already had twice as much science as most instructors try to get into a methods class. So we're really a step ahead here. As far as I know, we've implemented this curriculum across all campuses. Some of the campuses had more trouble getting the course established due to equipment costs, but most of the campuses are offering the course now.

THE STUDENTS

Dean Mehlinger is directly involved in a variety of activities across the Indiana University campuses. He described the students, faculty, and programs at these different sites, and shared his observations about some of the differences and the similarities among them. The following example outlines the type of student enrolled in the School of Education at Bloomington, and in the elementary program specifically, as contrasted with other campuses:

One critical difference is the age of the students. Bloomington is almost entirely a residential campus with few commuters—many fewer, than found at Ohio State and the University of Minnesota. Practically all of our students live on campus; therefore, they're almost all recent high school graduates. Bloomington has all the characteristics of a residential campus—good and bad. On the other hand, on any of the regional campuses, New Albany, the southeast one, for example, they have a lot of students who are more likely to be twenty-five years old rather than nineteen or twenty. Many of them have jobs, although New Albany does have more full-time students than some of the other campuses. They are most likely, especially if they're elementary teachers, young, married women with families who are spreading their educations out over time. In some cases, they are more serious students than those at Bloomington. Bloomington students, not just in education but across all majors, are often young people who are here enjoying college life in addition to studying. The students on the regional campuses generally expect to find teaching jobs in that area. The Bloomington students who choose to go into education are interested in recruiters from California, New Mexico—wherever. They're ready to go, and they will generally consider a job anywhere. That's not true of the regional campuses. It's a different kind of student body. In many ways, they're much more interested in cultivating collegiality among themselves. Some of the best-organized student teacher groups are on the regional campuses . . . better than here because our students are into sororities and fraternities and the little 500 student-alumni groups and all sorts of things. They have a different sense about why they're here.

Mike Cohen reinforced Howard Mehlinger's perceptions, stating that he enjoyed working with the older, more mature students on the Indianapolis campus.

I couldn't give you the average age in education, but it is probably five to ten years higher than the average of other undergraduates. They may have been working or they may change a major or they're women returning after having children. There are lots of older women returning to the elementary program. I had one class this semester where six people already had degrees. One was a young woman in her mid-twenties with an engineering degree from Purdue University.

One reason the students are good on our campus is that they're older and more serious. Students will challenge you . . . will raise issues. And they're opinionated. If you have suggested readings, they're willing to read them all. The responsibility they take for learning is incredible. And, of course, they've often had experience with their own children in school so that they aren't as inexperienced as the younger graduates. I don't think those undergrads are really ready for teaching—even after student teaching, they're not really ready to work with a lot of different students.

Dr. John Ray, the dean for Student Affairs and a veteran faculty member, further described the elementary teacher education student body at the Bloomington campus especially. We asked whether there might be differences between the students who attended Indiana University compared with those at Ball State University, Indiana State, or Purdue University:

Certainly, there's a lure to come here because it is Indiana University, *the* state institution. It is older than the other institutions and has a reputation for outstanding programs, whether in education, music, business, or whatever. So there is a certain something one might gain from graduating from Indiana University.

The six regional campuses are another distinct advantage. It's not uncommon for a student to start out, for example, at the northwest campus and live at home for a semester or two and then come to this resident campus. So this systemwide . . . statewide network is a great advantage because our program is represented as a statewide school. As you know, we do several things in cooperation with the regional campuses. We meet regularly with them. We plan our programs jointly so that a student can go from one campus to another easily— and, as usual, the students are pedominantly Indiana students.

Indiana ranks very low in comparison to other states in terms of those who go to college and the general level of education achieved. For years, Indiana was heavily industrialized, and students tended to get good-paying jobs rather than going to college. That pattern has not changed even though the industry has changed drastically. Indiana has a very high unemployment rate. Some cities, Anderson and Gary, for example, are among the highest unemployment rates in the country. In any case, the students who come here will come from mostly Midwest—primarily Indiana—hard-working, middle-class, and first-generation college families.

We also asked various faculty about their perceptions of the students in education. One faculty member, who has taught in the School of Education at IU for many years, described the student body as quite bimodal:

We seem to have one group of students who is very good and another group of students that is quite poor. I really don't know how to explain this. Perhaps the poorer students are coming to school basically to get a degree and they choose a college they think is easy. I don't know. Nonetheless, we do have a good number of students. I think education was the first choice of many of the top students, especially those in elementary education.

Other faculty reiterated this perception of the dichotomy between very good students and marginal students. We talked with Jesse Goodman, a professor in the School of Education, regarding his perceptions of students at Indiana, especially in contrast with students at other campuses where he had taught. He felt that there many academically able students were enrolled in the elementary program, but a few students did not appear to be highly motivated. While he acknowledged the generally conservative nature of students on campus, he indicated that given their youthfulness and lack of exposure to people who were quite different than they were, that they were nonetheless open to new ideas and new experiences:

They're fairly conservative. On the other hand, they're open-minded. Most of them are between twenty and twenty-two years old and have never really had to question their own cultural background or upbringing. That's one of the reasons I don't deal with theory *directly*. I try to raise theoretical concerns in the context of everyday educational realities. You have to take into account the students' backgrounds. I try to be sensitive to that. I find most of them are open to the new theoretical ideas I bring to class. They certainly don't leave the class thinking we've got to tear down the system or that capitalism is terrible. But they do come out thinking that maybe knowledge is not as absolute as they had thought . . . maybe there are other ways to think about teaching and the way students learn.

We asked students about their perceptions of one another as well as the faculty with whom they interacted. The following dialogue illustrates the limited number of older students in the elementary program as well as the lack of cultural diversity or, in this instance, what is viewed as cultural diversity by a recent high school graduate:

Student: I was surprised to see that there weren't more older students here. I transferred from Western Kentucky and there were more older students returning to school. Here the students are younger. Unlike Western, I'm one of the few married people here, so I feel as if I'm not part of the student body even though I haven't been married that long.

Zimpher: Are the students here mostly from Indiana?

Student: There are a lot of people from Chicago. And I'm surprised about the size of the Jewish population, although I don't mean that negatively in any way.

Howey: Is that positive?

Student: Yes. You think about things more. I think it's good because in my
             area we have no Jewish people and in our county there are no blacks.
             I lived my first two years with a Jewish girl and it was really differ-
             ent. We celebrated both Christmas and Hannukah.

Given the relatively parochial background of many of these students, we
asked whether they viewed the formal curriculum preparing them for teaching
as providing them with new and different social perspectives. We asked, for
example, whether any of the education faculty with whom they interacted
presented a radical perspective on schooling. Generally, these students questioned what we meant by *radical* as if the term itself was foreign to them. The
following discourse reflects this apparent lack of understanding of the politics
and economics of schools:

Student one: I haven't heard a lot of that. I'd like to know more about the
                school organization because we don't hear much of anything
                about contracts or . . .
Student Two: [interrupting] Yeah, I don't even know who you would apply
                to.
Howey: Aren't you getting a little worried about this?
Student Two: Yes.
Student Three: My husband's getting a lot worried about this [laughter].

The few older students whom we interviewed felt quite apart from many
of the younger students in the program. The following exchange is instructive
in this regard:

Zimpher: Do you find that the people in education with whom you are
              going to school are intellectually stimulating people as well as
              culturally diverse?
Student One: No. I don't know. One of the things that bothers me about them
              is that I feel I can't talk with them about anything that doesn't
              have to do with what's going on on the weekends. It's as if they
              can't think about the future. They can't constructively criticize
              and analyze a situation. For instance, we were talking about
              immigration and one student said she didn't know why we were
              studying it. I said it is important because you have to understand
              different values and their origins. Younger students don't seem to
              have deep roots or even a kind of belief in an idea or even to
              think deeply. I don't know if that's not intellectual. I guess that
              they just don't have much cultural diversity. . . .
Howey: Who are your friends in the program?
Student Two: It's really changed for me. Since I got married, I have a different
              outlook. Now I always sit in the front row. You find different
              types of people in the front row than you do in the back.
Howey: You used to sit in the back?

Student Two: Yes, with the sorority girls. The girls sit in their cliques and the few guys in the elementary education classes sit together. I talk with the lady who sits next to me in one class—she's a married mother returning to school—about things that go on in the community and that kind of thing. And then I go into a science class and the girls are talking again about how one of them is going to visit a guy at Yale for the weekend. You get a totally different perspective from one group to the next.

Student One: I think a lot of it is students who can't make it in the other schools turn to education because it is a little bit easier. The courses are not as tough as economics or accounting, and so a lot of business people turn to education. And a lot of sorority girls—not to put them down—use this program to get through school.

The elementary education classes we observed on the Bloomington campus were comprised almost exclusively of the traditional profile: college-age, white, female students. As was the situation in elementary education classes at all of the campuses we visited, males were a decided minority. Typically, in a class of twenty or thirty students, only two or three men were enrolled in elementary education courses. Few minority cultures were represented and, as we have indicated, few older students were enrolled. The students we observed at Indiana University were generally casual in their attire; however, several young women in the elementary education program on the Bloomington campus dressed quite fashionably. The students we interviewed were candid and not afraid to share criticisms as well as perceived benefits of the program, as the following interchange illustrated?

Student One: Some of the good professors here are too involved in research projects or other things to spend time teaching a college class. They don't have the time to prepare themselves for the class. If they did, they would be excellent. My biggest complaint is 'assistant professors'—graduate students [referring to teaching assistants]. To have any methods class taught by a graduate student is so unfair. A lot of them haven't even had teaching experience! They're just right out of school.

Student Two: This is the first time that they're teaching in a college class . . . one that they haven't even completed themselves. I feel like I've gotten short-changed in two methods classes and in an elementary school science course. I received an A in that class, but I feel that all they care about is that we get the assignments done just like their professor is telling them they have to do it—I feel like we gear our whole class around that.

Howey: Can you register a complaint?

Student One: I complained last semester about an AI to the professor. He told me to write my complaints in the evaluation at the end of the semester.

While some students viewed aspects of their teacher preparation as uneven because of the lack of experience of certain instructors, overall the students we interviewed were satisfied with their preparation. They invariably indicated that they believed they were prepared to teach and, as the following student observation illustrates, they also believed that the faculty was also the strength of the program. When asked for the best, most positive comment that could be offered about the program, one student replied, "You have teachers that absolutely make up for the rest of them. That can absolutely bring out the enthusiasm and creativity that drives you. That's what I like. We do have really good teachers who keep me excited about teaching."

We also met with a number of experienced teachers who cooperated with the elementary program during the student teaching and practicum phases. We asked whether they believed the students today appear to be better prepared to teach than they were formerly. Most responded that the prospective teachers from Indiana University *were* better prepared today. We also asked those teachers who had worked with students from other institutions how they would characterize Indiana University elementary teachers:

Teacher One: I think they are different from student teachers from other schools. One thing I have noticed is they are so enthusiastic.

Teacher Two: Of course, it depends upon the student teacher you work with in terms of how you see the program, but I've had excellent student teachers to work with. I'm amazed at how much know-how they have when they come into the classroom and how willing they are to try new things. Often, it's not something that you, the classroom teacher, have suggested that they do, but they do come to you with ideas and they want to try them. I think that's great!

Teacher One: I think they're coming out more and more qualified each day.

Zimpher: What is it that makes these student teachers better today?

Teacher Two: For one thing, I think they realize there's a lot of competition out there for jobs!

Howey: So they're working harder. Are they also prepared better?

Teacher Two: Both. I think they're taking their preparation more seriously. They're very serious about their careers . . . they really want to be teachers. It's the attitude, 'I've got to go out there and show that I can be a good teacher and I have to do it right away from the initial interview'. Even the resumes they send out show how serious they are. They're professionally done.

Teacher Three: These student teachers are very eager to do a good job for us. And they're very eager to learn to use our materials and the curriculum that we have in the classroom as well as their own ideas.

We observed the earnest nature these prospective teachers revealed to cooperating teachers as well and it frequently was coupled with a desire by these young people to help others, as characterized in the exchange below:

Zimpher: Why are you here at Indiana University, and why did you decide to become a teacher?

Student: I think I've got a lot of the qualities that can really help not only the students I teach, but society in general. I'm not going to change the world, but I sure can help. I think there's a great need for really good people, and I think I can contribute. I'm willing to make sacrifices financially if necessary. I don't know how long I'll stay in it. I don't know if it can grow with me, but I'm very serious about teaching.

The cooperating teachers with whom we visited also had some concerns about aspects of teacher preparation today, one of which had to do with the quality of general education of students in college today. While these experienced teachers believed that advances had been made in terms of the curriculum in elementary school and how to teach that curriculum, the broader knowledge they wanted in a teacher was seen as lacking, as illustrated below:

Howey: Is there anything that we're not asking that you might want to share with us about these teachers?

Teacher: I think the whole approach to training teachers is wrong. I think all people going into education should spend at least the first two years—or maybe more—in liberal arts. They should not make a decision before that time, or, if their decision is made, they should not go into the program until at least their junior year.

Howey: How would you feel about it if students spent four years in general studies only?

Teacher: It would be terrific. They ought to be out there competing in the classes with all the other people in chemistry and literature and history and everything else because we've got to have the best. They shouldn't be in professional courses only for education majors. Then, they should go on to the school of education for their methods courses, field experience, and student teaching. Maybe it will take five years.

Howey: This is an internationally known university. Do you find even in a university setting that these people are not liberally enough educated?

Teacher: Yes. Definitely.

Zimpher: Why is that?

Teacher: My students don't always know some of the basics in American history. They don't know . . . they haven't read basic works of literature. And it's not because they don't want to, they just haven't had the opportunity. The general studies outlined for them is weak.

THE FACULTY

As one would expect at an institution as large as Indiana University, the faculty represents a broad spectrum of perspectives and interests. The School of Education emphasizes research and development. Scholarly inquiry understandably is an important priority. In the 1984–85 Annual Report for the school, more than twenty externally funded grants were identified as associated with faculty in the school. An extended list of various honors accorded faculty for scholarship and service during that tiime was included. Further evidence of the research orientation in the school are in the various centers attached to the six departments in the School of Education. Seventeen different centers and institutes are identified on the Bloomington and Indianapolis campuses, including: The Center for Innovation in the Teaching of the Handicapped, The Clearinghouse for Computer Education, The Center for Urban and Multi-Cultural Education, The Computer Literacy Center, The Social Studies Development Center, and The Vocational Education Services Center.

Even in institutions with a research mission, faculty vary in their ability and commitment to engage in scholarly inquiry. Some are characterized primarily by their commitment to teaching or the time and effort they give to developing special laboratory activities for students. Some devote considerable energies to the outreach function of the university. Witness the following exchange with Professor Ed Buffie, the then chair of the Elementary Education Program Area:

Howey: Given some of the insights derived from recent studies of teaching, would you say that the teacher education programs at your institution have advanced?

Buffie: I would like to think so, but I just don't know. Clearly, there's a real problem with the findings of many research studies reaching the public schools and people in the public schools acting on the basis of research findings. Whether the research that has been generated has made our teacher education programs better . . . I don't know. I feel the way Howard [Mehlinger] does in the sense that all of us in the School of Education should be exemplary in terms of our teaching. And I believe that very deeply. We ought all to be working hard to be the very best models in terms of our own teaching. I think there are a couple of ways you can really advance the cause of teacher education in the classroom. One is to be outstanding in terms of your service commitment because you are out in the real world. You view things differently when you're out in the schools, particularly when you're working side-by-side with school people to help them solve problems. You learn a lot from that experience.

I also think you learn a lot as a result of research and writing. It seems to me however, a more balanced approach would insist upon exemplary teaching and then a strength in one area or the other . . . service or research and publication. Howard [Mehlinger] is moving in this direction. He has talked about that, and he clearly wants that to be the case. I don't think the faculty sees that yet. With the Center for Excellence in Education [discussed later herein] this will be a good vehicle for promoting that.

THE CURRENT ELEMENTARY EDUCATION PROGRAM

We are in the office of Duaine Lang, coordinator for field experiences in the School of Education. Professor Lang is well-known in the network of directors of field experiences across the country. He is a past president of the Association of Teacher Educators and has, for many years, worked to improve both the scope and the quality of field experiences for students in programs of teacher education. His office reflects his extensive involvement in this organization and a centerpiece on his wall is an award which he received from ATE for outstanding service over the years. Lang has been on the Indiana University faculty for almost two decades, and we thought that he was in an excellent position to provide an historical perspective on the nature and quality of teacher education at Indiana University having interacted with all of the teacher licensure programs over the years. Because of rather severe retrenchment in faculty and resources in the School of Education over a number of years, many of the alternative programs in teacher preparation have been discontinued. Thus, we asked whether he thought the program currently represented a quality effort, and he replied:

> Our program has been strengthened in both the general education requirements and also in the sequencing of professional coursework. The new state licensing patterns have contributed to this. There are some problems; it was a long process, and it involved a lot of teachers. Somebody in the state department wasn't writing this. The pre-student teaching experiences—the laboratory experiences—have made a significant contribution. The competency testing program is also beginning to show some results.

Professor Lang elaborated on some of the distinctive qualities of the current elementary program. He called attention to courses that were now clustered, whereby there was joint planning by professors representing different subjects, especially in terms of the field component attached to these courses which are offered in a contiguous sequence. Also, students have the opportunity to go through the program in cohort groups:

> We don't have the highest expectations for fieldwork in our required programs. The University of Evansville is probably better than we are, but they're only dealing with twenty students. I believe our program is quite rigorous and of high quality. Ours is one of the few programs in the state where the early experience requirement is *course* related. The expectations for what is done in schools grow out of the course in which students are enrolled. At the elementary level a lot of this came about because of Gerald Marker, because of his backing. It wasn't his idea as such, but when he was the undergraduate coordinator he advocated clustering the courses and making them a single experience. And that's a strength in the elementary program to the extent that it's forcing these instructors to share

the field experience time; in effect, to share the courses and their expectations for students in those courses with each other.

Lang continued his description of the program and the block or cluster emphasis:

> The elementary program has four clusters; in effect, four semesters that precede student teaching. When the students enter the program, they're engaged with work in educational psychology and this is clustered with a first course in literature. At the next level, they get into the science and math methods. Students take both of these courses at the same time, and a common field experience services both math and science. Then, at the 300-level, they get into the general methods work and the cultural diversity component of the program, the language arts and reading. There are four courses in this cluster where students have an interrelated experience in schools. At the 400-level, the semester immediately preceding student teaching, students take the second reading course, social studies methods, and the music and arts methods. These courses share a thirty-hour field experience and, instead of making a separate placement for each of these courses, we make one field placement. Generally, we can get all the students in a cluster within a single school building, which means that one professor, one of those three or four professors, will also have the responsibility for the field experience supervision.

The laboratory and field experiences attached to these courses vary. As we indicated, considerable diversity exists across this faculty. One orientation for these laboratory and clinical experiences is an effort to instill more reflective habits in these prospective teachers. This orientation is discussed by Jesse Goodman, who teaches social studies methods:

> In social studies, I focus on a *critical perspective* to empower teachers. I'm thinking in terms of the literature concerning the deskilling of teachers, which, to me, is combating the idea that experts should make educational decisions and teachers should mindlessly follow rules and implement curriculum that other people develop. From my perspective, we'll get better education if we try more seriously to empower teachers—to help them make more informed judgments and get them thinking and being more reflective about what they do and why and what's valuable to teach, and what's the best way to teach it. So, the course, from my perspective, is designed with some attempt to empower the students as curriculum developers and implementers, as thoughtful practitioners, as people who think about the social and political implications of their teaching . . . the hidden curriculum and what kind of unintended messages they want to send the students through the methods they employ.

As indicated, these field experiences vary in orientation and, on occasion, they extend beyond the school context as well. For example, Mike

Cohen described a planned field experience that had been built into the Children's Museum in Indianapolis and involved faculty from other campuses as well:

> We use the Children's Museum for some of our field experiences and that's interesting because it started here in Indianapolis. One of the Bloomington faculty members now uses it as well. One of the faculty members at Kokomo also uses it. What you have is a pilot experience at the Children's Museum which has evolved into a program where our students meet children from a school at the museum and spend the day going through the exhibit with them. Then, they go back to their schools and, on a one-to-one basis, develop instruction based on their experience at the museum.

While there is currently one basic program in elementary education, there are still variations and we would be remiss in sharing our story of Indiana University if we didn't speak at least briefly to the efforts of Professor James Mahan. For more than fifteen years Professor Mahan has coordinated teacher education options focusing on an appreciation of cultural diversity. He has designed programs for students to work with Native Americans, Latinos, whites in remote rural situations, and multicultural groups in urban areas. Mahan is intense in his commitment to preparing high-quality teachers to address the country's cultural diversity:

> I just don't see placing student teachers any place they want to go. I can start a project in Florida and know I could get enough students to justify the project, but I need to know why they want to go there. I could conjure up a program that would mandate learning Spanish and their cultural heritage down there with Cuban immigrants and build a strong rationale on paper, but I still think many of the students would be going because the beaches are there. I don't want to get into that kind of thing.
>
> There need to be cultural, educational, and sociological reasons for conducting cultural immersion projects. The students in my area work hard. Dean Mehlinger went to American Indian reservations with me in the fall of 1981 or 1982, and he spent six days visiting American Indian schools. When he finished, he commented that it was just like the Peace Corps and that these student teachers were really working! He stayed in dormitory isolation rooms with me where mirrors were sometimes missing and where the lavatories were less than three feet above the floor. Why? Because these boarding school dormitories were built for small children. One staff member brought him a piece of a broken mirror to shave by in one school and he cut himself on the shard. I thought it was perfect! It was just exactly what he needed to see. There was no swimming pool and no golf clubs. Of course, he's not that way himself. I went out jogging very early one morning, and he was sitting in the school lounge. No one was up at that time, but he was writing. He works like that, and I'll guarantee you he was out there at 4:30 a.m. that morning working on a manuscript.

We asked Dr. Mahan to elaborate on the prerequisite requirements to this multicultural program and whether his efforts, often-cited in the literature, were unique in terms of teacher preparation today, at least in the Midwest:

I think so, but there's no reason other places couldn't do it and some universities no doubt are conducting similar programs. But truthfully, when I go across that big Navajo reservation that's the size of West Virginia, I bump into few other student teachers from other institutions. An occasional student teacher from an Arizona or New Mexico institution, perhaps. . . .

In the Indiana University program, students take a course that consists of extensive readings about which they then write abstracts. They'll see motion pictures . . . we'll talk to them . . . we'll bring in ethnic minority consultants. We may assign certain shorter articles that they're to read and report on before their peers. We do whatever we can do to get relevant information before them. Then, about mid-spring, they must attend a three-day workshop, and, again, we will bring in consultants—within constraints of time and money. We have done a fairly good job of bringing them in—Hispanics, Native Americans. . . . Students complete the workshop, and, in one of the next two full semesters, they go to their sites to student teach. It varies from project to project, but at the end of each two weeks that they're out there, students prepare a rather detailed cultural synthesis report in which they list and describe the kinds of cultural activities in which they've been involved. They describe and interpret the two events that jarred them the most over the two-week period. These are not just student teaching projects where merely the geography changes. I think our reading requirements, our evening seminar requirements, our workshop requirements, and so on, cause uncommitted students to screen out of the project.

Jim Mahan's efforts, especially the experiences he provides students on American Indian reservations and in Latino projects, are well-known in a number of institutions. We discussed the extent to which students both from Indiana University and other campuses are involved in these projects.

When it comes to annual enrollment in the five projects, we've got about eighty Indiana University students—all kinds, not just elementary—in the project for next year and we are approaching a total of 550 Indian reservation student teachers served over the years. About 15 percent of the students annually are coming into the cultural projects from the Bloomington campus. Also, I've got twenty-two from other universities. For a long time, we've had students from other universities coming here. As our tuition rates increase, something I have no control over, people from out-of-state universities begin to be discouraged. But West Virginia, Buffalo, Miami of Ohio, Millersville, Ball State, and the University of Maine are some of those who have been with us for a long time.

Many students who have participated in these projects, as Mahan reported, stay on to teach there. But, regardless of whether they remain, they are impressed with and affected by these experiences. In the evaluations of the program we examined, the following comments by students were typical:

> As everything is winding down, I'm getting very sad. I've come to feel so attached to the people and their ideas—even just the feeling of being here. I hate to see it end. I feel as though I've just gotten started into the meat of things here in 'Beautiful Valley'. This has been a fantastic experience for me. I've learned just as much about myself as I have about Navajo life and culture. You were right—I feel that Chinle was just the right place for my student teaching. It has become home to me in many ways.

> My experience in Weslaco was one of the best, if not the best, experience in living of my entire life. It began slowly. The people at the agency were slow to accept me and the area was slow to accept me. Eventually though, we began to accept, understand, and even respect each other. I feel richer for having come here. I love the Mexican-American people and their culture and traditions. As a matter of fact, any day now I may become 'una Mexicana'. Now that I think of it, . . . *fantastic* doesn't even describe the experiences. It was just an extremely positive growing time.

> My experience in Nogales was more than I had expected out of a student teaching assignment. While in Nogales, one is not merely restricted to, or isolated by, the school. Rather, the community plays an integral role. This was especially significant and easily observable during the agency internship. The people were overwhelmingly warm to me. I think people here are generally more appreciative of people, and they enjoy showing that.

THE INDIANA PROGRAM: PAST

A number of faculty volunteered an historical perspective of the program for us, especially in terms of the numerous options for preparing elementary teachers that existed in the past. We found accounts of the demise of these options instructive and include a few of those recollections by faculty. Professor Buffie recalled some of these program options:

> At one time, a lot of energy went into our undergraduate teacher education program; there was a lot of creativity and a lot of diversity that we no longer have. We have a good program right now. Don't let my comments mislead you. We have a good program because we have *good* people. But essentially, we all operate independently; we don't have much interaction with other faculty. Occasionally we may have a couple of faculty that work closely together and so forth, which is quite different from what we've had in the past. We're not as distinctive as we once were. People still think of us as being distinctive . . . we may be living off past glories. Essentially we have one program here and it's the same for all students. That change occurred out of necessity and intent. [Buffie is referring to major cutbacks in faculty which occurred over several years, as well as the need to achieve less labor-intensive teacher preparation than existed in many of the earlier program variations.]

We, at one time, had five different programs for undergraduate elementary majors. We had a highly articulated program that covered three semesters, the Encore Program; we had the Professional Year Program; and a Professional Semester Program. In each of those three instances, faculty worked closely together and were responsible for the same group of students. For example, in the Professional Semester Program—the Block Program—there were five faculty who each taught two sections of fifty students and had complete control of the students' time. The students were all interviewed before they came into the program. We told them they had to be free between the hours of 8:00 a.m. and 5:00 p.m. so that students with part-time jobs after school were excluded. We had to have them from 8 to 5.

Frank Lester, a professor in mathematics education, also reflected on what the institution was like when he joined the faculty in the early 1970s:

When I came here, I was involved in the Professional Year Program, in which students were placed in a school for a full year and had all their methods courses taught to them in the school. In the elementary schools, to oversimplify a bit, half of the students would student teach all morning long and the other half would student teach all afternoon; when they weren't student teaching, they were taking methods classes. We saturated schools so that we might have twenty or more students in a school. It was very nice. You could have panel discussions with teachers on various topics and issues. We even had some of the students teaching pupils as part of the classes. I mean there were a lot of possibilities, and we achieved real integration across the methods areas. Many core presentations involved teams of us—social studies, math, science, reading, language arts— usually five or six of us. We would plan a semester, identify the common themes or issues, and decide how we could begin them in a different way. Obviously, there are drawbacks; such an approach is not very cost efficient . . . there's a low faculty ratio for the number of full time equivalent (FTE) students that you're generating. This cost factor led to the program's demise when the external money ended.

I was also involved in the multicultural program. Which was an attempt to prepare students to teach in multiracial, multiethnic environments including American Indian reservations. I also worked the Math Methods Program, which was very successful. In fact, it's still being used in about twenty institutions around the country. It was funded by the National Science Foundation, and the materials were developed here. For five years, we had summer institutes for college people to be trained to use the materials. We required then, as now, that all of our education students take nine semester hours of math in addition to three semester hours of methods course work. We integrated this so that as they were studying their math they were also getting methods work along with it.

We also incorporated what one might call an *immersion school*. We provided these schools with special equipment and support—we bought a full-time resource teacher for them—and we were there frequently. The teachers, the student teachers, and the children all loved it. We held 'math fairs,' and one was during the basketball sectionals. The state goes crazy over basketball. We held a math fair at one of our rural schools and it was scheduled during the finals of the sectionals where the high school was involved—and we outdrew them! We had three-pronged integration. First, was the emphasis on the math content they were learning; second, was on the pedagogy; finally, the fieldwork where concepts we would address on campus would soon be put into practice by the students in the schools. We were there often enough and long enough that there was change over time.

The faculty recalled with some fondness what appeared to be the salad days in teacher preparation, at least in terms of *diversity,* but they had multiple explanations about why this condition no longer existed. One reason, of course, was the considerable diminishment in the number of students and faculty. Another factor cited by some was an aging faculty, who, over time, was forced to attend to more conventional forms of scholarly inquiry in order to be promoted. There was the considerable impact of the sharp decline in external (especially federal) funds to support innovation in teacher education. A number of factors were more related to specific programs. Professor Lester explained the decline of the integrated math program in the following way, for example:

> The math education faculty was the first group who had a regular field experience integrated into their curriculum before the state mandated it because we thought it was a good idea. The students ought to be out in the schools, but it wasn't until the state said students must have regular and continuous field experience that everybody else got into the act. Well, this is a small community, and one of the problems that resulted from that mandate was that we overwhelmed the schools with large numbers of students.

Various faculty talked about the considerable decline in both students and faculty from the early 1970s. Professor Lang stated:

> There has been a diminishment of numbers in practically every teacher preparation institution across the country. Ours, though, is of a different magnitude, especially with regard to demographics. In 1971–72, we had about 2,600 student teachers. Currently, we have about 600 per year, at least from our Bloomington campus. I'm talking about *bodies* not placements. Also, remember that now we have seven different campuses that have elementary student teaching programs.

This diminishment in numbers of course cut across all licensure programs in the college. Professor Gerald Marker, in discussing changes in secondary social studies over this similar period of time, remarked, "In secondary social studies, to give you an example of how we changed, in the early 1970s, we took 350 students through the secondary social studies program on this campus. Now, we're putting about fifty or sixty through our program." Professor Mahan ventured his opinion as to why many faculty did not continue their involvement in efforts such as the above.

A big problem was that we were still hiring professors at that time, and the young professors were assigned to work out in the schools. Pretty soon the young associate professors were told that if they didn't have a number of articles written, they would not be promoted. So, they'd be clamoring to get back in the office, teach down the halls here, and then go back to the office and write. The budgets constricted and, as enrollment dropped severely, we began to hire fewer and fewer professors. Finally, there were no young professors to assist in the field-based projects and public school sites. In the last year I was in it, I was the *only* professor; we had four doctoral students teaching the methods courses and the school teachers were asking what had become of the faculty that was supposed to be working with them. I understand those are headaches you'll get at any university.

Dr. Lang may well have identified the primary reason that the range of program options declined in the School of Education at Indiana.

Over the years, then, as the number of the students diminished and there were fewer faculty, our faculty just simply got tired of work in the field. It's a lot tougher out there—that's what killed most of the projects—they were predicated on faculty being out in the field and it's not only tough work but there's not enough reward after the grant runs out.

A continuing retrenchment has been evidenced in the faculty and in the funds to support programs at Indiana University for the past fifteen years. This downward spiral, however, appears to be coming to an end, as Gerald Marker, who served as an associate dean to more than one dean, observed:

Central Administration has been involved in long-term decrease in the size of the School of Education and its budget. Central deals with a lot of data and one of the things they look at is our cluster credit hours. Our credit hours are divided by our total budget—they do that to everybody—and, of course, in many ways this is too simple a formula. For a long time, however, we were the most expensive credit hour on campus—higher than social work, optometry, almost everyone. We have, over time, cut back considerably. In some ways, we can still be seen as overstaffed if you look at the kind of courses we teach relative to what other people teach. We appear expensive. So, they have systematically cut our base budget. It was happening in 1970 through 1972, when I was in the dean's office, and it happened every year I was there except Howard's [Mehlinger] first year as dean, when he negotiated as part of his agreement to become dean for a no-base budget cut during his first year. We've had a base budget cut every year in the $200,000 to $250,000 range. Their goal for the School of Education is 100 faculty—at one time there were almost 200 faculty. They want the faculty to stabilize at that number and we are almost there now.

Thus, Indiana University has seen a continuing reduction of faculty over the years and the diminishment of programmatic options into a more singular approach to prepare teachers. This current approach, while not especially distinctive, rests on a competent faculty and their high-quality involvement in this program. Clustering courses, continuing field experiences, and school cohort groups are programmatic features. Once the plateau of stable faculty numbers is reached, which Professor Marker observed is soon approaching, then what does the future hold for teacher preparation at Indiana University?

PROGRAMS AT INDIANA UNIVERSITY: THE FUTURE

Several planning efforts in the school currently look to the future. Committees have been formed that recommend new directions in both the elementary and secondary programs. Professor Anna Ochoa's leadership in this regard is widely acknowledged by her colleagues. Ochoa is the current director of Undergraduate Studies on the Bloomington Campus. She shared the following with us regarding her committee, which is concerned with elementary teacher education.

> It's been an exceptionally good committee—people with a lot of commitment spending a lot of time. And their recommendations span the whole program, . . . which is not to say they're exhaustive, but they extend all the way from changing admissions standards to capping program enrollments. We've looked critically at general studies and at the professional studies. There is a recommendation for an academic area of concentration. The idea of a fifth year program was dismissed fairly quickly—more quickly than I would have.

In addition to these emerging efforts to redesign teacher education within the School of Education, recent changes have been made in admission standards, as Professor Ochoa noted. The required grade point average for admission to education has been raised, and students are now required to pass basic skills tests as well in terms of reading, writing, and mathematics. When these tests were first administered, almost 20 percent of the students were screened out of the program. Thus, these efforts appear to address the concern expressed by some over the bipolar distribution of students. Also, in our discussions with Dr. Anya Royce in the provost's office, we were informed that the admissions director had dramatically sought increasingly higher SAT scores of incoming freshmen within the last five years. She indicated that Indiana University was increasingly drawing more students from the top one-third of their high school classes. The School of Education as well as all other schools appear to have benefitted from these recruitment and standard-raising efforts. In checking data shared in a recent self-report to the NCATE, evidence suggested in excess of 80 percent of the students in education graduated in the upper one-half of their high school graduating class, and this figure compared favorably with other professional schools on campus.

Understandably, the dean of the School of Education is, in many respects, at the forefront of planned changes for the future. In this concluding

section discussing possible future directions for this major school of education, we concentrate on a number of ideas and concepts expressed by Dean
Howard Mehlinger.

Many faculty are currently involved in critically examining future directions for teacher education and the ideas espoused herein by the dean will,
in the final analysis, most likely rise or fall to the extent by which they are
also embraced by the faculty. Dean Mehlinger readily acknowledges this.
Nonetheless, he appears to bring a unique perspective, or at least emphasis,
in terms of the mission of the School of Education in the major *state* institution. In these portrayals of different programs of teacher preparation, we are
stressing different or distinctive qualities that might inform us about the way
to advance teacher preparation; therefore, we have chosen to focus on this
dean's particular vision for his institution which he is approaching on multiple
fronts. Certainly, what appears to be the centerpiece for planned change in the
future at Indiana University is the proposed Center for Excellence in Education. Mehlinger spoke to the origins of this concept:

I was asked to take this job in 1981, and, in turn, I asked two conditions of the
president and vice president. This school had been in a steady retrenchment since
1972. Every year its base had been cut. Every year it had faculty lines reduced.
We had approximately 200 faculty lines in 1972. This year in Bloomington we
had approximately 100 lines. So we've been steadily cut, and it would be foolish
to claim that this erosion has been done easily or without the cost of quality in
particular areas. It has varied a lot. Some areas have been hurt more than others.
Morale was very low when I became dean, and I agreed to take the job knowing
full well that there was going to be more retrenchment. Something had to be done
about faculty morale. It was very low, and it was not likely to rise very quickly
unless we did something.

These were the two conditions for my accepting the position: first, I wanted
at least a year's breathing space. If further faculty retrenchment was necessary
because we were out of sync with the average student/faculty ratio in the university, fine, but I had to have a year's breathing space while I began to get on top of
this organization and see what kind of changes were, in fact, needed. That was
condition one. It was readily accepted. Second, we had to do something about the
incredible physical conditions. Not my own; this is a fine office. I'm treated very
well. But as you walk through this building, you will see a fifty-year-old building. This used to be the laboratory school. Some of the restrooms are still
designed for first and second graders. The building is safe. It's well-maintained.
But it's a lousy building for a modern school of education. One of our strong
areas in this school is in Instructional Systems Technology. About half of the
faculty who are in the program—it's entirely a graduate program—go into
corporate training sites. The day they walk out of the door they enter better facilities than they were trained in. . . . It's incredible. . . . And they said they would
do their best.

My tenure began about the time that the state was about to have a budget
deficit. The state ordered no new university buildings because the demographics

indicated that enrollments were declining. So, after about a year, I went to see the president and asked how the building plan was going. He told me they hadn't made any progress on it and he didn't think that we were going to be able to do it. But, he told me if I could figure out a way to do it, I could go ahead. So I began having meetings with people to see what we wanted to do in education; to redirect the focus of education. Over a period of about a year of study and with help from a lot of different people, we devised the Center for Excellence in Education.

The school needed to do something to change its image of itself and its image on the campus. When you walk onto this campus, you're not here very long before you begin to sense there's something about the School of Music that's extraordinary. You go to the Musical Arts Center and someone hands you the program of activities for the week and you see a whole host of things, and you know there's something about the School of Music that's very special. People want to be attached to the School of Music even if they're not musicians, because that's the jewel of the crown as far as Indiana University is concerned. And the School of Music doesn't have to promote itself. Everybody knows about it.

The School of Education doesn't feel that way about itself. People really ought to know that the best teaching—people who have proprietary ownership of teaching—are the people in education, and we ought to have the best teaching facilities. So, I thought this so-called center would be first a facility of the first order to reflect the state-of-the-art technology to enable teaching. And if my dream is fulfilled, it will be a spectacular facility, and it will be a facility used across campus.

Therefore, we have this initial vision of this physical facility representing the very best in terms of communications technology and their applications to instruction. Mehlinger went on to illustrate the next steps employed in getting faculty to think about the type of facility that they wanted.

The first step was to form a faculty committee and to ask, after the new building is built, what will we do with it? It can be anything we want. We asked faculty to share their best dreams. We sent out a questionnaire to the faculty. Fewer than one-half, perhaps only one-third, even bothered to respond. And so we began to check it out, thinking it was kind of strange. The faculty said they thought nothing would happen. The university wouldn't do this.

The faculty committee then made appointments with every member of the faculty to fill out the questionnaire with them and listen to their complaints. And still the attitude was that this simply wasn't going to happen. That was, I think, in 1982 or 1983. It took an entire year to talk with everyone because it was so difficult to get the faculty to take it seriously.

Now you find in the faculty—now that Congress has appropriated the money and it looks as if we'll get substantial money from the private sector—the belief that it's going to happen. Now the faculty have said to the Long-Range Planning Committee that they can't go any further with this building until the committee asks their opinion.

Dr. Thomas Schreck, formerly dean for Student Affairs and currently director of External Relations, worked very closely with Dean Mehlinger in developing the Center for Excellence in Education. He talked with us about the history of the center at some length and shared many of the efforts that occurred outside of the university in order to promote this concept:

> I think it is important to tell you the way we announced the concept. The Lilly Endowment provided the center with a $65,000 planning grant. Some of it was earmarked for writers to help us convey our ideas and clarify for others what we were talking about. Some of it was expended in travel to talk to those who might help us in various ways. The first announcement of the proposed center took place in Washington, when the president of the university, the state superintendent, and other key administrators hosted a Congressional Breakfast. We told our Congressional Delegation what we were trying to do, and we asked for their help. We told them the center was unique. We've seen technology centers in education, but we haven't seen anybody who's really trying to rework a whole school, a whole university—and to interface with the state's public schools. The Washington announcement was followed by the governor's breakfast press conference where we brought in the CEOs of major corporations and other leaders from around the state. It was really a who's who in the state.

The lobbying efforts in Washington resulted in an appropriation of $6 million under Title V, Section 501 of the Human Services Authorization Act, Public Law 98–558. The authorization states that the federal government's share for the cost of this facility would not exceed 50 percent. Currently, approximately $10 million in federal funding exists. AT&T recently announced they will form an alliance with Indiana University "to pursue the application of technology to the educational process." The agreement calls for an expenditure of $7 million in equipment and human resources to create this state-of-the-art facility.

Tom Schreck elaborated on his conception of what is embedded in this soon to-be-built facility.

> Howard [Mehlinger] and I both acknowledge that it is first a facility—but it's more than that. It's a concept. It is very difficult to tell somebody what is going to happen at the center. When you put together a facility that rich in terms of technology in a cooperative venture with a corporation like AT&T, a vendor who does more than supply equipment and who is committed to continuing research and development, couple that with the faculty of the total university to bring about educational reform . . . that's exciting! The center can be on the cutting edge of the application of technology. Putting a student in front of a 'drill and practice' personal computer isn't the answer.
>
> We have been working to build a teaching facility. It will house the School of Education, but it will really be a university facility that will cut across schools and colleges . . . there will be other faculty involved, although they may not all be physically located there. You can bring faculty into networks. There will be teaching facilities there that will be utilized by other schools and other disciplines. For example, the business school is interested in offering a statewide graduate program in business. The center could be used for this purpose.

One thing that caught the fancy of the federal government was the notion of private partnership, a partnership with a major corporation. Second, and I think this has made it appealing to the private sector, it is not a School of Education venture to reform K–12 school curriculum *alone* or even to reform teacher education internally or to take on the training of school leaders in this state. And I think school leadership is a critical issue. We are going to work *cooperatively* with the state and local districts. To make the center work we need a true partnership. You take a quality faculty who have good skills and know pedagogy, they know how students learn and they know how to build curriculum, and you wed them with people who know a lot about technology. For example, how do you get people from the Bell Labs to work with people at the university to develop the concept of laser technology for instruction?

Two of our faculty are extremely interested in building a simulation lab for field experiences. . . . Think about the Department of Defense—we've had some preliminary conversations with them—they've spent *billions* on simulations. Why can't some of those resources flow back into education? It's about time we employ the best of the applicable technology they've developed and we've invested tax dollars in.

You soon realize that the best teaching facilities are not in schools; they're in corporate America. We went, for example, to Cincinnati where AT&T teleconferences to more than sixty regional locations three times a week through interactive video. They offer courses comparable to graduate courses for their employees in sales, promotion, and everything else, out of a central location with two-way interaction. They have a student tracking system and a student registration system that is most likely better than any university in the country has in place. They literally load the course offerings on computer and then take reservations. They have the course filled, and nobody ever comes to Cincinnati.

Gerald Marker, in discussing the need for more diverse and robust laboratory experiences in the teacher preparation programs at Indiana, underscored the importance of the Center in this regard and extended upon Schreck's observations:

I think the center's going to give us an option, which I hope we pursue, to replace some of the field experiences with simulated laboratory experiences. I think we're going to get the equipment and hardware to do it. There are lots of exemplars from practice that students can analyze and learn from. The inefficiency of the field experience is related to a lot of those things over which you have no control . . . what the students are going to see and do . . . it's so labor intensive. But if you had, in the can, thousands of samples of real world classrooms and examples of teachers illustrating a wide variety of concepts, then students could learn from these if you had the hardware to do it.

Schreck described the way the center is intended to interface with schools throughout the state and the coordinate campuses, and he outlined the possibilities for curriculum development and instructional improvement in the schools:

If you want to improve schools, start with content reform . . . the curriculum itself . . . what's being taught in our schools. States such as this one are going to increase English and math requirements. We need to look at the materials being taught, the content, as well as how it is being taught. The role the teacher currently assumes in the classroom is going to change with technology. Because of our eight-campus system and our existing technology, we are well-positioned. The next step is to link the K–12 schools through the eight-campus system. Dean Mehlinger is continually meeting with the State Superintendents' Association and the State School Boards' Association, the principals, and other leaders to keep them abreast of what we're doing. He routinely meets all over the state with groups of ten and twelve superintendents. The day we offer linkage, a number of schools will probably expend whatever it takes to participate. Even if they need to get new monies; they'll raise the money locally to tie in.

One brochure which describes the proposed Center for Excellence in Education summarizes essential features of the center as well as its general mission and immediate priorities.

The Center for Excellence in Education will be a model facility—one of a kind in the nation—affecting instruction provided to children, youth, and adults in a wide range of formal and informal settings. The Center will conduct research, produce educational products, train educational leaders, and develop effective management practices.

The Center will feature the application of technology to education. The Center will encourage partnerships among schools, universities, businesses and industries, and private and public organizations. Successful educational reform requires that responsibility be shared appropriately. The Center, an example of cooperation among various sectors of society, will demonstrate how linkages among groups are developed.

The Center's mission is broad, touching on all instructional settings and age groups and nearly every subject area. Initially, the Center will focus on problems affecting the performance of elementary and secondary schools.

THE SCHOOL OF EDUCATION AND ITS MISSION TO THE STATE

Mehlinger enumerated other priorities for the School of Education beyond the Center for Excellence in Education. Yet, this proposed center is instrumental in a number of ways in achieving these priorities, such as maintaining a strong coordinate campus arrangement and linking these multiple campuses to the needs and problems of K–12 schools in Indiana. Dean Mehlinger talked with some passion about his conception of the mission of a state university relative to the schools in the state.

People ought to decide what they're going to do in professional activities or any other kind of activity; they ought to assess their strengths and weaknesses and what they do best. To use a basketball metaphor, since this is a town that likes to talk a lot about basketball, if you're 7'1" tall, you don't pretend you're a point guard and dribble between your legs. You get under the basket and stuff the ball through the basket. Indiana University has certain characteristics that embrace both strengths and weaknesses. One of the characteristics is that we have a system of campuses all over the state in which we can help people become teachers, and we can work very well with a lot of public schools—better than almost any other university in the country.

And I think we have a responsibility to do that. We're a state university. The taxpayers expect us to serve the state of Indiana. We went through a period of time where we were dazzled by federal money and dazzled by federally supported programs. I'm not saying that to blame anyone because my own prior work here was director of a research and development center in social studies, and my principal exposure to Indianapolis was through the Indianapolis Airport. I rarely went into the city. I ran experimental projects all across the nation. It was a marvelous way to work. But it didn't do much for Indiana.

One of the first things that I learned as dean was that the General Assembly was less than fully impressed with what the School of Education was doing for the state of Indiana. They didn't see that their investment in our research and development work was having much payoff for Indiana. My own judgment was that not only were we doing some dumb things with regard to our own clients who were paying many of our bills, we also weren't being very good stewards for the university. This *is* a marvelous world-class university, but it was not very tightly linked to Indiana schools.

I once asked Bill Hadley, who is the chief lobbyist for the Farm Bureau and by reputation the most effective lobbyist in the state of Indiana, what would happen if the Legislature tried to close the School of Agriculture at Purdue University? He just smiled and told me that they wouldn't dare because within twenty-four hours they would close the Legislature down. They'd have combines, tractors, and plows parked all over so the legislature couldn't get in the door. He said that he'd have 90 percent of the farmers in the state right outside the capitol. I then asked what would happen if someone tried to close down Indiana University's School of Education. He just smiled and countered, did I think schools would shut down? Would superintendents march on the Capitol with their teachers? Would school boards be in the streets with PTAs?'

The dean shared with us his assessment of public education in the state of Indiana and what he believed the governing and administrative powers of the university thought the School of Education's role was in relation to those schools and their needs.

In this state, the public schools are not as good as they ought to be. The School of Education ought to be very concerned about the quality of schools and concerned beyond merely giving speeches about it. Now, I'm reasonably effective at giving talks to Rotary Clubs about the quality of our schools, but when it comes to devoting ourselves to improving the quality of schools, our performance has not matched our rhetoric. The university sort of floats above the schools. It's a world-class institution without worrying very much about the quality of the seniors coming from those high schools into the university. That is a mistake. Our president knows that and our trustees know that.

This cycles back to the Center for Excellence in Education. The center, if all the pieces come together—and that's always uncertain—will be an extraordinary facility for demonstrating ways that the university—we in the School of Education are the main bridge but not the only bridge—can contribute to the schools.

I cannot judge other schools of education. I can only comment about our School of Education. When I became dean, relatively little work was going on in schools. Of course, scholars were doing individual research, not unlike the Arts and Science faculty. Many of our faculty operate on an international and national scene. Some are very active in their professional organizations. But when you added up these individual pieces, there wasn't much that was having a substantial impact on education in this state, which relates again to my notion about a professional school. If a professional school isn't somehow having an impact on schooling or on the clients it serves and if it doesn't have a major segment of the faculty who work cooperatively in training those clients, then we are not much different from an Arts and Science faculty—and that's not what a professional school should be.

We questioned whether he might be placing a disproportionate emphasis on activities at the state level to the exclusion of the national and international responsibilities of a major research institution. For example, Indiana University is not part of the Holmes Group, a consortium of major, research-intensive institutions dedicated to making major changes in teacher preparation with an avowed purpose of moving teacher preparation to the postbaccalaureate level.

There are criteria for which institutions can belong to the Holmes Group, and one rationale for this consortium is provided by Professor David Clark, now at the University of Virginia, who at that time was on the faculty and a former dean at Indiana University. He is widely respected for his general contributions to teacher preparation and helps us understand the Holmes Group initiative. He shared with us what he thought was a misconception by many in terms of the mission of the Holmes Group:

I hate to see the proposal of the Holmes Group reduced to arguments over whether you can put together an outstanding undergraduate-level teacher education program. That isn't even an issue. Of course you can. Everybody knows that. You can put together an outstanding teacher education program at any level and in different life spaces . . . spread over four years or five years or a fifth-year program. The issue is rather what sort of hopes for generalized reform might we have for teacher education over the next twenty years. Those who argue that the hope is [for reform] institution by institution, don't understand the nature of the change process in the field of education in my opinion. And that's the reason that I'm interested in the Holmes Group Consortium. I'm interested in it not only because it asserts what could be a relatively high-quality program, but also because it does so within a framework that might allow for change in the general status of preparation for teaching nationally. It presents a reform movement that would be possible for some groups to get behind.

I'm not all that sanguine about the future of the Holmes Group Consortium, but I think it's our best hope at the present time, and we desperately need to demonstrate that we can do something. Most people don't believe that things are going well in the training of teachers.

In this regard, then, the leaders of the Holmes Group put forth restrictive criteria so that a collective commitment across institutions could be made to a specific set of priorities. Gerald Marker recalls discussing admission to the Holmes Group with Professor Clark:

I said if the group would give just a little bit we could stay in; if they would allow us to run a postbaccalaureate program but also continue to run an undergraduate program if we've got a good one that meets a lot of the needs of state schools. He told me that revolutions are not led by people who compromise. They could not compromise. If only two schools commit to the consortium that do it, then it should be two schools.

With this background, in mind we can better understand Mehlinger's agenda for the School of Education at the national level on the one hand and Indiana University's not being in the Holmes Group on the other:

Certainly, we have a national agenda. It's not the Holmes Group, but we have a national agenda. I also hope that the Holmes Group succeeds. In fact, I wish that there was a way that I could play a role in the Holmes Group. But that's not possible as things stand now because we would have to state that our intention is to abolish undergraduate teacher education, and we're not going to do that here. Leaders in the Holmes Group have created a strategy that the best way to make major change is to take only those who buy the whole package—I think that's a long-shot strategy. Nonetheless, they are the best judges of that.

If they had not chosen that as a strategy, however, then we would probably have participated because we intend to have a graduate teacher education program. But it won't be the only program at Indiana. It's very important that our faculty participate in national efforts, including efforts that are viewed as reform movements. We are working with the Goodlad network, for example, on partnerships with school corporations. The faculty find part of the excitement of creating such a partnership is the fact that they will be participating with faculty and groups with similar concerns in other states. But that won't be the only network we'll be participating in. We'll join other groups as well. . . . We expect to be very active in programs relating to better preparing school principals, for example. That's one area in which we will be extremely active.

In addition to the development of the Center for Excellence in Education and employing this as a primary vehicle to work closely with the state department and school districts throughout the state of Indiana, Mehlinger has

assumed leadership in two other forums designed to advance teacher preparation in the state of Indiana. One of these was the formulation of a coalition of
key institutions preparing teachers in the state of Indiana called the Coalition
of Teacher Education Programs (COTEP); the other is the Indiana Association
of Colleges of Teacher Education (IACTE). Professor Gerald Marker was
released from his administrative responsibilities to serve as the executive
director of COTEP, and he convened the steering committee for this group as
well as various cross-institutional faculty committees (from each of the six
institutions) to develop recommendations for the improvement of teacher
preparation. He was confident that some good would result from this strategy
for improvement and assured us that it was not a top-down approach that was
driven by the ideas of a small group of deans:

> I've coordinated something called the Coalition For Teacher Education Programs.
> It's a Lilly Foundation-funded project, and it's an attempt by six institutions [four
> state schools and two private schools], who prepare a large number of teachers in
> this state to come together around a set of recommendations for improving their
> teacher education programs. When it's over I'll go back to teaching in the
> elementary program.
>
> These institutions are committed to some shared standards. They want to de-
> velop a set of recommendations for themselves, not for other people, unlike other
> commissions that propose what other people should do. COTEP's trying to de-
> cide what it should do, and the deans committed themselves to working together.
> Obviously they had involved faculty, and they have to stay away from recom-
> mendations that they felt either didn't have a chance on their campuses or in
> which they themselves didn't believe. They will go back and tell their faculties
> they really believe in these ideas and I think they should consider them. That's
> really all they committed themselves to do. That's all they could do. They're not
> naive enough to think that they can sign for their faculties on anything. So they
> aren't going to do that.

Dean Mehlinger exerted leadership recently in IACTE. While he felt
compelled earlier to initiate the COTEP consortium, he was optimistic that
this association might contribute as well to enabling teacher preparation. He
shared with us the strategy he employed upon assuming the presidency of
IACTE in 1986:

> In essence, I wrote a 'Dear Colleague' letter to other deans in the state and I
> gave them three facts that reflected the political situation in this state. This letter
> addressed national reforms—the Carnegie Commission, the Council on Basic
> Education task force reports, and so forth—but, basically, the effort was to draw
> attention to the politics at the *state* level because, quite frankly, that will affect us
> far more directly than the Holmes Group or anything else. So I reviewed with the
> deans what the governor and the state superintendent were saying, and I identified
> the groups who inform teacher education legislation in the state. We can either lie

low and hope the whole thing passes us by in a year or we can get off our tails and actively promote our own reform.

When I assumed this presidency in March 1986, we had an executive committee meeting, and I told the executive committee I wanted to try one idea. Every president ought too be entitled to one outrageous idea and I wanted their permission to do it. They were understandably hesitant, but told me if I fully developed the idea they'd consider it. At the April meeting of the executive committee, I gave them more information. The idea is essentially a 'deregulation' approach that asserts good teachers can be prepared in a wide variety of settings—large or small, or private or public, or research or nonresearch. It doesn't mean that we are doing a good job in all these settings, but that it *is* possible. And if we don't believe that, then IACTE is kind of a funny organization because we all represent different institutions. In effect, we'd be admitting that some of us can't do it. So then what would we do? Right now the state tries to apply regulations and often we pull a very thin sheet over a lot of factors that don't fit at all. The state sort of turns its head, blinks, swallows hard, and lets it go.

I wanted to shift the focus of accountability to the outcomes, to publish the results of the outcomes—like a licensing test and like successful performance during a probationary period. Teacher preparation is conducted in different ways, which is all right as long as the outcomes are achieved. They weren't sure about my idea, but said I could present it to the full membership. Whether the ideas themselves are all that original or innovative is not the reason I'm sharing this with you; I want to underscore that reform at the state level is ultimately more interesting—maybe not more intellectually interesting to the profession—in terms of having impact on teaching education. What we do at the state level will be far more significant in my judgment than what we do at the national level. Therefore, anything that prevents us from working well at the state level is an annoyance or an obstacle to overcome.

Howard Mehlinger shared with us the various documents he had either collected or written for his IACTE colleagues and elaborated on the deans' reactions to these proposals:

I thought the chances were highly likely that people would listen politely and then vote it down overwhelmingly because the fear of changing from what we do now is always great—sort of leaping into the unknown—and I thought there would be all kinds of reasons given not to change. Surprisingly, a substantial number spoke favorably of the general concept; good questions were raised about our ability to manage certain aspects, such as the year-long probationary period. I know some other states have tried and had problems. A subcommittee has been formed to work on some of the most problematic aspects of it. But I'm more optimistic about the proposal now. I think there's a chance we might be able to do this.

Essentially, what the proposal says is that there really ought to be only three tests. One 'test' is more of a public disclosure sent to the state. It addresses who is admitted, what SAT scores they have, and other indicators of students' academic aptitudes. It also addresses what students do when they get into the program—what courses they take and so on—and the number and types of students enrolled and type of faculty. If you offer a program for math teachers and you don't have any math teachers, you just say so. Then, when prospective teachers are searching for a position around the state, they aren't misled. Next, we ought to include the performances of students on the statewide test, which has been law for at least a year, and finally, their success in the so-called probationary period.

Consequently, people who look at our disclosure statement will know just how good we are based on the information that will be on file with the state. If, in fact, you deviate from your public statements, the state can hold you accountable. Second, the state will continue to improve the kind of test it's currently giving. Now when students finish an approved program, they don't get a license until they sit for the test, which determines whether they earn the state license. But, while taking a test appeals to the public, the ultimate test of a competent teacher is still performance in the classroom. So let's add on something like a probationary year where the state looks at the performance and decides whether the person is sufficiently qualified. Again, the performance of our students should be public information. Occasionally, the state would publish the test scores and the performance rates in the probationary year by institution, so we'd be held accountable for that. Then if you did a lousy job, the public would know about it, and you could be put out of business. Right now, with the current regulation system, all we know is that *all* of us are approved and, we suspect that there're some programs that aren't very good.

In summary then, we have a dean who, along with his faculty, has envisioned bold new directions for his School of Education and who has been involved in initiatives on a variety of fronts to achieve that vision. It is clear that he sees a relationship between his proposed Center for Excellence in Education, the involvement of his coordinate campuses (for that matter all other institutions of higher education in the state preparing teachers), and fundamental improvement in K–12 schools as well as in teacher preparation. One final illustration underscores the future agenda for the School of Education, at least from Howard Mehlinger's perspective:

The governor wants Chinese widely offered in our schools. Whether that's a good idea or a bad idea, the state will probably invest in this because leaders have a notion that learning Chinese will increase our competitive advantage economically. With the INTELLINET system that the state's going to install, it will be possible to deliver *Chinese* instruction to every school in the state of Indiana, in three or four years. Indiana University has excellent language facilities. This is something the university can do to help the state in a major way through our special resources in languages and through the center.

And so, not only can we make it more interesting for our faculty and draw better students, both graduate and undergraduate, but we can also be viewed by the state as doing something appropriate for the state; in turn, this will help justify educational funding. Right now the state doesn't believe that the School of Education is as important to educational reform as I think it is. Our faculty may think it's unfair or wrong that state officials think this way, but you don't change that perception by simply asserting that it's unfair. You've got to demonstrate to people that you make a difference. So that's my agenda.

6

Conceptually Coherent
Alternative Programs

Who Comes to East Lansing?

The history of the Lansing area is a story essentially of the settlement of the Northwest Territory. Initially, it drew settlers because of its farm land. Today, the metropolitan area of Lansing is populated by nearly one-quarter million people. Its economic base includes business, industry, and agriculture. The "premium vehicles" (Buick, Oldsmobile, Cadillac) operation for General Motors is headquartered here, as is the Motor Wheel Corporation, the world's largest manufacturer of styled wheels and a leader in technological research. Other large, industrial corporations are based here as well, including more than 400 industries and another 5,000 businesses within the region.

As a cultural center, it is obvious that the Lansing community cares about the performing and creative arts. In the heart of downtown Lansing, a family can attend performances of the ninety-member Lansing Symphony, visit the Capital Center for the Arts and other galleries, become involved in nationally recognized theatrical groups like Boarshead and the Civic Players, and attend dramatic and musical events at the new Dart Auditorium on the community college campus.

Lansing's support of education has been enduring as well. From the travel bureau perspective, "A university town has a special feel. Michigan State provides more than football Saturdays and the thrill of Big-Ten competition. It helps focus community concern and effort on education and the influx of more than 40,000 students adds vitality." Lansing also hosts a downtown community college, the Cooley Law School, the Great Lakes Bible College, and the Business School at Davenport College. In addition, Lansing is served

167

by eight local school districts, including the Lansing City Schools totaling in excess of 100 elementary, middle, and high school buildings available to sustain the field experiences of students in the MSU College of Education. Finally, Lansing is a hub for transportation. It is convenient to Detroit and Chicago, and Canada and the Great Northwoods are within easy reach as well.

What are the undergraduate students like who come to East Lansing to study to be teachers at MSU's College of Education? They are almost all white and, in elementary education, almost all female. They are almost all college-age students, as opposed to a nontraditional or older population, and almost all from Michigan. One faculty member told us:

> I was surprised that the students were parochial. I thought coming to a big university they would be worldly and cosmopolitan and appreciative of other cultures and understanding of ethnic groups. And I don't find that, generally speaking. There are a few exceptions in each group, but I was surprised. I come from a small church school and I can understand why my perspective, at times, was narrow. But here, these students are in this big university where you've got everything from all kinds of places . . . but they're from Michigan. That's right. Michigan people.

We found this profile confirmed in our observations and in the data we analyzed. Certainly, efforts have been made to attract a more diverse student body, but they have not been as successful as some would hope. The students acknowledged their parochial nature as well. When asked about their backgrounds and their selection of MSU, the students told us repeatedly that they graduated from high schools across Michigan. One student observed: "It bothers me that there are no black people in the entire program. I've only had one black girl in all my classes. I don't know why." The same student, a male, made further observations about the gender imbalance in the program: "In terms of gender or race, a lot of us realize that we have more biases than we thought. And we're able to work on them. I was pleasantly surprised at being in a class of forty women! But, where are all the black students?"

In summary, then, Lansing, with its pastoral and agricultural roots, fits in many ways the land-grant origins of the university and to some extent is a typificiation of the MSU student. While a portrait can be drawn of an easy environment, nonetheless an international institution of considerable stature operates within this pastoral setting.

What Defines MSU?

By its own assessment, "three words—tradition, diversity, and beauty—characterize Michigan State University." MSU was founded in 1855 and in 1862 became the model for the nation's seventy-two land-grant colleges established under the Morrill Act. Since then, MSU has dedicated its resources to the triadic land-grant mission of teaching, research, and public service. The university houses fourteen colleges, three of them graduate professional schools, and provides study programs in more than 200 academic majors in the liberal and fine arts and in the sciences. Beyond elementary education, the larger student body understandably represents more diversity. Undergraduate students are enrolled from every county in Michigan, every state in the nation, and 100 foreign countries. More than 3,000 minority students are enrolled in undergraduate programs.

MSU characterizes its campus as one of extraordinary natural beauty and certainly these visitors concur. Numerous treed areas, with a profusion of flowers and lovely roadways, pedestrian walks, and bicycle paths weave their way through the very spacious natural setting, which is the 5,000-acre campus of MSU. The university is also a leading residential campus, with twenty-seven separate facilities, gothic and ivy-covered or of contemporary design, wherein many of its 40,000 students live as well as learn.

MSU has many rich traditions. For example, it was the first university to sponsor national merit scholarships, and now has more than 400 such merit scholars studying on campus. Additionally, in excess of 600 students are enrolled in its Honors College. Ten students have won Rhodes Scholarships in the last thirteen years. Faculty have distinguished themselves as members of the National Academy of Sciences, and are recipients of Fulbright, Gugenheim, and Danforth Fellowship Awards. They are sponsors of many scientific breakthroughs and scores of research projects. They are contributors to powerful technological innovations such as the new electron microscope. The university has also been a significant sponsor of the performing arts. The Wharton Center for Performing Arts is a showcase for an impressive array of performers in music, theater, and dance. There is an artist-in-residence program at MSU and the Kresge Art Museum and the MSU permanent collection are manifestations of the university's commitment to the arts. The institution is further characterized by a considerable international outreach program begun twenty-five years ago and flourishing today in developing nations throughout the world.

The MSU College of Education is more than seventy-five years old, has approximately 150 full-time equivalent faculty members, and offers programs in nearly seventy different teacher and school personnel certification programs. It also has a comprehensive graduate program in school service, higher education, and other social service areas. The college is divided into four departments including: Educational Administration; Teacher Education; Counseling, Educational Psychology, and Special Education; and Health Education, Counseling Psychology, and Human Performance.

The college has two nationally known centers for research on teaching and teacher education which warrant description. The Institute for Research on Teaching (IRT) was created in 1976 to conduct research on teacher thinking and decisionmaking. It was funded by the National Institute of Education and in 1981 was given a second five-year contract. Its three major missions are to conduct a coordinated program of research on teaching; to provide synthesis and analysis of research on teaching; and to disseminate research findings to other researchers and practitioners concerned with educational improvement. Particularly, the institute has focused on problems of practice, teacher collaboration and planning in conducting research, and the multidisciplinary nature of research. Four alternative teacher education programs in the college have served as laboratories for testing the results of IRT research and as a source of new issues for study. As findings emerge that suggest new directions for teacher education, they are incorporated into the MSU teacher preparation program and subsequently evaluated. As our scenario of MSU unfolds, we see repeatedly the interactive relationship not only of the faculty members in terms of their IRT assignments, but also the symbiotic relationship between the research conducted in the IRT and the implementation and study of teacher education at MSU.

A second and more recent opportunity for MSU has been the federal OERI funding of a National Center for Research on Teacher Education (NCRTE). This center, formerly located at the University of Texas—Austin, has been funded for the concentrated study of programs in teacher education. As such, this new center at MSU has as a critical emphasis the study of the way teachers learn to teach throughout their careers in a variety of formats, particularly focusing on acquisition of teaching skills in mathematics and writing. The comprehensive agenda of the center should further contribute to MSU's reputation as a leader in the study of teacher education. These two initiatives make obvious the College of Education's commitment to research and development in teacher education.

Another development which has intimately drawn in the energies and investment of faculty members in the College of Education is the creation of the Holmes Group Consortium, a network of research institutions. Comprised initially of twenty-nine institutions, this consortium has now grown to almost 100 major schools and colleges of education who have agreed to participate in a reform agenda in teacher education. The initiative has developed under the leadership of MSU's dean of the College of Education, Judith E. Lanier. Multiple and sustaining references to Dean Lanier are made as our descriptive portrayal unfolds. Suffice it to say that her leadership in the initiation of the Holmes Group, the publication subsequently of a document called *Tomorrow's Teachers*, which outlines the Holmes Group's agenda, and her diligent work in formulating the engagement of almost 100 research-producing institutions toward the goals of the Holmes Group give MSU a particular perspective on and important place in the reform of teacher education.

Numerous MSU faculty members have contributed to the development of an agenda for the Holmes Group as well as that for the National Center for

Research on Teacher Education and the ongoing research efforts of the IRT. This combination of engaging in national issues of reform in teacher education, producing research on teaching and teacher education, and pioneering planned variations in teacher preparation is abundant evidence that MSU's College of Education is pivotal in the landscape of teacher education nationally. Within this energized environment, we attempt to describe the nature of teacher education in the College of Education at MSU.

Alternative Approaches to Teacher Education at MSU

The MSU College of Education, by its own account, has been committed to improving educational opportunities for K–12 children and youth over the many years the college has been in existence, complemented by a second major goal of creating and continuously revising models for educating teachers. Taken together, these two goals allow for the purposeful integration of research, development, and teaching, which ensures an ongoing and qualitative response to the needs of teachers. The dedication to scholarly innovation and dissemination in teacher education stems from the belief that the combined resources of the College of Education, the IRT and the NCRTE can address the challenges and problems of teaching and teacher education effectively. The commitment to provide leadership is in keeping with the mission of the college and the land-grant philosophy of the university.

As a consequence of this commitment to quality and choice, the College of Education has designed alternative programmatic approaches to teacher certification that are: (1) conceptually organized to respond to enduring problems that professionals encounter in their work; (2) firmly grounded in research; and (3) carefully designed to incorporate the collective wisdom of teacher educators in bridging the gap between theory and practice.

Thus, in addition to the Standard Program designed for students seeking either elementary or secondary teacher certification, the college offers four planned variations in teacher education programs to which students may seek admission. These four alternatives are characterized as offering:

1. special attention to the major challenge of fostering *academic learning*;
2. special attention to the major challenge of teaching in *heterogeneous classrooms*;
3. special attention to the major challenge of promoting personal and social responsibility (*learning communities*); and
4. special attention to the major challenge of professional decisionmaking under conditions of multiple and competing demands and expectations (*multiple perspectives*).

A number of the faculty we interviewed spoke about the development of the alternative programs. One of the first alternative program coordinators,

Professor Glenn Berkheimer, recalls the initiative taken by the current dean of the College of Education, Judith Lanier:

> Judy Lanier at that time was not dean, but she was chair of a committee that was looking at various views of teacher education. It became obvious to her and to people on the committee that there wasn't one view of what teacher education ought to be, but several. After a great deal of discussion, the faculty together with the administrators concluded that probably the most powerful programs would be ones that were put together with faculty that believed the same things about what teacher education ought to look like. This approach carried the assumption that a consistent, articulated program is much better than one that is not, and that this is most likely a powerful factor in turning out quality students.

Cassandra Book, now assistant dean in the College of Education, also recalled: "Judy [Lanier] convened a group of faculty here in the college to examine teacher education and to explore the best way to train teachers. And they fought and argued and concluded that no one best way exists. They then decided that they had better come up with some alternatives that they all agreed upon." At that time, Judy Lanier had written a paper, "The Functions of Schools," which served as a stimulus for the alternative programs. Groups of faculty formed around the various themes represented in this paper, as well as other perspectives they brought to the dialogue. Different faculty congealed around a theme and often worked together for several years to pull it together. Dean Book noted that today, "the four alternative programs are conceptually organized and thematically based so that they come out of a sense of . . . what we do know about teacher education and what the missions of schools are. Those concepts pervade each of the alternatives and their individual development."

Joyce Putnam, professor and coordinator of the Multiple Perspectives program, also reflected on the long history of the college's involvement with alternative programs which stemmed from the original federally funded Triple T project. This project ultimately was converted to a project called EEE (Excellence in Elementary Education). Cass Book concurred: "This college has a long history of alternatives. We had the Excellence in Elementary Education Program, the Elementary Intern Program, the Secondary Education Pilot Program [SEPP], the CBTE Program. We are systematic about the way we are going to differ and what we are learning from these different programs."

What has emerged, from the vantage point of Perry Lanier, a professor and coordinator of the Academic Learning program, is a set of different perspectives, problems, and themes which confront teachers:

> If you're interested in diversity, the Heterogeneous Classrooms program works around that. That's built around problems that teachers are predictably confronted

with. Learning Communities feeds off of another set of problems, which is teachers always having to decide what to do with an individual versus a group. They build their core courses around the individual and the group and the responsibility a teacher takes for that. In Academic Learning, we key off of what the teacher is confronted with when deciding what and how to teach, content of teaching and methods. That's the way I cast the difference.

Laura Roehler, professor and coordinator with professor Bruce Burke for the Learning Communities program, described the development of alternative programs this way:

> Initially, the courses for each program were written and developed by people who self-selected to work in that program. During the planning year, when we wrote the curriculum for the Learning Community, we had collaborative working groups negotiating what the curriculum would be, what the foundations courses would look like, and so on. We knew that we had to meet state certification requirements. We had to meet all regulations. But, we took a lot of time to think through what the program's philosophy and the way the propensities of Learning Communities would be treated in the courses. And we knew, also, that times change and that people come and go. Since that time, we have added a lot of new members to our faculty, but at the outset, the hope was that the curriculum and the sequence of experiences within the curriculum would be internally consistent with the philosophy of the program.

Faculty members evidently selected programs because of their own affinity with what was emphasized in those programs. As Laura Roehler recalled:

> I was attracted to the Learning Communities program because I was interested in the culture of classrooms. I was interested in the classroom as a community, and a theme that runs through all of the language arts content I teach focuses on children as 'makers of meaning' within the several intersecting communities in which they live, including the community of their classroom.

At this time, prior to further anticipated changes consonant with the Holmes Group's agenda, the College of Education's Program in Teacher Education can be characterized as four alternatives plus one standard program. Students select programs for a variety of reasons according to Dean Book:

> I talk to them and I hear them talk about their choices in selecting programs that are consistent with their views of themselves as teachers. There are some students who choose a certain program because of the way it expands their view of how they want to see themselves. But, for the most part, I think they enroll in programs that reinforce their existing beliefs of what a teacher does, or what they most want to prepare themselves to do. Also, sometimes, they tell you that advisors and faculty are influential in their decisions.

Students we visited with concur with the dean's assessment. For example, one student observed that while enrolled in TE 101, "Exploring Teaching," students were discouraged from entering the standard program: "I know a couple of people in the class who recorded 'standard' when they filled out these forms. The instructor asked why they were filling in standard and was something wrong with the other programs? The answer was always that students had to work or do other things. In these alternative programs, you have to go to class when they offer them." Still other students perceive a greater challenge in the alternative programs that may not exist in the standard program: "In TE 101 we got a preview of each of the pilot programs, and we could choose between those and the standard program. The standard looked awful, so it was among the others."

Professor Donald Freeman, after talking to a number of students over the years in his role as program evaluator for the college, observed that:

> Practical considerations probably play a major role in students' decisions to enroll in the standard program in preference to the alternatives. Ease of scheduling required courses is one example. Because of the format of the alternative programs, students are often required to take a given course during a particular term and at specific times during the week. In contrast, students in the standard program typically have a choice of times and terms in which to enroll in required courses. This flexibility is particularly appealing to students who have a lot of requirements to satisfy in their major field of study and to those who are eager to complete the teacher certification requirements in the minimum number of terms.

These choices also are apparent in a study of belief statements of students enrolled in the alternative programs and the standard program. Freeman observes, "My feeling right now is that there may be some distinction between students who go into alternative programs versus those who are in the standard program, rather than major differentiations of beliefs among students enrolled in the alternative programs."

In summary, a picture is gained of a faculty committed for some time to the development of alternative teacher education programs; a program leader, now the dean, who originally stimulated and provoked faculty dialogue about multiple perspectives for teacher preparation; a faculty engaged in collective program development efforts that eventually emerged around different orientations to teacher preparation and that allowed many other faculty to assume leadership roles at the program level; and a student body capable of discriminating among choices about the way they could be prepared as teachers. As one student concluded: "The whole alternative program issue is the result of research that's going on, and my impression is that what's happening at Michigan State right now in terms of the alternative programs is putting us in the forefront of education."

The richness across these programs and the distinctive aspects of each program will be the primary focus of the remainder of this descriptive portrayal of MSU. But because the nature of alternative programming at MSU is complex, broad in scope, and difficult to describe accurately in its variety, we thought that it might be helpful to trace, however briefly, the nature of one alternative program (how its program theme emerged, how its courses are structured, and some of its unique attributes) before moving to a characterization of the alternative programs totally.

HOW DOES AN ALTERNATIVE PROGRAM MANIFEST ITSELF?

The Evolution of the Heterogeneous Classrooms Program

The Heterogeneous Classrooms program prepares teachers to teach effectively in academic areas while focusing on the needs of the diverse youngsters that comprise a typical classroom. Teachers do not treat individual clients in isolated settings but rather deal with complex and heterogeneous groups of human beings in schools within a democratic, pluralistic, society—a society committed to educating all of its citizens. According to program coordinator Professor Richard Navarro, this program is committed to equity and to preparing teachers to work with diverse students:

> The distinction that needs to be made in our program is between preparing teachers who have some knowledge and background about diversity—which we believe all the programs provide to different degrees in their school and society course and their emphasis on equity—and focusing on preparing teachers who are attempting to have significant impact on schools with underrepresented populations, children who are academically at risk, and handicappers. We are continuing to do the former and striving to achieve the latter. And that is the difference.

Students characterize the program similarly: "the people in our program are more aware of individual differences. They're not so quick to stereotype. People in our program are more aware of biases and how they can challenge them; even if they have biases themselves, they can change them."

When asked whether the program points more toward cultural differences or learning differences, students and faculty typically respond, "Both." According to a student:

> Academic, cultural, social—you can have identical twins and chances are very likely they are not going to be identical in ability. We have been doing little things in a seminar that show what type of a person you are, as part of the feedback process for our field experiences. I really had to work on teaching tactile learners, because I'm a visual and audio learner.

The themes of equity and diversity are integrated into a series of on-campus and field experiences, which students enroll in a sequential fashion.

In the alternative programs approach at MSU, common course numbers are employed, but they are also labelled by letter to distinguish the course as it pertains to each particular teaching strand. For instance, in the standard program TE 200, "Individual and the School," is described as follows:

> Major psychological factors in the school learning-teaching situation; concepts in human development related to problems in the school situation; teacher's role in motivation, conceptual learning, problem solving, and the development of emotional behavior, attitudes and values, learning of skills, retention and transfer; and measurement of student abilities and achievement.

In contrast to this rather general course in the standard program, TE 200B, which is used for Heterogeneous Classrooms is called, instead, "Educational Psychology of Individual Differences in Classrooms." It is described as follows: "Educational psychology foundations of the range of diverse capabilities and characteristics found among school children and the implication of these differences for instruction." While faculty members typically have a particular affinity to one program, they may offer instruction across programs in a matrix arrangement. For example, a faculty member may teach Educational Psychology in more than one program, but will teach it differently to accommodate themes emphasized in that program.

The Heterogeneous Classrooms teacher will complete a total of fifty-four professional education hours moving through a series of courses including educational psychology; individual differences; a school in society course; several courses on the teaching of reading and children's literature; a course in methods of mathematics; social studies, and science; a course on evaluating learning environments; a course on equity and stereotypes; and a course on exceptional children. There are numerous laboratory and practical experiences and all of this is preceded by a course required for all elementary majors called TE 101, "Exploring Teaching." As we indicated, in TE 101, students are required to visit at least two programs to assist in determining for which program they will ultimately apply. We asked what, if anything, particularly characterized the Heterogeneous Classrooms cadre of students that we interviewed. Students typically responded that their interest in cultural and learning differences was unique.

The student who selects Heterogeneous Classrooms also engages in a series of field experiences supported by a "proseminar," which is offered concurrently with the field experiences. In the proseminar, student cohorts are provided opportunities to develop critical generic teaching skills (such as classroom management) and are provided time to discuss and integrate new information, research findings, and fieldwork experiences. Furthermore, the Heterogeneous Classrooms program field dimension places students in school classrooms for six terms. Beginning with half-day placements once a week, students move in graduated steps toward increased classroom contact and greater instructional responsibility. The field sequence culminates in the closely supervised student teaching term in the senior year.

Distinctive Features of the Heterogeneous Classrooms Program

Each of the program coordinators and the faculty members who were interviewed spoke to the distinctive features of their respective program areas. Richard Navarro singled out the field experiences as a major distinguishing feature of Heterogeneous Classrooms:

> Students begin in the field the first quarter they start the program, which is one of the big differences from the standard program. The alternative programs also have distinctions that attract different students. Multiple Perspectives conducts much of its course in the schools. Learning Communities, as the name implies, puts a great deal of effort into developing a community experience with faculty and students. In the Heterogeneous Classrooms program, the emphasis is on preparing teachers to work with students with different learning needs, and so the idea of being able to enter a program that focuses on diverse learners is attractive to another group of students.

Navarro again underscored the interest in linking teachers to heavily impacted areas with students who are at risk academically and socially: "The students are highly committed and interested in working in these situations, but then they exit the program without a clear direction of where they're going to teach to deal with these students." Navarro wants to make the commitment to the program explicit by looking more closely at the nature of the student's placement at the culmination of the program.

A second distinctive feature of the Heterogeneous Classrooms program (and the other alternatives as well) is the integration of themes throughout the courses in the program and the ability to reinforce particular concepts as the program evolves. One way this is accomplished is by offering a foundations course early in the sequence and also at the program's culmination after student teaching. In Heterogeneous Classrooms individual equity issues are addressed in the beginning program and larger social issues are dealt with at the end of the program.

Another distinctive feature of the program is that its focus is on the learner. According to Navarro:

> The other programs, are really focused on the teacher . . . teacher as decision-maker, . . . teacher as leader, . . . teacher as expert in academic subject matter, and so forth. But, we're really focusing on the student coming from a diversity of backgrounds and abilities and skills, which is something that's distinctive, and the students pick up on right away. That's one of the reasons why they come to us.

We were told the faculty were focusing on specific issues and concerns, such as ensuring more diversified placements of their graduates at the culmination of their programs, continuing work on integration in courses of their themes, and continuing to stabilize faculty involvement in the program. In this vein, a number of faculty members noted that some individuals in the college had been with the program from its inception, others have joined recently, and still others have moved on to other areas.

Our focus now moves away from the particulars of one of the alternative programs to the distinctive features of the alternative program arrangement generally. We hope that, as this description unfolds, each of the remaining programs in the college will be described adequately enough to allow the reader to visualize the diverse nature of these four alternatives.

WHAT IS DISTINCTIVE ABOUT THE ALTERNATIVE PROGRAMS' APPROACH TO TEACHER EDUCATION?

Introduction

Perhaps the most comprehensive statement about the distinctiveness of the alternative programs was presented to us in the reflections of Henrietta Barnes, chairperson of the Department of Teacher Education:

> What is different and most powerful, regardless of the conceptual basis of any of the programs, is that there is a major purpose or a theme that allows each program to select the content from all of the various disciplines that contribute to one's understanding about teaching. So, the theme of a program, regardless of what it is, might be any number of themes that one might select; I don't think the particular themes that we've selected are the distinctive character at all, but the fact that we have programs that carefully select content to support a given theme, and build that content in a *cumulative* sense. We do try to provide foundational knowledge, carry along basic concepts into each of the courses along each of the programs, so that there is a cumulative impact of the knowledge that we're trying to promote, including dispositional knowledge, attitudes, moral and ethical issues, decisionmaking, as well as knowledge about how one goes about teaching subject matter, how one thinks about learners, how one thinks about the schools and interactions with other professionals.

Barnes added other distinctive features of the alternative programs: "They are *articulated* between campus coursework and field experiences, with very strong efforts to help students be *reflective* about the activities in which they are engaged." She addressed yet another important feature of the programs, which she referred to as a disposition toward professional knowledge:

The difference is, I think, that they [the students] come to believe that there is a professional literature, that there is professional knowledge, and that they have acquired some of it. That seems to be what they tell us. They feel competent and confident, they know that they have some knowledge they can draw upon and they attribute that knowledge to the program. People in the standard program who are asked similar kinds of questions don't feel as confident, don't believe they are as competent, and what they do know they attribute to their experiences in classrooms as student teachers. They attribute it to the workplace.

Finally, Barnes noted another distinctive feature of the alternative program under the designation "learning how to teach." "What we're talking about is overcoming the preconceptions of what teaching is by creating a powerful enough intervention that has its roots in practice yet brings together theory and practice in ways that inform each other." This emphasis on learning how to teach is a notion embedded in the research agenda of the IRT, a focus of the emerging R&D Center for Teacher Education, and a common interest of faculty members in the alternative programs at MSU.

We illustrate these and other distinctive features we observed to describe more fully the alternative approach to teacher education embedded in the MSU program.

The Distinctiveness of Themes

Numerous faculty corroborated the view that the theme orientation is critical to the evolution of the alternative program approach. According to Joyce Putnam, the faculty began their dialogue on program development by focusing on a theme. In the case of Multiple Perspectives, the theme was "the teacher as a decisionmaker," and it integrated three other functions of articulating philosophy, identifying goals, and matching philosophy and goals with program activities.

The Academic Learning program prepares teachers to teach school subjects effectively while focusing on the academic requirements and the intellectual underpinnings of particular disciplines. This program is based on the assumption that teachers need ever greater understanding of the critical bases for knowing and selecting appropriate skills, concepts, and principles to be taught while exploring the boundaries and conditions of knowledge in their own disciplines in addition to seeing the relationship of one's discipline to other disciplines. Glenn Berkheimer, the first coordinator of the Academic Learning program, spoke to its thematic evolution:

The Academic Learning thrust met my value system. I believe that teachers just don't teach, they teach content, and that whatever the content is, it has to be specified and must be taught directly. I believe that a generic methods course doesn't work. You don't teach language arts like you teach science, and you don't teach math like you teach science. Therefore, if you teach generic methods, then you're assuming that the students are wise enough to use those methods in the context of the subject areas, and we know that's not been true historically. If you're going to meet individual differences and if you're going to teach fifth-grade students addition and then multiplication, you have to know content. You have to meet individual differences, but you have to know the content to do so. I don't think you can meet individual differences unless you do, which was part of our problem with individualizing instruction. One of our great problems in our schooling occurs when we start teaching subject areas that require more background than teachers have.

Thus, this program has a major orientation toward knowledge in the academic disciplines, an understanding of the structure of the discipline, and a combination of knowledge of discipline and knowledge of pedagogy.

The current coordinator of the program, Perry Lanier, elaborated on this concept of academic learning:

The best way for students to learn subject matter knowledge is through conceptual orientation, so we emphasize that. Taking that view does two things. It optimizes their learning subject matter knowledge, and it has a natural spin off of not learning trivia. Clearly, we expect our teachers to have an orientation toward the development of concepts versus rules, directions, and procedures. There will be differences in subject matter because the concepts in mathematics are fairly abstract. And so, to develop those conceptually, we have models for them, be they pictures or concrete objects. We have chosen tasks that are intellectually engaging; that are not rule bound, but rather push for understanding.

Thus, Professors Lanier and Berkheimer represent an orientation toward the academic disciplines that stresses conceptual understanding and that has evolved out of the research done on naive theories and student misconceptions. The Academic Learning program confronts these misconceptions and teaches teachers to teach correct concepts.

Again, themes explicated in a particular program may also be emphasized to different degrees in the other three programs, as a professor in Heterogeneous Classrooms explained:

Our primary theme is individual differences. I think of it a little more broadly as cultural diversity, but the main idea is that there are individual differences within an elementary school. I think we are probably no more committed to individual differences than people in the other programs, but we're certainly much more aware of them as the theme and as a focus.

Obviously, some themes require more emphasis in some programs than others. The same could be said for the focus on misconceptions and preconceptions in the Academic Learning program. Certainly Linda Anderson's focus on metacognition in the course she teaches for the Heterogeneous Class-rooms program focuses as well on misconceptions, even though this is a predominant theme of the Academic Learning program.

Here we have depicted themes that are embedded in particular conceptions of teaching; conceptions of teaching that are research-based and experientially studied and that represent the values of the professors in the programs. The affinity of faculty members for their specific programs is represented by Andy Anderson, a professor in the Academic Learning program, who commented:

> We start from, in part, a conviction about the nature of schooling and, in part, a pragmatic need to limit the program according to our available resources. The conviction about the nature of schooling is that teaching does have an essential purpose—mastery of academic content. The essential purpose of the program, then, is the students' mastery of academic knowledge in the four areas that we have necessarily selected for concentration: English/language arts, science, social studies, and mathematics.

The Distinctiveness of Dispositions

In our conversation with Henrietta Barnes about the development of the alternative teacher education programs at MSU, she spoke of the concern for dispositional and propositional knowledge, with reference to Israel Scheffler's work on orientations to teaching. We asked her what meaning she attached to the term *dispositional*.

> I'm thinking of habits of mind, ways of thinking about children. For example, a beginning teacher in Multiple Perspectives (which is not necessarily focused on equity issues) told me that she took a job teaching sixth grade in an inner city school. She said that when she started, she wasn't afraid at all to go in and teach. She knew what to do. She said, 'These kids are just kids. I know that they can change. Now, their behavior was really bad, but I knew they could change.' That's a disposition toward students as learners who can grow and change, and the teacher is the facilitator. This way of thinking is not embedded in all course experiences for teachers everywhere.

Professor Barnes continues, "I think that all strands have a philosophy that coordinates with the theme that has to do with attitudes and beliefs about learners and about yourself as a teacher and the interaction between them." She provided us with a particular example of the Learning Community design, which has its roots in Joseph Schwab's notion of learning communities. The Learning Communities program prepares teachers to teach school subjects effectively while focusing on the concommitant need to promote personal and social responsibility among students. It is built on the assumption that schools have to assume increased responsibility for developing qualities needed by citizens in a complex democratic nation. Consequently, the Learning Community program emphasizes personal and social responsibility and prepares future teachers to create opportunities for both personal and cooperative learning in classrooms. The Learning Communities teacher is described as one who possesses certain perspectives toward the school curriculum, the learning environment, personal and social responsibility, and rationale processing. These perspectives are expressed in propensities, defined as internal dispositions toward acting in a specific manner. Desired propensities in this program include: (1) adopting a holistic view of the instructional process in which managerial decisions are integrally related to pedagogy; (2) seeking integration of subject matter content as a cornerstone of the curriculum; and (3) using the school and community as resources for teaching and learning. These propensities are manifested in particular dispositions or habits of behavior which Henrietta Barnes referred to as dispositional knowledge.

Barnes further discussed dispositions in contrast to what she views as limitations in the standard program:

> The tendency in the standard program is to provide the students with too much knowledge, which is not covered in depth nor learned in terms of what implications it might have for them with regard to teaching and their roles in the classrooms. Consequently, dispositions probably aren't taught because they're not embedded. They're not infused. The focus is on knowledge. You can say you need this attitude or that attitude, but there's no opportunity, over an extended period, to practice certain things and get feedback about where you're on target and where you're not. That is the difference between the knowledge-base approach, which is a traditional program, and an alternative program, which reflects dispositions.

Thus, students perceive themselves not only as having a professional knowledge base guiding them, but as having been synthesized and internalized so they are now *disposed* to behave in certain ways as a result of relying on that knowledge base.

The Distinctiveness of Reflectivity

Embedded in the notion of dispositions is that of reflectivity as manifested in the various programs. Reflectivity is a particular disposition toward the teaching and learning process. The ability and willingness of education students to engage in reflective processes is a concern of faculty. Joyce Putnam, after interviewing one of the student teachers in the Multiple Perspectives strand, observed: "It was absolutely incredible to me the extent to which the student was able to be reflective." She continued:

> In every course, in every area, she had very specific things that she thought could improve and things she would do differently, including not teaching a particular unit until a later time or starting earlier or building prerequisites or using entirely

different materials—a whole variety of things that showed she was reflective about the subject matter as well as the children and where she was going through specified goals and objectives.

Henrietta Barnes pointed out that reflectivity needs to be implicitly addressed and drawn out. "For example, if the student hadn't been asked those questions, I don't think she would have been able to talk so explicitly about her classroom experience." Putnam particularly recalls times in the program when classroom teachers asked her why the students were required to engage in certain activities in the schools:

> We want our people to be reflective and begin to articulate their reasons for doing things, and one of the ways they learn this is by asking what the reasons are for what they do. Practitioners have reasons for things they do, but they sometimes need time to reflect because their rationale has been internalized and may not be readily recalled. That is why we have the student teachers ask what you think about some of the observations they've made about your teaching or comments, so that the next time they come back, they could tell you *why* you do or think certain things. The teachers reported that our student teachers ask them about aspects of their teaching that had become automatic; they have to stop and think about them and ask where it came from, why they are doing that, how did they get there? We ask the student teachers to give classroom teachers time to reflect so they don't feel defensive about information they have internalized but can, given time, reconstruct.

One of the students in the Academic Learning program talked about reflectivity in this way:

> I like these classes a lot, they're theory-based and a lot of it is up to the individual. Some people in our classes think this is all common sense, and I think they're mistaken. True, a lot of what you get in a class like this is not new, it's not earth-shattering, but if you take the time to pull those things that are in the back of your mind up to the front of your mind and really look at things you think you already know, you put them in perspective and in the proper place that they should be to start out as a teacher. I think that's challenging.

The concept of writing journals has evolved to encourage students to be reflective in the Academic Learning program as well as in other strands. The journal is kept in a loose-leaf binder so that pages can be exchanged, taken out, or handed in. While the journals are not evaluated or assigned grades, they are assigned as a way to develop writing and thinking skills, as a basis for communication with instructors and other students, and as a way for students to understand themselves as learners. Journals are read from time to time, responded to, and shared with other students in the Academic Learning program. Journals and the proseminar activities that allow students to share thoughts constitute explicit program dimensions to encourage reflectivity.

The Distinctiveness of Campus/Field Articulation

Each of the campus/field relationships and articulation of program goals in the alternative programs is distinctive. We illustrate this first by introducing the Multiple Perspectives program, which has not as yet been addressed in our portrayal of teacher preparation at MSU. The Multiple Perspectives program examines the various and often competing purposes of schooling: "Students have opportunities to learn something about the multiple functions in schools and the teacher decisions that relate to them." The other teacher education alternatives allow for more in-depth study along a particular function of schooling. The emphasis in this program is teacher decisionmaking. Attention is given to decisions regarding instructional design, instruction, individual differences, and group development. The program reflects expectations for teachers with regard to (1) learning in academic disciplines, (2) personal and social responsibility, and (3) appreciation for learners that exist in a diverse society. In this program, "teachers are decisionmakers who must balance these competing demands on the school." In the Multiple Perspectives program, the designers wanted not only students to work in schools but teacher educators to work in schools as well because, as one professor stated,

> It's important for our students to be in schools to learn the theory, to examine research findings and principals that we're going to teach them, and to struggle with the same tensions that classroom teachers do in terms of putting those into practice. If we teach students in isolation, nothing will change because we've been doing that for years.

Accordingly, the Multiple Perspectives program provides for entry into field sites early on and consistently throughout the student's program. Through a cadre of field instructors and selected cooperating teachers in the school, the Multiple Perspectives program is continually integrated with actual school experiences. The program has negotiated with schools to take its thirty-five students on a saturation basis two days per week. In exchange, faculty members from the Multiple Perspectives program provide staff development to the schools selected for this exchange and teacher candidates spend two periods per week providing small group or one-on-one instruction to students designated by the principal and teachers.

Already we have noted the orientation toward reflectivity embedded in the Multiple Perspectives program and the encouragement of the undergraduate students to be reflective in these field experiences. The goal is to achieve some mutuality in reflecting on practice by the preservice students and by the experienced teachers in the field. The Multiple Perspectives program wants to work with teachers who will "take seriously the study of their own practice in ways that will contribute to the field." According to Professor Putnam, the Multiple Perspective program supports interaction with the field as follows:

A student in any term of our program is learning something in class and hearing what it is and *why* that's important to them as a professional teacher. They frequently see models of that because of teaching a class or other kinds of demonstrations that our faculty do. Then they go into the field and they try it themselves. So, all the field assignments, everything our students do in the field, is coordinated with their coursework, the labs, and the courses our students are taking. The field instructors either have been to those classes or have studied the coursework in our weekly staff meetings. The field instructor's job is to reinforce and support the program content with the students in the field.

Putnam also reports that the content they focus on in their science methods courses is the same science curriculum taught in the Lansing School District, ". . . so the cohesion in the curriculum goes into the field." The focus of the methods course, however, is on teaching for conceptual change.

A similar portrait can be drawn of the field experiences in the Learning Community program. The development of the field component in Learning Community begins largely with microteaching experiences and moves to full-time student teaching in the following manner, according to a faculty member in this strand:

> The students are paired. We try to start them in the field right at the beginning and put them in a microteaching situation. We give them lots of support so we're trying to model one of the principles we believe in: give them lots of support but with challenge. We want to challenge them, but with enough support to acclimate themselves to instruction. And we gradually shift from microteaching to teaching. Two of our students are in a classroom on two days and two other students on another day, so there are four of them in a room this term. Then next term it drops to just one person in a room at a time. In the fall, they're in the classroom they're going to student teach in, and they start becoming acclimated to the supervising teacher and then they do their student teaching. So, it's a carefully planned field component. We make certain it has logic and continuity to it.

Laura Roehler, a coordinator of Learning Communities program, considers the nature of field experiences in this program a continuing challenge.

> I want to establish a closer link between what goes on in the field and courses. When we're out in the schools, the teachers are either neutral about collaborative learning or they're doing a little bit of it, and our students sometimes have difficulty seeing the integration or application of some of our concepts.

Field supervisors in Learning Communities report that they supervise their students at least once each week at both the junior and the senior level. One field supervisor observed:

> We don't expect them to be doing everything well. They do not have to show us their best lessons when we walk into the room. . . . My sense is that they want us

> to be there. I missed a lesson on Monday and I walked in and they said, "Oh, you missed our lesson." That told me a lot. They want us there.

Another field supervisor speaks to the impact of continually supervising these students from one course to another as follows:

> I told Laura [Roehler]—she had a reading course last term and she talked about modelling very explicitly—that the students were at the point this term where they can try those ideas she presented. They can do the writing part and now they're trying it out with the kids, really trying it week after week until they can do it smoothly. They begin to apply what they're learning immediately but then it's the next term when they really get a chance to practice and begin to grow.

With regard to Heterogeneous Classrooms, one faculty member illustrated the nature of field experience with reference to one of the goals of the program, which is that students experience unintended bias.

> There are two ways you can experience it. I don't think we're going to have our students live with families in the slums of Lansing, however. The other way is to show them how to think about classrooms and what goes on in classrooms, so they can now begin to see things that they couldn't see before. That, in turn, forces them to reflect on their previous assumptions of the way classrooms were organized and how certain inequities were created or perpetuated. When students are asked to analyze texts, with regard to curriculum bias they may come to realize things they never had. Or, you show them there are ways students sit in the classroom by gender and look at seating patterns and displays, task allocation, teacher/student interactions, discipline; then, they go into the hallways, the cafeterias, and the playground and examine systems of interlocking relationships. They come back the next day, ashen, and tell you they had no idea there were so many ways in which children segregated themselves and teachers either encouraged it or did nothing to the contrary. There *are* ways you can get them to think about the hidden aspects of school life, and they *can* experience these in field observations.

As a final illustration of the articulation between campus and field experiences, we study the nature of field experiences in the Academic Learning program, particularly with respect to a program currently evolving with funding from the Office of Educational Research and Improvement to develop what Perry Lanier refers to as the mentor teacher concept.

Another faculty member, Cheryl Rosaen spoke to field experience in this strand in general:

> We just started addressing our students' process of learning to teach and how they come to understand the concepts we're trying to teach them. One of the things that makes this program distinctive is the idea of the way experience is used and thought about in the "learning to teach" process. Unlike some of the

other programs that assign students to a classroom early in the teacher education program, we feel there are a lot of disadvantages in being out in the schools. Of course, there are advantages, too. Now we're beginning to think through more thoroughly the way we can, if we increase the time spent in the classroom, do it in a way that we think will make sense to our students. What we're seeing is their understanding in a course and then getting into a classroom and finding out that even if they understand all of that, it doesn't apply. It doesn't fit. They can't use it here. We're trying to build a bridge that is helpful to our students . . . that will help them see how the framework of thinking that we're trying to teach them actually fits in with real life, instead of having them think it's too idealistic and it doesn't help. We're having them understand that it's a way of thinking through the real issues that they come across in schools.

The teacher mentor program should enable the program's capacity to work more intensively with teachers, so that teachers and students can talk more intelligibly about the theoretical framework of the program and its applications in the classroom. Anderson and Rosaen are attemtping to integrate this approach in their curriculum methods course, as Rosaen related:

This is a new approach in the sense that we're not only addressing our course content in ways that will overlap the concerns our students have about their own teaching, but also working with cooperating teachers in a way that they can talk to students and help them understand their thinking and why they're doing it. We're helping the students begin to look at what they're seeing in classrooms in ways that will help them understand how students understand content, how teachers make decisions, and how those come together, instead of someone just seeing this miraculous classroom functioning or this bad classroom that's not working well without a way of thinking about it.

This conceptual orientation is a hallmark of the mentoring program. Specifically, mentor teachers in this project are involved in the following:

1. providing support and guidance to Academic Learning students in specifically designed field experiences (including student teaching) over a two-year period;
2. interacting with university faculty to learn about the Academic Learning program;
3. reviewing recent research on teaching and learning in the teacher's particular subject matter area and exploring implications of the research with faculty and Academic Learning students;
4. reacting to field experiences in order to help program faculty design experiences that help students use recent research and make sense of real classrooms;
5. guiding Academic Learning students' learning about those aspects of teaching that can be learned best from field experiences rather than from university study.

This will allow earlier, more sequential field experiences, wherein students would be assigned to teachers who understand this conceptual orientation. One of the mentor teachers elaborated on this plan:

> I have one teacher who will work with me throughout her student teaching year. She's already been with me two terms, and she'll be with me two more terms. In the winter term, she observed me teaching social studies; but, prior to my teaching something, she interviewed the children with regard to their preconceptions of the subject I was going to be teaching. After she observed me teaching, she conducted postinterviews, asking students' conceptions. Each time, she wrote summaries of her interviews with me and with the children, and I responded. The next term, we switched to the science discipline and, at that time, she was involved in the teaching and I did the interviewing. She had to do at least four total group activities.

Students in the Academic Learning program are knowledgeable about the rationale for the current progression of field experiences:

> They're giving us a cushion—confidence, knowledge—so that we can walk into the classroom knowing a little bit more about what we're looking for and what we're doing. If I had gone in last term, I wouldn't have known what to do. They would have told me, but I wouldn't have known why, because I wouldn't have had enough understanding just last term, and this term, too, it's a clearer view . . . of what it is I need to know. Sure, you're going to learn it if you go to the classroom. You get it dumped on you on a regular basis. But this way you go in with a more secure attitude and orientation toward teaching.

Another student concurred:

> If we started out our first term going into a classroom, sitting and watching for fifteen hours a week without a lot of background, a lot of people would be looking in the wrong places. They would be looking and saying, 'Aren't they cute?', or 'Look at what they're doing. Isn't that neat?' And they may be getting some things out of it, but I think the majority of people starting out would not have the background to synthesize and study what the teacher is doing and why, and the significance of some of the things that are happening in the classroom.

With the assistance of the mentoring program, then, students are able to see how children and teachers are dealing with the concepts they have been studying in classrooms in a more effective, regular, and sequential manner.

In summary, a number of distinguishing characteristics constitute the nature of field experience and the relationship of field experiences to programs across all four of the alternative programs at MSU. Regardless of the time at which students are placed in the field—at the outset, as is the case in the Multiple Perspectives program, or on a deferred basis, as is the case in the Academic Learning program—the field experiences are cohesive, sequential, and extremely intentional. Faculty have designed specific activities, assignments, and tasks, which students are obliged to conduct in schools. There are systematic observations of these students and a variety of instruments are employed to assess their assignments. Almost all courses are linked with experiences in field sites. As well, many courses provide developmental laboratory experiences which approach reality through videotaping, simulations and games, and peer teaching. Also, faculty contribute to related staff development activities in the schools because there appears, across all four programs, to be a paucity of teachers who understand and practice all of the notions ascribed to in the various programs.

Supervision is intensive in each of these programs. Field supervisors are sometimes faculty members and sometimes graduate or part-time staff hired specifically for this task. These supervisors report that they are in schools weekly and that they see the students who are assigned to them once or twice each week. Often, their assignments allow them to follow students from one quarter to the next, and from one course to the next, so that their experience with the students is cumulative. Some problems exist, however, in the supervision of field experience students, including costs and the amount of travel time to visit schools that are often located thirty minutes or more from campus.

Nevertheless, our understanding of the nature of field experiences at MSU suggests that the observations of education students are systematic and organized around specific assignments and objectives. Students are encouraged to be reflective in thinking about the nature of their classroom experiences and to exercise inquiry skills. For example, we were advised that students in the Multiple Perspectives program conduct a research project during their senior year, which is usually field-based. Students are often paired or work in groups during their field experiences. This is certainly the case in the Learning Communities program, with its group orientation and concern for a supportive environment for students in the classroom.

Each of the programs also appears to use student feedback in refining these field experience activities. Furthermore, because supervisors follow students over time and across courses and can observe whether the content offered in the courses is apparent in the student's practice, this allows field supervisors to provide feedback to faculty. Faculty know the content of each other's courses and, therefore, are also able to look for manifestations of that content in the experiences of their students when they are in schools, which they frequently are. As well, in some of the programs, the courses on campus actually study the curriculum being used in the school sites. Although all of these characteristics are not present in each of the options and some are emphasized more than others depending on the program's orientation, these appear to be the main distinguishing features of field experiences at MSU.

Distinctiveness Through Integrated Structure

Recall that Henrietta Barnes referred to integrated structure as including articulation between campus and field, which we have attempted to demonstrate;
articulation between and among courses; and the creation of groups of students that interact as they go through the program experience, and therefore
become known by a set group of faculty members who work together in a program. Here we demonstrate the way Barnes's notion of integrated structure
manifests itself in several of the alternative programs just as we did with field
experiences.

We move on, then, to integrated structure as exemplified through the
sequential nature of the course experiences. Particularly, we refer to this as a
developmental sequence apparent in each of the alternative programs in the
way in which courses are articulated one with another. In our discussion with
Cassandra Book, she observed that the standard program meets all the criteria
of state requirements for certification, but lacks the organization and clear
view of the teacher that is desired. In contrast, she notes, the alternative
programs reflect designs wherein the faculty members have worked together
to create "courses that build upon one another, are sequenced in a manner that
makes sense to them, and are studied constantly to see whether sequencing of
activities and material is appropriate."

Dean Book noted as well the influence of students moving in cohort
groups as, in some ways, ensuring a developmental sequence in the courses.
She observed:

> When I teach TE 305A, I have to know what was taught in 205A and 201A, so
> that I can build on that and don't repeat what's been done there; and so I don't
> contradict or, if I contradict, that I do so knowingly and we can talk about this
> because those students hold you accountable all the time. They've heard this
> material and they are together as a class. It's not just one person challenging you
> . . . they're *all* challenging because they've learned it together and it's been
> reinforced so the level of scrutiny and the public nature of our teaching is
> important.

A further illustration of curriculum cohesion comes from the Multiple
Perspectives program. Joyce Putnam recalls that they put the curriculum
together over time from rather technical to higher-level kinds of decisions so
that the concepts that were to connect in any given term still connect and that
concepts from one term connect to the next term. She provided an example of
this cohesion:

> This instructional design model is taught in the first term of our program. We
> want the students to use it just like it's taught, but we start adapting it immedi-
> ately. Something that's fine for an individual student in reading must be altered
> when teaching a reading group. In the third term of the program, they take a

science course and what looked like a technical approach is not seven different models of planning at all. It's the same model of planning that you teach them to adapt. We've determined what adaptations must be made, and we teach those very clearly. So, we now have a program that we've developed that has a cohesive curriculum, and we work to keep it in place.

A curricular device used in the Academic Learning program to ensure cohesiveness is that the same individuals who teach some of the early courses in the sequence also teach some of the later courses. One example is the interval between TE 200, which is an exploration of individual differences in the classroom, and TE 450C, which is a school in society course. These two courses, and two other courses in the program, are ones in which the faculty have spent particular time focusing on cohesiveness. This curriculum sequence is as follows: The first course is TE 200C, wherein the concept of learning for understanding and conceptual change is introduced. Then, developmentally, the students take 205C, which is curriculum for Academic Learning, wherein the concepts of learning for understanding and conceptual change are extended into the disciplines. These two courses serve as a conceptual foundation for the methods courses and for organizing seminars and work with students in the field during student teaching. The third core course is TE 406C, which is on interdisciplinary inquiry; finally, the culmination is TE 450C, "School and Society."

Each of these alternative programs has some thematic or conceptual design, and the task, as Joyce Putnam so frequently reiterated in our visits, was to approach these themes or concepts developmentally over time. In each of the programs, the articulation of programs has been reinforced by a sense of collegiality, sometimes in student cohort groups, sometimes in student/faculty relationships, or sometimes in terms of faculty who work closely together.

Thus, we examine briefly how collegiality contributes to integrated structure. We look first, at student collegiality. A great deal of student identity is found among the various strands. Students refer to themselves as being participants in a cadre, meaning that students enter a program in a group and in a cycle, so that all of the students beginning a program in the same quarter have a particular cadre number, such as cadre 2. In three out of the four programs, students enter the program during the autumn quarter; in Heterogeneous Classrooms, they enter during the winter term. Each of these alternative programs has gone through a number of cycles and one of the programs is now up to its fifth cadre. These become, in essence, a student cohort group. This is the same cohort group which Cass Book referred to earlier as the group of students who keep the professors honest and on target because they move through the program together and they speak in a unified voice about the nature of the curriculum.

Perry Lanier also spoke to the effects of these cadres:

One thing you might not get anywhere else is that we attempt to have a sense of identity. We do a lot of socializing which keeps the students together and thinking as a group; and because they take a lot of classes together, that does happen. We interview them and send them a letter of admission stating who their advisor is early in the fall term. We invite all of the faculty and people who will be working with the student teachers . . . we think that's an important thing. . . . In the spring, we have a party for the juniors. At the end of their student teaching, we have a reception for them. Last year, I had it at my house, of probably sixty-five graduates, nearly fifty were there, plus many faculty. So, when they leave, they know the faculty and the faculty know them.

Joyce Putnam had recently presided over the same kind of function for the students in the Multiple Perspectives program. She had more than 100 students, faculty, and cooperating teachers at her home.

Aside from the social aspect woven into each of the alternative programs, a form of academic socialization is found as well. Each cadre develops its own personality. This is, in part, determined by the student cohort group and what happens to that cohort group as it moves through the program.

We asked students to describe their relationship with the faculty members at MSU. One student responded: "Very good. Most of the faculty members are very eager to help. If I go in with a question and they don't know the answer, they'll find it and get back with me." We continued this dialogue by asking about the availability of the faculty; that is, were appointments necessary? One student responded, "I just drop in." Another student said, "Forget office hours." Another student said, "It is a first-name basis,"—if not in the classroom, certainly during their office visits. Students also reported to us that during their TE 101 experience, wherein they were required to visit alternative programs, they had access as needed to the program coordinators and to the faculty members as they pursued their inquiry into the various alternatives.

Joyce Putnam spoke to the faculty/student relationship:

When you work with the same students over time, you get more of the kinds of strokes that teachers in classrooms in schools get because you can talk to the students. They get to know you. They really give you the kind of feedback that says you're doing a good job. That doesn't happen when you're teaching one class for ten weeks and see them for a total of thirty hours and then you don't see those students again. They've gone on. You don't have the chance to develop the same type of relationship. Also, we are able to develop social relationships with a set of colleagues who have some like-mindedness. They get strokes from students with whom they're working as well. There's also a sense of accomplishment because they've invested a lot.

Henrietta Barnes concurred:

The faculty continue to work in the strands because they're getting smarter, and they feel like they're accomplishing something; whereas, if you teach the same methods course over and over to a series of students coming through, it becomes an assembly line. You always see them at the same point. You never see the finished product. You never see what cumulative impact you have. I think that's discouraging.

As chair of the department, she acknowledged, as well, the pressure associated with these alternative programs. People who are not fairly open and fairly secure are not able to be successful in these programs because the work is very visible. "You are accountable. When you make a mistake, everybody knows it, and the students tell you; maybe some of your colleagues also let you know. So, some faculty will not teach in these programs."

Still another perspective on collegiality at MSU is the students' observations about the class size. One student compared it to Central Michigan, in that while MSU is much bigger than Central, he was surprised that "my classes are so much smaller because of the different programs. I think recruiters for prospective teachers like that—that we have so much attention given to us. Our largest class is about twenty-five to thirty people."

The kind of collegiality established among the students, and between the students and the faculty, is in many ways mirrored or modelled in the relationships of the faculty one to another. We look later on in this portrayal at the nature of faculty load, commitment, and interaction, attempt to describe the labor-intensive nature of the alternative programs and the time and effort required to sustain them. The large number of meetings and interactions necessary to support programs of this type along with the other multiple assignments and responsibilities that faculty members in this type of institution carry reflect this intensity. Regardless, we can cite numerous examples of faculty collegiality. The students are aware of faculty communication and the manner in which programs are designed and sustained. Both faculty and students exhibited considerable pride in their specific programs, yet no unnecessary competition was evidenced. Rather, coordinators of programs worked together for the betterment of the overall program. For example, Joyce Putnam relayed the following about the decision to support Perry Lanier's mentoring program: "We talked about that from the beginning, that it was important to do that, and we voted to support the mentor program if he didn't get funding for it. We agreed we would do less in the other programs to allow him to get started. It had to do with keeping all things viable and the quality there."

Consequently, as one example, the faculty members meet and collaborate on all the programs and support improvements in programs even if not their own. Problem solving works in the same personalized way in that when courses need reviewing, the course coordinators discuss this individually with faculty members. They discuss these issues with each other and they use student feedback, all of which weaves into the sense of collegiality supporting integrated structure.

The Distinctiveness of Utilizing the Knowledge Base

In this section, we illustrate the way in which the research orientation of the faculty, the conceptual underpinnings of their own study, and the theme development of the four programs have reinforced the utilization of these bases in the curriculum of each alternative program. Clearly, the use of the knowledge base is an extension of the notion of the development of themes, dispositions or propensities, reflectivity, and the nature of field, campus articulation.

Recall that Henrietta Barnes described the manifestation of the knowledge base as the way in which students come to believe that there is a professional literature, that there is professional knowledge, and that their students have some of it. To illustrate, we look first at the Heterogeneous Classrooms program and a conversation we had with several faculty members regarding that program. One faculty member observed that the focus of the early courses in the program was to emphasize classroom diversity and help prospective teachers see "that so much more goes on in the classroom that they may not otherwise understand and that if we're concerned about education and providing access to the content for all of the students, including those with diverse characterisitics, it's not something to be shunned but it is an important part of classroom life."

One professor described an attempt to change the assumptions prospective teachers make about teaching and schooling as follows:

> The course I teach focuses on the in-school factors that may contribute to students having difficulty in school—cultural differences, social class, race, gender, handicapping conditions—anything that might explain why some students experience difficulty. I also look at the social context in which teaching occurs and some of the ways in which teachers *unintentionally* create and perpetuate inequalities in the classroom as they interact.

In Linda Anderson's class, she looks at ways students misunderstand the content that is being taught: We're trying to teach them how students think about and understand what the teacher is trying to teach them. So our focus in these courses is around the social context of learning and the conceptual understandings of learning, which has enormous benefits for students with diverse characteristics. Teachers may, unintentionally, help to create the conditions in which the students with diverse characteristics start to have trouble.

Anderson also engages preservice students in a metacognitive process of making connections between their prior knowledge and their new knowledge by monitoring their own comprehension. Compare these examples in the Heterogeneous Classrooms program with the main ideas articulated in the

Academic Learning program. As Andy Anderson described it, "in particular, I'm thinking about the research on cognitive psychology, cognitive science, wherein researchers have some agreement about the kinds of problems that children have when they try to learn and the nature of understanding." This orientation relates to a set of convictions about the nature of knowledge and, particularly, the misconceptions or preconceptions that learners have about a given content area that have to be changed before real learning can occur. We were given a number of examples from this branch of cognitive psychology, and the following illustrates the primary conceptual orientation of the Academic Learning program.

Professor Glen Berkheimer provided this example of student misconceptions about knowledge, using kinetic molecular theory:

> All matter is made of particles. Particles are constantly moving. There are empty spaces between the particles. A major misconception has to do with children having great difficulty in thinking in terms of empty spaces. So you ask them what fills those empty spaces. They say—air, dirt, germs. But then you ask what happens when a bar of copper is heated. The particles get larger, according to the students. They are visualizing that those particles are touching and the particles get larger, whereas the scientific conception is that the particles move faster and therefore the bombardment increases and the *spaces* between the particles get larger, not the particles; the particles do not get larger. Perhaps that gives you some feel for a common misconception of students in this area. If they carry that misconception through, then they lose the whole dynamic of molecular motion, and they won't be able to understand the foundations of chemistry.
>
> You have to identify the *most important* misconceptions. Students are full of misconceptions. You must determine which ones really prevent further learning —you have to know your subject very well—and then you conduct hands-on activities, everything you can do to confront and counter their conceptions. Essentially, the Academic Learning program shows how all the ideas within a particular theory are related . . . I have the students do a content analysis, do a conceptual map of a topic, and then I work with them to help them see which of the concepts *are* most important. We do research on misconceptions, but we also find it very effective to think about which are the most important concepts and which are hierarchical.

Generally, students were aware of the conceptual, theoretical, and research bases such as the above being conveyed to them in their courses. At every turn, we found students cognizant of some of the research going on at MSU. Students even queried us about the nature of our own research and inquiry. For instance, in asking students how they came to know about teaching, we asked, "would you call your field experiences trial and error, or applying theory to practice?" A student responded, "I wouldn't call it trial and error." And another student said,

A little of both. You have to use some trial and error because you have to experiment and find out what works for you and for your students, and I don't think when you first go into the classroom everything is going to work. From my program, I learned that it's really a process—to learn how to teach is really a process . . . teachers aren't born. You have to really learn. And theory, of course, plays an important part in this.

Repeatedly, the students referred to the orientation toward inquiry in their programs. Students told us that they read research articles. They couldn't always remember names of specific scholars, but they knew names were there and that the faculty used these frames of reference. They did not say that the notion of learning to teach was basically experiential or that the professors brought in only stories about their own experiences and that was how they made sense out of things. Rather, they reiterated time and time again that professors brought in theory and research and there seemed to be a discernable confidence among the students about the existence of a professional knowledge base. Students were exposed to multiple approaches, if not multiple theories, and they had experience in testing out certain theories. Several students we interviewed challenged us when we used the term *trial and error* for they believed that it belittled their knowledge base. They preferred the term *experiment*. They said, "we experiment when we go in the field and we try different ways; some work, and some don't." They portrayed themselves as teachers thinking about their own thinking as teachers, a perspective of which Linda Anderson would be proud. As Henrietta Barnes indicated:

> What we're talking about generally is overcoming preconceptions about teaching by creating powerful enough interventions that have their roots in practice and bring together theory and practice in ways that inform each other. That's what has to be done if we're going to change those preconceptions into affirmed practice. Hopefully, by discarding some preconceptions that are not so good and building new schemas, teachers have to think carefully about what kind of sequencing and structure to put into it.

In these alternative programs, then, multiple perspectives on learning how to teach are found, but the focus of these programs is to use the best contemporary knowledge about teaching, often generated by the faculty members in their research roles, to inform the nature of these programs.

Degree of Rigor

In many ways, a discussion of the degree of rigor, or degree of difficulty, of the program of instruction offered in the four alternative programs can be referenced through perceptions of the student body. We are aware already that most of the students in the alternative programs consider themselves very special groups, sometimes referring to themselves as *unique* or *different*.

We have characterized them as mostly white, often middle-class, primarily female, and somewhat parochial in their perspective. We have also attempted to capture a sense of energy among the students in the way they talk about the process of becoming teachers.

What we have not been able to highlight yet is the level of sophistication we found demonstrated among the students in terms of their thinking about a career in teaching and their studies for this. For example, we were particularly interested in one student's account of his education studies because he had been a psychology major at another college and had already completed two years majoring in psychology. We asked if he had taken the discipline of psychology and tried to relate it to educational settings, and if that had been worthwhile. The student responded, " . . . for what psychology's worth. You have to take psychology with a grain of salt, because you can explain things under a lot of different rationales. But yes, I applied what I learned about people in pyschology to how I deal with various types of situations." We probed further and asked him about the theory base in his program and whether it presented a particular perspective. He responded without hesitation, "I'd say humanistic, as much as anything. The faculty are really cognizant of people and their backgrounds and how their backgrounds affect the way they learn, and how their culture affects the way they learn. And they have been continuously building that awareness in us, and when you get out of the classroom, it shows."

We also talked with students about the job market, and one of the students shared a resume. They used the term *resume*, and they spoke about the development of a resume as if it were a common procedure for undergraduates. Again, these students are also able to articulate the rationale for their program. The following remarks are from an Academic Learning student about her program:

> I am pursuing a career at the middle-school level, and I looked at all five programs. I was impressed with Academic Learning because it looks at the academic discipline very deeply, at the misconceptions children have, and at the ways we want to change their thinking. I thought it was interesting to look at teaching from that perspective. It wasn't just concentrating on a subject, but concentrating on the way students think about that.

A number of students spoke to the perceived difficulty of their various programs. During our interviews, we spent time with students in both Heterogeneous Classrooms and in the Academic Learning program. In a discussion with a few students regarding the Heterogeneous Classrooms program, we asked if the program were a difficult one. One student responded:

> I think so. It's kind of competitive. Being in the same group with the same people all the time, just with the people that you sit with all the time—everyone shares their grades. It's almost like you have to keep up. I'm sure everybody doesn't feel

that way, but, I was surprised when I got into it just how dedicated everyone really is.

The students reported that they do a lot of reading, not only from textbooks, but from articles and chapters from certain books, and "a lot of excerpts from research." When asked about the nature of intellectual discourse among the students, one student responded: "It's high. I've found that with certain friends in the group, that a lot of times we'll just be going to the mall, or whatever, and we'll bring up something, a problem that somebody's having in a classroom, and we'll really get into an intense discussion about the possible ways to solve that problem."

Still another student, when asked to compare courses in general studies to education courses, responded:

> If I were to take an engineering course, I would probably fail the first one and they would kick me right out of that college, because physics, all those numbers, they're not interesting to me. I don't like them. I don't care about them. And I don't think I'd do it. But, if you put an engineering major in the classroom, I don't think he'd last more than a week with those screaming kids. . . .

We asked another student how she felt about that, and she responded, "About screaming kids? I love screaming kids."

In another exchange about intellectual challenge or rigor of the courses compared to other major programs, we talked to a student who had been involved in business management. The student reflected:

> I think my record a couple of years ago is comparable to my record now. I think if there was a sense in which I've been applying myself as well in business, maybe my attitude would be different. But I breezed through all those classes without doing very much work. In these classes, I'm definitely finding challenge. I'm not bored.

Another student added:

> It's not so much a challenge as such. It's a challenge, definitely, but I've never taken classes except in philosophy, which I loved (one of my minors is philosophy) where I've sat and I've concentrated—thoughtful concentration. My mind really is thinking about things I would never have thought about, and it's really—it's not just theories and stuff, but it's more than that. It opens up your mind.

We found evidence, as well, that students picked programs not only because those programs met their belief system about teaching, which has been conveyed to us in a number of conversations, but also because they thought they would learn more. For example, one student observed:

I thought I would learn more about the subject matter in which I was interested. I thought most of the material in the other programs would be common sense after I had experience in teaching awhile. I wanted to learn how to teach my subject area, and my program is geared to conceptual change. And what I've come up against is a basic question of how do teachers form these misconceptions in the first place? Part of it is that the teachers don't know enough about their fields to answer students' questions or they give them misinformation. I have a lot of questions about the elementary level. Why aren't teachers more specialized at that level? Why do they expect teachers to be good and expert in every field?

Not only does this appear to be a reflection of the intentionality of the student's choice, it is yet another example of the sophisticated level at which the students reflected on their programs. In summary, we found that the students were articulate, prideful, eager, and energetic; that they could reflect on the nature of their choice in the alternative programs; and that they valued the professional knowledge being conveyed to them.

Faculty Commitment

Another dimension of life at MSU concerns the degree of faculty involvement in the programs and concomitant responsibilities sustained by faculty members. Most faculty members are on nine-month contracts and may access support for a fourth quarter of instruction in the summer, or they may use that time to participate in either international teacher education programs or in the seven-year rotation of the leave-with-half-pay sabbatical. During any quarter of a faculty member's service in the college, a typical teaching load is two courses, and advising graduate students in independent studies. Several faculty have a half-time appointment in the IRT or, perhaps now, the NCRTE. Program coordinators are usually given a reduced instructional load to compensate for increased nonteaching duties. As well, we learned that in the Academic Learning program, faculty members also supervised the students in field settings. In other programs, full- or part-time field supervisors are hired or doctoral graduate assistants serve in this role.

Faculty members not only conduct research as a part of their own research agenda, or an agenda in the IRT or the NCRTE, but also integrate that research knowledge in their classrooms as well. In some instances, they use the alternative programs as a focus for their research. Some faculty members teach in more than one strand.

Beyond this designation of faculty teaching load, faculty members are involved in various strands by virtue of their commitment to the philosophy espoused within that strand. One professor observed:

What was satisfying to me, was finding a match between what I philosophically agree with and how comfortable I feel teaching in that program. So, Heterogeneous Classrooms wasn't the first program I looked at, but it was the one that I felt most comfortable in. I think they've done a good job, not just artificially stating their theme, but trying to find faculty who can identify with it.

I'm very much learner-focused, yet I think that in this college, you've got people who are very concerned about teachers, and what they do and think about as teachers, and how teachers focus. We have others who are very concerned with community, and how those things come together, and those different interests start falling out in terms of the different programs and specific interests of the faculty.

Another faculty member reported that "There's been a real effort from the beginning to bring in faculty who really are consistent with the philosophy of the program." And another professor elaborated, "I think it's very growth-producing for us as faculty, because we can give lip service in the other programs to diversity, but these students are constantly testing my behavior as it relates to diversity . . . because I cannot just give lip service to it. I have to demonstrate daily that I value it, and I recognize that."

Consequently, faculty are attached to strands because they have a philosophical affinity to that strand and, because of this affinity, are able to model that commitment to the students in their teaching. As one student reflected about one of his professors: "I learned a lot about teaching from him, by what he did, what he modelled." We tried to examine, as well, the commitment it took to *sustain* these programs. We asked one faculty member, particularly, how often the faculty met to talk about the programs. The response suggested considerable work. The professor noted:

We have a fall meeting and usually once a quarter we have a meeting of the entire group. Then, specialized groups such as those with 250B classes, meet with the field supervisors before they start on their field assignments so that they understand what the field assignment is all about and how they can help the students. The field supervisors inevitably start getting feedback that there's something wrong here or there, and informal meetings are held so that I can deal with students or modify things as they happen. We also have quarterly meetings where we discuss things, but then it's institutionalized enough that people know what they're supposed to do, and they have a set of tasks that they've outlined. It's a matter of coordinating with the people that are directly affected and making sure that those things work. They're also other subset meetings of the whole program, so I might be involved in other meetings with people who are teaching other methods courses, and the field supervisors the next quarter, when I'm not teaching in the program. . . . Also, we have periodic meetings to review the content of a couple of courses with other people in the program to see if it makes sense— where you are and what you're thinking. To have that type of meeting is very helpful.

This suggests that for some faculty at least, there are endless rounds of meetings. Joyce Putnam shared that every Wednesday afternoon, from 1:00 p.m. to 5:00 p.m., she and other faculty members met with field supervisors.

We were also impressed throughout our visits at MSU by the fact that faculty were generally accessible, usually around the campus and seemingly always involved. It is easy to understand, when trying to sustain the kind of articulated, integrated structure to which Henrietta Barnes referred, that frequent meetings might be necessary. These observations led us to look at the relationship between faculty commitment to programs and instructional load and faculty research, which is our next topic.

Relationship of Faculty Research to Program

Already we have introduced the goals of the IRT and the new R & D center. Several faculty members stated that part of their time is committed to conducting research in one of these two agencies. Certainly, a review of the catalogue of IRT products confirms that faculty are deeply engaged in research. A review of faculty contributions to professional journals, and particularly those faculty involved in the undergraduate programs, further reinforced that these are active researchers.

As well, in classes we observed, we found faculty members discussing findings from their own research with students. As one faculty member observed of two colleagues,

> they are both in the IRT and jointly conduct research, so that the research findings are the same. So, what they bring in terms of research to the classroom overlaps a lot. It's just that when it's presented, it's presented within a different context. I'll give you a study done by a professor who taught in Heterogeneous Classrooms, Learning Community, and Multiple Perspectives. His study shows that students do think differently.

Not only is this an illustration of the way faculty members use research in class, but that faculty members also use the programs to study the alternative strands. In talking with two professors who work together, one discussed their research this way:

> We work together, but we have different lines of inquiry although they are related. We have separate projects and, in fact, because we are both interested in writing and we read each other's work, we try to further our knowledge of the field. We draw on the same body of knowledge. My work has been with the problems of planning for instruction and a lot of collaborative research with teachers. The other professor is essentially looking at culture . . . so it's a different interpretation. As a result, I'm interested in response as a research question; and, for me, the issue of how to respond as a teacher or as a peer is far from settled. I've opted not to prescript the responses, but rather to make that problematic for our students.

Notable in our several observations of and discussions with faculty is rhetoric that reflects inquiring professionals constantly testing hypotheses, defining terms, and analyzing data. Our image is of Sharon Feiman-Nemser walking through the hall carrying the Second Handbook of Research on Teaching with a question about the use of the term *disposition* referred to in one of the chapters. She was actively engaging other people in conversations about the nature of the term *disposition*, and this went on each time we saw her that day. Even in the evening, at a social gathering, faculty were busily engaged in dialogue on the nature of a particular research problem. As Perry Lanier observed, "There's clearly a research integration in teaching," and then he proceeded to discuss Andy Anderson's use of misconceptions and the approaches of a number of other faculty members who share their research regularly in classes. Henrietta Barnes also discussed various faculty members' research in connection with the programs:

> Over time, they are doing more and more of their own research in connection with questions that come out of the work in these programs, and I think that's good. There's a whole line of exciting research, and I think it fits in and helps the program. And all of us get to know about it and it is a real opportunity to share.

Much of the research effort on programs sustains, as well, a general approach to program evaluation, our next consideration.

Program Evaluation

According to a report prepared by Don Freeman, who is the director of the Office of Program Evaluation, such evaluation at MSU is an ongoing, cooperative endeavor involving a number of individuals and groups throughout the college. The Office of Program Evaluation was established in 1980 to coordinate the evaluation of all the undergraduate programs to provide an information base for the continuing development and improvement of programs. It also provides technical support to individuals in the various programs who are sustaining program evaluation and, finally, contributes to research on teacher education. In each of the program areas, a program evaluator was attached on a fourth-time basis, beginning in 1980, to sustain the evaluation effort. As such, Freeman described the nature of evaluation in this way: studying the programs to see what changes occur between program entry and program exit across three general categories of student outcomes: (1) acquisition of professional knowledge; (2) confidence in teaching performance; and (3) educational orientation and beliefs.

At the moment, the focus for evaluation across programs has been largely in the area of explicating the nature of student beliefs. Study of classroom performance also occurs. Freeman noted, "each program has an elaborate set of instruments that they use during the field experience. We've looked at those collectively and decided that everybody's still committed to the evaluative instruments they use in their programs." Therefore, an attempt has not been made to do an across programs assessment of teaching performance to date. As well, the development of measures for professional knowledge is moving developmentally. Joyce Putnam stated that some are attempting to design a test for professional knowledge at the culmination of the Multiple Perspectives program. Some discussion has been held about the use of the National Teacher's Exam as a measure of professional knowledge, but only on an experimental basis. Beyond this, numerous archival documents exist about the nature of evaluation and the documentation of the *development* of the programs that are available for anyone who wishes to study the nature of the evolution of each of the four program areas.

WHAT SUSTAINS THE
ALTERNATIVE PROGRAM APPROACH?

The commitment to the land-grant goals of research, teaching, and service are readily observable in the MSU profile. The College of Education is overtly committed to research. IRT's ten-year history, the proposed research agenda necessary to present a successful proposal to the Office of Educational Research and Improvement for the funding of the R & D Center for Teacher Education; and the long list of contributions by various faculty members to the knowledge base of teacher education through journals, books, monographs and research papers are evidence that this college and this institution are committed to scholarly inquiry. Add to this the necessary energy to sustain four alternative teacher education programs, all of which are highly integrated with local elementary and secondary schools, and we have a portrait of faculty commitment that truly extends to the broader professional community, to the school community, and to the student community.

When looking for explanations of what sustains these alternative approaches to teacher education when such efforts have wanned at other institutions, at least three somewhat different but compatible conditions appear to have allowed program experimentation to prosper at MSU, most notable of which is the collective commitment of the faculty to research and development in teacher education. Notwithstanding is the role of the coordinators who provide leadership for the four alternative programs. Finally, and importantly, the priorities of the current dean in the College of Education have contributed to this. Few institutions have entered into planned variation in teacher education, certainly not studied it over time. In the case of MSU, these alternatives were discussed as early as 1978, institutionalized by 1981, and were thriving into the 1986–87 academic year. What is the explanation for such momentum?

The Faculty

Throughout this scenario, we have attempted to document in multiple ways the level of commitment the faculty in the MSU College of Education have to the alternative programs' perspective. Clearly, many faculty designed and implemented these programs through endless hours of discussion, documentation, sometimes argument, but ultimately resolution and commitment to a particular theme or focus. Not only were faculty the critical actors in the design of these four alternative programs, they are the teachers in these programs. They teach multiple courses within strands, and some faculty members teach courses across strands. Still others have tirelessly taken on the leadership role as program coordinators. As several faculty members attest, sustaining these programs requires quarterly program area meetings, annual meetings to review the nature of the curriculum, sometimes biweekly or weekly meetings to calibrate the articulation of one course experience to another, multiple contacts with field participants in the program, and, finally although not unimportantly, individual student advisement. In the sheer measure of time, these faculty members have made a considerable investment in the maintenance and extension as well as the vitality of these alternative programs. Part of this has to do with quality scholars who either see opportunities to engage in research in these programs or the need to adapt their research to teacher preparation. As one faculty member opined, "I think the reason that the dean spent the money that she spent to have senior faculty teach in the undergraduate programs was, in fact, so that the teacher preparation program would reflect the research."

We also asked students how they felt about the nature of research as it is embedded in the undergraduate program. We are reminded of the Academic Learning student who earlier stated that institutions such as the IRT and the NCRTE are putting MSU at the forefront of education.

We asked at what cost were these students at the forefront. Did they feel like guinea pigs? Their response, "I think it's great! At times you might feel like a guinea pig. But it's not a bad feeling. I hope that it all works out for the best." Another student, in response to our question about this research atmosphere, said: "I feel very special having professors talk to you and then reading books they've written that are of national scope. That and also by talking to outside sources and the fact that you [as researchers] are here studying our program. A lot of people are going to be looking around here."

Another student asked if we were conducting our study so we could implement some of the ideas in our schools. This sense of curiosity was apparent when we interviewed the first group of students. They wanted to know what our areas of research were and what line of inquiry we were developing—fairly sophisticated questions for college juniors.

We asked Henrietta Barnes the degree to which the faculty believed they were in the forefront—as the students observed—in terms of innovation and utilization of the knowledge base in teacher education. Barnes responded:

> I don't know if they feel they're in front; sometimes they feel they're not—they know the problems are considerable and that sometimes they feel they are not doing as well as they should be. But I feel that when they talk with others outside of here they tend to get positive feedback. Recently, two people said something to the effect that they felt we were doing a good job. Faculty are always a little bit surprised by how they are viewed, I think. They're certainly not humble, but they don't necessarily feel that what they're doing is the best that could be done.

In some ways, this is the most telling observation we heard during our visit to MSU. This is clearly a success environment where what manifests itself in practice is also codified in national, respected research journals. And yet there is the sense in which these faculty believe they could do better, the sense that more experimentation and inquiry is necessary. Such a vision feeds any outlook on the future.

We were, of course, curious as to the disposition of the College of Education at MSU regarding its decision to join the Holmes Group. On each occasion when we asked this question, looking for some indication of the future of the preservice alternative programs in teacher education, our question was met with a sober response and one that clearly acknowledged how deeply embedded this commitment is to alternative approaches to teacher education. In a discussion with Don Freeman and Cass Book, Book observed:

> I don't know that we will continue to offer undergraduate teacher education here. I don't know that we'll continue to offer it in these formats. I think that there is a sense that they have been very good. That they have progressed. Clearly, our students coming out of them are good, well-prepared. Clearly there's a difference, from what interviewers tell me—superintendents, people who work with our students. So, I think there will continue to be a commitment to alternatives, although it may change in format. It may be preeducation courses that provide alternatives. Or maybe there will be alternatives at the graduate level. I'm just not sure.

Freeman inserted "I'd be shocked, given our tradition of alternatives, if we didn't pursue this. . . . It may not be any one of the four that we have right now, but some other kind of theme or alternative themes will be presented. I'll be shocked if we don't have alternatives that students can pick from."

To these comments, Book added:

> I'd be not only shocked, I'd be disappointed because I think that we've invested a lot in these options and faculty commitment and enthusiasm are so high. You've got to take not only what happens to students but what happens to faculty, and my observation is that we have faculty who really can converge on one of these

programs, invest a lot in it, be able to work together so that they are strengthened and their teaching is invigorated. I see a positive staff development effort that has occurred as a result of these programs, as well. And not everybody stays—some people decide this format is not for them, or they teach tangentially to it. . . . There's some of that, but, for the most part, we really have gotten faculty excited about teacher education.

We close this section on the faculty with our own observations. This, by several criteria, appears to be a highly productive faculty. They come to work early and stay late. They occasionally host other faculty, students, and teachers in their homes. They engage in research and publish on a regular basis. Even at the end of May, as the academic year was coming to a close, they were generous and gracious in the time they gave to us. They gave us energy in a studied, dispassionate way. They are accustomed to studying programs, and they are accustomed to having their programs observed. They knew that was what we were doing—studying them and studying their programs. They wove us into their busy days with little trouble.

Teaching and research are generative activities. Faculty approach their task with a sense of optimism and inquiry. One of the most energetic faculty members with whom we spoke, Andy Anderson, teaches a course in curriculum once a year, which means that when he sees additions or changes he wants to make, he has to wait one year to implement them. Thus, he observed in the spring, "For the first time, I feel we have a conception of curriculum and what teachers and students need to learn and what teachers have to do in schools that's going to fit together. I tend to be optimistic this time of year! I said that last year, too."

We observed this attitude repeatedly at MSU. People work hard, people experiment, students give feedback, faculty receive feedback, and they begin to think immediately about revisions, about changes that can be made effectively, about fine tuning the entire process.

The Coordinator's Role

Each of the four alternative programs has a program area coordinator or co-coordinators. In many cases, this is not the coordinator who began with the program, or even the leaders who surfaced during the theme discussions between 1978 and 1981. We had the opportunity to speak with each of the coordinators and their names were often brought up in discussions with faculty and students. Each of these coordinators sustain multiple responsibilities, and Laura Roehler helped us list their duties. She began by acknowledging, "I think we have a group of people who are really dedicated to the concepts which underlie this program." She noted that she and Bruce Burke have one-quarter of their respective loads committed for coordination and that a program documenter also has one-quarter of his time released. Both teach regularly in the program. Roehler's research is related to the content of some of the courses she teaches in reading. Beyond that, she noted: "We handle scheduling. Each term we examine our evaluation data and make changes— using this feedback—scheduling changes or moving courses around that seem to be more appropriate. . . . We are starting a new one-hour seminar and I handle that and all the field placements. I'm responsible for all the field courses and the student teaching." This list is added to by Richard Navarro, another coordinator, who identified seven different types of meetings he engaged in relative to his program over time. Richard also observed that the *consistency* of leadership is critical to developing and refining a focus for these programs. Perry Lanier added his observation on this role:

> There are some frustrations in that you're not in an administrative role where you can assign people, yet these classes need to be covered. So, you negotiate with particular individuals informally. They formally sit down with Henrietta [Barnes] to work out their assignments for the year. That quasi-administrative responsibility—just being able to request people's time—is sometimes frustrating for me. As coordinators, we also attempt to monitor the program and collect the syllabi each term in all courses that are being offered to the students to share aims and objectives.

Regardless of the frustration Lanier suggests can occasionally occur, especially when negotiating faculty assignments, he definitely enjoys the informal nature of his responsibility. He observed:

> The quasi-administrative role I have as a coordinator gives me more degrees of freedom than I had when I was in the administrative chain, because I can go directly to faculty members and their respective chairs and try to get someone to work on it, although it doesn't always work. I enjoy the latitude I have.

Coordinators can avail themselves of the same opportunities as other faculty members. Laura Roehler and Bruce Burke, for instance, as co-coordinators of the Learning Communities program, are preparing to take sabbaticals. Other coordinators have involved themselves more directly in the overseas program, but it is still difficult to avail themselves of the same amenities as other faculty members because of the program coordinators' ongoing responsibilities. As Joyce Putnam observed:

> We've discussed the coordinators' responsibilities, trying to be clear about a procedure that would let us in and out of these roles. It is different than being just a regular faculty person here. For example, one of the opportunities in our department that you have is to teach overseas and in the graduate program. It's difficult for me to do that, although I want to. But more important, it's difficult not to be present when you're in charge of a program. I think also leadership styles have something to do with that.

Thus, we found the coordinators expend much time in these programs which did create some tension. As Don Freeman observes of both Joyce Putnam and Cass Book "Joyce [Putnam] publishes and does research in about the same way that Cass [Book] does—out of her hide and certainly not with the kind of available time and energy that others can bring to the task. But she gets the recognition, I think, that she deserves in the coordinator's role because people recognize what a demanding role that is and that the whole fate of the program is built around that."

Henrietta Barnes observed:

> The most difficult part (of sustaining alternative programs) is providing the coordination and leadership. From my perspective, the hardest job is getting people who can and are willing to do this—that's the hardest goal. Like Joyce or Perry, Richard or Laura and Bruce. It's difficult because you have to give up some of your agenda. Also, it's very complicated. You have to work with a lot of people on a lot of levels and as you know much of it is political. There aren't many people who can do that. Or will do that. And I think that's a critical need and it could make or break the programs.

Finally, Book's observation on Joyce Putnam:

> The one thing that I think is a really serious problem, if anything is, is the development of leadership. Joyce [Putnam] and Richard [Navarro]—they're going to be burned out. We've had people burn out in the program. Glen Burkheimer reached the point of saying there were other things he wanted to do and he was tired. That's not a criticism at all. It is draining to coordinate those programs. Last night, Joyce had a party for the students in the program with their cooperating teachers, and it was just terrific in terms of what obviously has happened to the staff in the elementary school. We're impacting a lot of people along the way, but at what cost to her? Joyce said that the night before renewed her enthusiasm so much she thought she could continue for another year!

Leadership from the Chair and the Dean

Henrietta Barnes is a pivotal figure on the landscape of alternative programming at MSU. As Putnam recalls:

> Henrietta [Barnes] was put in as chair the fall that we were really at a point of having to make a decision about whether and how we were going to go ahead with the programs. In terms of getting us started and getting people to talk to each other and getting documenters and many other things like that—in all the initial efforts—her leadership was very helpful. We probably got the programs piloted and through the system the second time because of her leadership and the support she could provide as administrator in the department.
>
> As new programs start, you fumble along because you don't know where all the pieces you need are, so, when we ran into problems, we would go and talk to

Henrietta. She was also very helpful in terms of the coordinator. . . . There was a tension between allowing the coordinators to work together so much that all the programs looked alike and letting us work together enough so we could be colleagues but maintain different programs.

Throughout our visits, the observations Barnes made regarding the distinctiveness of the program and her obvious command of the overall structure was impressive. Many acknowledged that the attributes of leadership were manifest in the person of Henrietta Barnes. Similarly, it was acknowledged that the genesis of alternative programs at MSU can be traced to Judy Lanier. In every historical account we heard, the chronology would begin with Judy Lanier's role in convening faculty members, facilitating committee discussions, assigning responsibilities, assuring the contributions of the faculty, acquiring leaders who could guide the piloting and subsequent implementation of the program, and ensuring the stability of leadership for them over time. As Cass Book recalled:

This college has a long history of alternatives . . . but we also have a dean who is obviously very committed to undergraduate teacher education. The faculty sensed that immediately. Virtually all of the people in the IRT teach in at least one undergraduate program. Teacher preparation is not something you avoid doing—you are expected to do it here, and I think people pick up that spirit and enter teaching in the programs with that spirit, knowing full well that the dean is very committed to this.

When asked if Judy Lanier offered certain kinds of incentives to engage people in these activities, Joyce Putnam recalled,

I don't think that she offered incentives from that perspective. She stressed the need to discuss alternative positions. . . . She provided the leadership that allowed us *not* to have to agree but to identify the similarities and differences that we held and to take positions about those. You were supposed to be clear about the position that you were taking and not forced to say how you fit with other people. It was an exciting time to be here!

It was, as well, Lanier's leadership that initially engaged the research faculty in the undergraduate program to institutionalize the programs as regular programs and not alternatives that operate outside of the system, to create the leadership role of program coordinator, and to provide cohesion and stability over time for faculty members to form like-minded areas focusing on a particular theme or conception of teaching.

From all observable perspectives, Lanier is a hard-working and dedicated professional. Her work schedule appears to know no limit by day of week, or dark of night. Her days in the office run into her evenings at home, where she graciously entertains a host of visitors drawn to MSU. She is referred to repeatedly, respectfully, and often with affection by those we visited with for having the necessary knowledge, energy, and passion to motivate a faculty. She continues to write, conduct her own research, and speak widely in national forums. Although many have contributed, the Holmes Group has evolved through her leadership in many ways. Her service to other major national committees is widely acknowledged.

More important in terms of the alternative programs, she had a vision that this faculty would be best served, as would the profession, by the development of programs representing alternative perspectives on teaching. She has contributed substantially not only to initiating planned variation in teacher preparation but to sustaining these variations over time. Thus, this aspect of leadership is unique to Judy Lanier and evident for many years now. The alternative were possible at MSU to an extent because of research initiatives already in place and because of the commitment of a great many talented faculty. However, they were enhanced considerably by the energies of the dean of the College of Education, Judith E. Lanier.

7

Cross-Program Analysis: Progress, Problems, and Promise

INTRODUCTION

As we indicated in Chapter One, the institutions we selected guided what we studied and reported on in our descriptive documentaries or cases. We were looking for manifestations of "best practice," because there is a considerable lack of comparative cases that attempt to consider the way different institutional contexts interact with programs preparing teachers. Through a cross-institutional analysis, we have been able to evolve not only positive but troublesome practices and conditions associated with preservice elementary teacher education in the six institutions studied. Again, we emphasized the positive attributes in the individual descriptive cases or documentaries, due to the nonconfidential manner of our reporting, and we examined practices and conditions more critically and generally across institutions in this chapter.

Obviously, given the nature of our selection process, the limited number of cases themselves, and the geographical region, we cannot and did not expect to make generalizations with regard to the nature and quality of preservice education in the United States. Observations, interviews, and document reviews, however, were quite congruent with the AACTE-sponsored RATE studies; nationally stratified probability samples conducted in ongoing survey research. We also participated as members of the RATE research team and refer to those studies in this chapter. We can make comparisons among and between these six programs representing different institutional types, and these observations can enable well-grounded research questions and hypothesis testing for study across a greater number of institutions. This was the ultimate intent of our inquiry.

Before proceeding with the cross-institutional analysis of common strengths we observed and concerns we noted in these institutions, we should briefly review our data collection and analysis procedures. At each of the six sites visited, we followed these data collection procedures: (1) we collected a series of taped interviews, field notes, documents, and other relevant artifacts; (2) the results of taped interviews were transcribed, and field notes and other documentation collected during the site visits were orginized; and (3) we read all of the institutional transcripts, field notes, and other documentation, and independently identified the common themes and salient concepts that evolved during our review and analysis. Eventually, these themes and concepts were confirmed or validated through triangulating the accounts of faculty, students, and other persons interviewed at the site, as well as through a variety of documents including a check against institutional bulletins describing the programs, professional journals and technical reports, and other fugitive material. Chapter One outlines our major research questions, which focused on curriculum, faculty, students, and programs. We review findings in regard to the first three areas herein and discuss programs in Chapter Eight.

INQUIRY INTO THE NATURE OF CURRICULUM AND CURRICULUM ORGANIZATION

We observed multiple instances of *articulated* and *integrated* curriculum, including: the relationship of the professional education curriculum to the arts and sciences curriculum; the relatedness within the professional education sequence of one course to another; the flow from campus experiences to field experiences and back to a synthesis of the two; the cyclical nature of curricula wherein faculty who are knowledgeable of each other's goals and content, highlight different points of view as well as complement one another; the construction of programs from goal statements to *clearly specified objectives* and program modules, as is the case in Toledo; and across programs the prevalence of *themes*.

We turn to these in reverse order, beginning with the nature of themes, recalling Henrietta Barnes's observation as MSU: "We have programs that carefully select content to support a given theme and build that content in a cumulative sense." The Heterogeneous Classrooms program, for example, reenforces themes embedded in the concept of heterogeneity by offering a foundations course early in the professional sequence and also at the culmination of the program, after student teaching. Issues of equity are addressed individually at the beginning of the program and in terms of larger social concerns at the culmination of the program.

Jim Johnson, at the University of Toledo, observed that the thematic *articulation* of the curriculum from one course to another is enhanced in that "public" modules are available to students at the outset and they can "see in advance the performance objectives and some indication of the kinds of classroom activities in the form of evaluation." The articulation of curriculum from one course to another was also underscored in the spiral nature of curriculum as shared by Judith Smith at Luther College, Kay Stickle at Ball State, and Ben Thompson at UW-Eau Claire. Students at several campuses were also appreciative of the integrative, interrelated, and holistic approach to elementary curriculum modelled for them in their courses and provided unsolicited testimony in our interviews with them in this regard.

The *developmental* nature of the curricula in each of the six institutions was observed in multiple instances. The ordering of courses and related activities was characterized in the related nature of field experiences beginning with observational experiences and moving to more intensive and protracted teaching experience. It was also seen in some instances in the degree to which the curricula moved from a focused and technical perspective of teaching to multidimensional perspectives reinforcing more artistic conceptions of teaching; it was observed in the introduction of concepts, revisited more indepth later.

At Ball State University, this sequence of activities is constructed to flow from the *freshman* through the *senior* year. At the University of Toledo, it is characterized by an introductory career decisionmaking course; moves through general pedagogy, educational psychology, and skill orientation; and then proceeds through methods of teaching in the various disciplines. The manifestation of the CBTE program at the University of Toledo allows students to move through the program in a "block format" wherein four hours every morning are devoted to a particular disciplinary block, including time in that four hours to eventually work in the schools as the quarter progresses.

Developmental sequence in some instances appeared enhanced, as well, by a sense of *shared ordeal*, the collective experiencing (typically in student cohort groups) of a particular "rite of passage" or difficult experience the students share. At the University of Wisconsin-Eau Claire, Ben Thompson describes the fact that it is not unusual for students who have completed—or more aptly, survived—the junior block to celebrate in a variety of ways. He notes that block parties are common and that students frequently silk screen T-shirts indicating they have survived the "block."

At Ball State University, we observed this same sense of shared ordeal. In the EXEL program, approximately 20 percent of the students drop out in the freshman and sophomore years. Those who remained appeared dedicated to pursuing teaching as a career. In the EXEL program, certain courses further sorted "the women from the girls." These experiences were identified by students as the higher-level reading and language arts blocks. Typical reactions of students to these courses before they entered them were apprehension and fear of failure. During the sequence students reported working very hard, putting in many hours outside class. Afterward, students demonstrated considerable pride in having shared in and passed through this "ordeal."

Luther College has a shared ordeal experience, as well. Prior to the professional education sequence, students experience the Paideia requirements and the requirements to prepare a senior paper. Students provided assessments of Paideia similar to that of the language arts block at Ball State University.

Thus, in all these programs, attention to the scope and sequence of courses in the professional sequence was common. These programs refute the allegation that teacher education programs are largely an unrelated set of courses, designed and taught by faculty independent of their colleagues, taken by students equally autonomous and in any order they desire, and culminating in a single school experience (student teaching) that, in many ways, is conceptually and chronologically distant from the earlier experiences. This could, in part, be attributable to the fact that these were elementary programs which call for coordination among faculty from various disciplines and that they were designed as distinctive "alternative" or experimental programs.

Cautions and Concerns

Several programs evidenced obvious shortcomings as well as the above-mentioned advantages. The conceptual coherence, curricular interrelatedness, and faculty collegiality which evolved from philosophical consonance about conceptions of teaching and learning was, in some instances, "unraveling at the seams." A strenuous workload involving multiple responsibilities mitigates against continuing faculty collaboration. As a result of our investigation, we have developed an "I can carry water up the hill once, . . . maybe twice," hypothesis. The creation of alternative program designs is a stimulating, growing time; we can speak from our own experiences as program developers. It appears this program development is in many ways organic, evolving on broken fronts, stimulated by dialogue, debate and culminating eventually in some fundamental philosophical harmony. The program builds on existing strengths and distinctiveness. It is carried forward by visible leadership among faculty as well as administration and a growing sense of group identity.

Innovation is difficult to sustain, as the change literature has repeatedly demonstrated. It may be even more difficult for the same faculty to *repeat* the process of designing coherent programs. These programs tend to live an extended life, albeit always changing somewhat and with these changes not easily discernible to an outsider. As a case in point, given the very considerable effort to evolve a highly innovative and parallel set of alternative programs at MSU, it will be interesting to see how broadly and readily faculty can or will make the transition to a Holmes Group postbaccalaureate pattern of similar options.

A number of factors also militate against student cohort groups, including the transient nature of the student population, their not infrequent heavy work experience and their intermittent patterns of enrollment.

Notwithstanding the efforts of faculty in several of these programs, there remain major problems in terms of the articulation of curriculum with both faculty in the arts, sciences, and humanities and those in K – 12 schools. Ultimately, questions of curriculum hinge on the nature and quality of the *content* and of the opportunities for *learning how to teach*. The broader teacher education literature informs us well with regard to these latter concerns.

Alan Tom (1987) quotes Henry Holmes in his cogent critique of the Holmes Group Report, *Tomorrow's Schools*:

> The burning question . . . seems to me to be not the question often debated among university teachers of education: 'Shall a master's degree be required of prospective secondary-school teachers?', but rather the question: 'How shall the work for the master's degree that ought obviously to be required of most prospective secondary-school teachers be so conducted that those who attain it may carry in to the schools technical competence that can keep itself alive, a professional philosophy that will endure and grow, and a cultural and scholarly foundation that will make them bearers of light to the youth they teach?' (p. 432).

Thus, Tom employs irony to make the fundamental point that it is not structural change (although we have tried to illustrate the cruciality as well of program design considerations) that should fuel the Holmes Group dialogue but debate about the nature and quality of the curriculum.

The venerable Harry Broudy (1984) argues eloquently that those preparing to teach should demonstrate the same type of cognitive ability and career commitment as those students in engineering, law, and architecture. He sees this commitment as calling for "genuinely professional" preservice and postgraduate teacher education. He underscores that the nature of intellectual bases in the general studies is the challenge for teacher education.

We in no way underestimate the magnitude of these challenges regarding the nature and character of general as well as professional studies. In the final chapter, when we offer a few modest recommendations, we suggest what we believe to be some serious omissions in professional studies and how better links to transform at least the nature of *preprofessional* studies might be achieved. We examine relationships with schools later in this chapter, when we respond to the research question concerned with the nature of opportunities for learning how to teach in schools.

INQUIRY INTO CONCEPTIONS OF TEACHING

To what extent were the curricula observed driven by clear and agreed-upon conceptions of schooling and teaching? Different conceptions of teaching were manifest to various degrees across institutions. For instance, the competency-based teacher education program at the University of Toledo is reflective of a behavioral psychology perspective with specific sets of teaching skills embedded in modules. The general assumption is that the acquisition of increasingly complex skills over time contributes to an effective teacher. This notion is different from the multiple conceptions of teaching, which exist in the programs of planned variation at MSU.

At MSU, one can look across programs to see that these programs reflect distinctively different departure points, if not emphasis in teaching, such as (1) learning in academic disciplines, (2) personal responsibility and social community, and (3) appreciation for diverse learners that exist in a diverse society.

At Luther College, the conception of a good teacher is embedded first in the notion of a well-educated person and an appreciation for "classical" education as reflected in the Paideia experience. The student is also given a foundation that is cross-cultural and that speaks to non-Western as well as Western influences on the American experience. The intent is that students appreciate a historical value system and are reflective about the values of others. From this rather classical conception of the educated person and, subsequently, the educated teacher, the Luther College education faculty's prevailing conception of teaching, as with the University of Toledo, focuses on the necessary *skills* of effective teaching, including basic communication and human relations skills, clarity of presentation, organization, and the individualization of instruction. This is not unlike the prevalent characterization of a teacher as disciplined, well-organized, and well-planned at the University of Wisconsin-Eau Claire or Ball State University. These two institutions particularly see themselves as "providing the basics." For instance, at Eau Claire, one student describes the program as "really showing you what's going on, so you don't have to sink or swim, . . . so that when you are a student teacher . . . you know what works and what doesn't and what's expected." Both students and faculty at Ball State University acknowledge a materials-oriented, hands-on conception of teaching, as one student reported, "I know that if I hadn't had these experiences at Ball State I wouldn't realize how important hands-on experiences are, how important that we do things really creatively."

Jesse Goodman at Indiana University discussed reflectivity, a common concern we heard among faculty there, in terms of assuming a "critical perspective":

> From my perspective, we'll get better education if we try more seriously to empower teachers—to help them make more informed judgments and get them thinking and being more reflective about what they do and why and what's valuable to teach, and what's the best way to teach it.

In discussing conceptions of teaching, we should also address the topic of *teacher dispositions*. At MSU, Henrietta Barnes offered a definition of teacher dispositions: "I'm thinking of habits of mind—the ways of thinking about children and all the alternative programs have a philosophy that goes with the theme of a combined set of attitudes and beliefs about learners and about yourself as a teacher and the interaction between them."

Cautions and Concerns

We return to alternative conceptions of teaching and learning, and the nature and mission of schools, in the final chapter when we discuss the definition and nature of *programs* of teacher education. We take the position that programs should be explicitly embedded in theoretically sound and research-supported, or at least hypothesis-generating, conceptions of teaching and learning framed both in the realities of and ideals for schooling. Numerous conceptions of teaching exist from which to select and creatively complement, if not meld together, program frameworks. These conceptions of teaching and learning are embedded in such disparate disciplines as the cognitive sciences, social psychology, psycholinguistics, perceptual psychology, counseling psychology, developmental psychology (child, adolescent, and adult), and cultural anthropology. They reflect forms of discourse and inquiry as manifested in expert-novice studies, research on metacognition, conceptual learning, classroom ecology, linguistic analyses, epistemological and ontological analyses, stage theory, group and communication theory, critical theory, and action research. They are represented in theoretical frameworks which can provide thematic structure and allow the identification of key dispositions for programs, such as put forth by Art Combs (1974) in perceptual psychology; Norman Springthall and Lois Theis-Sprinthall (1983) in developmental psychology; David and Roger Johnson (1985) in social psychology and cooperative learning; Benjamin Bloom (1981) in cognitive psychology and mastery learning; Gary Fenstermacher (1986) in philosophy and practical reasoning; and Zeichner and Liston (1988), Carr and Kemmis (1983), and Zimpher (1988) in terms of generally promoting a disposition for inquiry and reflection.

This list could easily be extended. The point here is that regardless of some thoughtful planning relative to conceptions of teaching in some of the programs we visited, far too great a reliance remains on behavioral psychology and skill and practice orientations to teaching in others. "Student teaching" still is embedded in notions of assessing performance through periodic evaluative snapshots framed by debatable criteria of teaching "effectiveness." The conception of teaching as primarily cognitive and problem-oriented in a highly complex environment could receive more attention.

Contrast "the demonstration of specific competencies" orientation with Koff's (1986) elaboration of Fenstermacher's view of professional competence embedded in practical reasoning:

> This view of teaching assumes that teachers can think and that in fact they do so while they are teaching. The actions these teachers take result from their practical arguments. A practical argument consists of a series of premises. It includes a

value/belief premise (e.g., it is good/better to . . .), a set of empirical premises (e.g., if I do this, then x will result), and a situational/perceptive premise (e.g., this is the appropriate time/place to . . .), and it culminates in action. Teachers can articulate these arguments. Specifically, a competent teacher is one who can articulate the practical arguments on which his/her actions are based. The competent teacher exemplifies quality and excellence in teaching and at the same time exemplifies professionalism in teaching, in the sense of profession as action or activity directed toward service aimed to some valued end, some public good. (p. 4)

This concept of a professional teacher appears distant from the current prevailing concept. However, if *programs* were framed for prospective teachers to provide evidential bases for their actions and decisions from their very first experiences throughout a well-delineated laboratory and clinical training (as we recommend in our final chapter), would we not move over time in this direction? We do not want to deny the importance of demonstrating core teaching abilities, but rather underscore that it is the when and the why in the problematic nature of planned events in the classroom that are the critical questions for the teacher to consider and reflect upon.

Beyond this, we are most concerned with the lack of attention to a *critical* perspective in terms of the nature of teaching and the mission of schooling. Michael Apple (1987) has represented the critical perspective well over time and brings this perspective to bear in speaking to the "crisis" in education today:

> The supposed crisis in teaching and in education in general is not an isolated phenomenon. It is related to a much more extensive structural crisis in the economy, in ideology, and in authority relations. As I have argued in considerably more detail elsewhere, we are witnessing an attempt to restructure nearly all of our major cultural, economic, and political institutions to bring them more closely into line with the needs of only a very limited segment of the American population. Thus, we cannot fully understand why our formal institutions of education and the teachers and administrators who work so long and hard in them are being focused on so intently today unless we realize that economically powerful groups and the New Right have already been partly successful in refocusing attention away from the very real problems of inequality in the economy and in political representation and shifting most criticism to the health, welfare, legal, and especially educational systems. In technical terms, there has been a marked shift from a concern for 'person rights' to those of 'property rights' in our public discourse. (p. 331)

We believe our prospective teachers need this broader critical perspective. Maxine Greene has eloquently called for more attention to art, music, dance, poetry, and literature in the preparation of teachers in order to develop a more critical pedagogy. She illustrates the way our cultural literacy can contribute to this perspective:

Of course we want to empower the young for meaningful work, we want to nurture the achievement to diverse literacies. But the world we inhabit is palpably deficient: there are unwarranted inequities, shattered communities, unfulfilled lives. We cannot help but hunger for traces of utopian visions, of critical or dialectical engagements with social and economic realities. And yet, when we reach out, we experience a kind of blankness. We sense people living under a weight, a nameless inertial mass. How are we to justify our concern for their awakening? Where are the sources of questioning, of restlessness? How are we to move the young to break with the given, the taken-for-granted—to move toward what might be, what is not yet?

Confronting all of this, I am moved to make some poets' voices audible at the start. Poets are exceptional, of course; they are not considered educators in the ordinary sense. But they remind us of absence, ambiguity, embodiments of existential possibility. More often than not they do so with passion; and passion has been called the power of possibility. This is because it is the source of our interests and our purposes. Passion signifies mood, emotion, desire: modes of grasping the appearances of things. It is one of the important ways of recognizing possibility. . . . (p. 427)

Finally, we should underscore the relationship between a conception of teaching serving as a conceptual framework and the derivation of a reasonable number of dispositions. Jim Raths and Lilian Katz (1985) refer to what is called the "Goldilocks" problem; namely, that the use and adoption of ideas may well be related to their size. That is, some ideas or concepts are too small or too specific in "conceptual size" and others are too vague and general to be well-implemented. The laundry lists of behavioral objectives manifested in many teacher education programs represent the "too small." The conceptions of critical pedagogy or practical reasoning could well illustrate the "too big"; that is, unless the latter are translated into more of a "just right" set of dispositional behaviors that would thread through programs. They suggest, perhaps, no more than ten such dispositional behaviors. Raths and Katz illustrate this concept of dispositions in the work of Doug Heath (1985), a developmentalist, and Art Combs (1979), a perceptual psychologist, in terms of the way they translate their theoretical constructs into a reasonable number of dispositional qualities that could provide focus and continuity to a *program* of teacher education. In this regard, the work of Howey and Strom (1986), in their attempt to delineate the requisite human qualities desired in teachers, is also instructive.

INQUIRY INTO OPPORTUNITIES FOR
LEARNING TO TEACH IN SCHOOLS

We have differentiated the experiential bases of curriculum from other curriculum organization characteristics not because the nature of field experience is not deeply embedded in the curricular configuration of these six institutions but because of the particular emphasis in each institution on the nature of field experiences and faculty involvement with the schools. In each institution, field experiences began early in the student's program and continued sequentially through the practicum or student teaching experience. Students and faculty invariably report valuing the experiential base of the program. Short of explicating the field experience design in each of the institutions we visited, we attempt to provide some flavor of the nature of field experiences, the various purposes they serve, and the nature of faculty involvement with schools.

Clearly, the field component of the University of Toledo's CBTE Program constitutes a significant distinctive feature of the college's program. The field experience begins with a career decision course, which is typically taken during the freshman or sophomore year and extends through the methods block and student teaching. At Indiana University, early and continuous field experiences are embedded in the programs and as Duaine Lang observed, they contribute as well to curriculum integration and a form of faculty teaming:

> The expectations for what is done in schools grows out of the course in which students are enrolled. . . . And that's a strength in the elementary program to the extent that it's forcing these instructors to share the field experience time; in effect to share the courses and the expectations for students in those courses with each other.

This commitment to early and continuous field experiences is evident in the Ball State University program as well, where students engage in early and sequential field experiences. As one student summarized:

> I've been teaching, in one respect or another, for four years now, and, by this time, I can just jump right in and start in on everything that is necessary for a successful lesson right off the bat.

With regard to MSU, the early and sequential nature of field experiences varies in different programs. A faculty member describes the Multiple Perspectives program:

> So, all the field assignments, everything our students do in the field, is coordinated with their coursework. . . . The field instructors either have been to those classes or . . . our weekly staff meetings. The field instructor's job is to reinforce and support the program content with the students in the field.

An exception to this early and continuous field experience is the intentional delay of field experiences in the MSU Academic Learning program, as Cheryl Rosaen elaborated:

Unlike some of the other programs that assign students to a classroom early in the teacher education program, we feel there are a lot of disadvantages in being out in the schools. Of course, there are advantages too. Now we're beginning to think through more thoroughly the way we can increase the time spent in the classroom. We do it in a way that will make sense to our students.

As such, the Academic Learning strand has designed a mentor program wherein supervising teachers in the field can be knowledgeable about the emphasis on student misconceptions and conceptual learning and relate these experiences to their classroom. Clearly, the range of field experiences in these programs, the early and sequential nature of these experiences, and the relationship between college instruction and the nature of field experiences are reinforced and facilitated by faculty involvement with the schools.

We do not have a good gauge to assess the precise nature and quality of the various school experiences across these six institutions as embedded in an array of school sites and as engaged in with a range of teachers and teaching styles. Our study did not allow for such investigation beyond some general assessment of the scope of these experiences and the perceptions of those who participated in them. Based upon what we saw and heard in these programs, opportunities designed for learning how to teach might well be better in many situations than generally acknowledged. Programs remain, nonetheless.

Cautions and Concerns

We do have substantial literature that addresses the strengths as well as the shortcomings of these experiences generally. The research of Griffin (1983), Schlechty (1985), and Zeichner (1987) are especially instructive in this regard. The pioneer efforts of Shulman (1985), for example, in underscoring fundamental differences in the thinking and perspectives between beginning and more experienced teachers has helped to spawn further research into these differences and how they are best bridged. This work is further buttressed by expert-novice studies in other domains.

The work of Berliner (1986) and Broudy (1985) has enabled us to think more coherently about the nature of laboratory and clinical training, and we elaborate briefly on Berliner's notion of a scientific laboratory in our recommendations in Chapter Nine. We found a paucity of well-conceived laboratory experiences and only a few examples of clinical training as generally defined in other professional training. In the latter instance, we refer to testing a student's understanding of theory by asking her or him to apply theoretical propositions or principles to particular situations.

Resolution of the problems here may call for fundamental conceptual alterations. Some would say paradigm shifts are needed in the way planning experiences for learning how-to-teach can occur—not only by those in K–12 schools, but by college-based teacher educators. This is an evolving agenda of major proportions, but other related anachronisms and political, social, and economic problems exist.

One such anachronism is our application instructionally of electronic information and communications technologies, especially in laboratory, clinical, and internship or student teaching experiences. The ever-increasing sophistication of many of these technologies and the cost attached to each abbreviated generation of development constrains state-of-the-art application. Yet, use of these technologies in many sectors is widespread. Not so in teacher education. The use of microcomputers in laboratory simulations or as tools for communication between faculty and cooperating teachers and student teachers, the use of interactive television in selected K–12 classrooms, or even amplified telephones appear largely foreign concepts. Considerable vision in this regard was demonstrated by Howard Mehlinger at Indiana University and a few others as well, but our notions about teaching and learning to teach remain basically person-to-person endeavors thereby contributing considerably to a serious problem in teacher preparation, its labor-intensive nature.

The problem is partially tied to the understandings and attitudes of many faculty caught up as they are in a world as distant from reflection as it is from the above technology. The problem is partially one of lack of support for education—the underfunding of teacher education. As tentative and dated as data are in this regard, more is apparently spent on the education of a public school student annually than the preparation of those who teach them (Peseau and Orr, 1979).

Thus, the fuller delineation of laboratory and clinical preparation for teaching, surely, has major economic and political implications. We cannot justify expenditures for such training if we cannot articulate such training and provide a far better rationale for it than we currently do. To rationalize present practice primarily in terms of unrealistic workloads is self-defeating. The intransigent stance of many faculty to change of any sort in institutions across the country should not be defended.

In summary, we saw numerous examples of faculty as competent and creative classroom instructors. Their devotion to students and the time they spent with them, even in a highly person-oriented profession, was most impressive. The RATE studies substantiate this commitment to students across a much larger sample of institutions. We were, also, in every institution we visited, impressed by faculty who appear to be on the cumbrium edge of their discipline. Yet, in many instances the distance between what is known and available to enable learning and what is actually employed tends to be considerable. We appear to do relatively well with what we have and therein lies a major part of our problem. We are like the self-made golfer who has achieved more than a modicum of success. Such a person is unlikely to step back and "unlearn"—start again so that he or she can acquire a more appropriate grip, stance, and swing. So, too, are we as educators reluctant to change. How do we incorporate new understandings, new visions? At the very least, we must find time to stand back to think about the conceptual underpinnings and attributes of a program. Our final chapter attempts to provide basic grist for doing just this, but first we look more closely at faculty and students.

INQUIRY INTO ISSUES RELATIVE TO FACULTY

The faculty included in our study can be portrayed in multiple perspectives. As we have indicated, these are essentially kind and caring renderings of a group of people who exhibited considerable commitment and enthusiasm for their roles as teacher educators. We begin with an insider's view of the professoriate, generated largely from the case studies, including an analysis of their perspectives about faculty ethos, their involvement in program, and demonstrated degrees of leadership in promoting program innovation. We move then somewhat more externally to the critique of others, typically scholars who have studied the professoriate over the last several decades, to frame issues and areas of concern that might well apply to our population of faculty, and to identify where further inquiry is needed.

In the six institutions we visited, we examined faculty ethos. The characteristics of faculty ethos are often mirrored in the perceptions of students as well, including: a sense of pride, the ethic of hard work among the faculty, caring for students, and finally, faculty collegiality.

A Sense of Pride

The sense of pride and accomplishment surrounding each of the elementary programs was apparent. No one institution stands apart in terms of this pervasive characteristic. Ben Thompson was illustrative of the sentiment about the University of Wisconsin—Eau Claire program: "Today, teachers criticize their teacher preparation programs. You don't hear doctors criticizing medical programs. So if we don't have pride in what we do and where we've been, how can we expect anyone else in the world to do that? On this campus, we have a lot of pride."

Pride was also reflected in the long history of the development of the competency-based program at the University of Toledo, of the experience over time at Indiana University with alternative programs and in the intensity of faculty effort at Luther College, and certainly in the alternative programs at MSU. At Ball State University a sense of pride was frequently and readily apparent in both the students' and the faculty's comments. As Kay Stickle observed, "We started with our pride, and we put in little things as we could." The EXEL program was founded by a cadre of faculty bound by their commitment to provide the best they were capable of for students. This commitment is still obvious today and permeated our observations. Dean Kowalski summarized: "We have a lot of good people here, and I really believe that our undergraduate programs have been as successful as they have because of the type of faculty here who have devoted most of their careers to working very closely with our young students."

An Ethic of Hard Work

Recall the admonition that the chairperson of Elementary Education, Ben Thompson, laid out for new recruits at the University of Wisconsin-Eau Claire. He took fierce pride in telling them, "If you come here, you're going to work, and you're going to be flooded with students all day."

UW-Eau Claire likely illustrates the extreme in their commitment to students. The extent to which faculty *should* be "on call" is surely contestable; nevertheless, there did appear to be a considerable commitment to students in all institutions which we visited. Beyond that, there is evidence of considerable faculty time devoted to a variety of other tasks at these institutions as well. At Eau Claire, the teaching loads of the faculty were extremely heavy, including major responsibility for field supervision. At MSU, the dimensions of teaching and service were tempered by acknowledgment of time needed for program development and research. Here, a faculty member in any given quarter might actually teach only one or two courses, but be heavily engaged in research and development projects related to the IRT or the National Center for Research on Teacher Education, for instance. However varied the institutional mission, faculty invested long hours in their work. The situation was exascerbated somewhat at Ball State University and the University of Toledo, where university norms and expectations with regard to teaching, research, and service have changed since many of the professors initially joined the faculty—a shift to more knowledge production but with not as yet a major decrease in instructional load. Because of the considerable consequences of load and expectations for the education faculty studied, we revisit this issue later.

Personal Caring for Students

A majority of faculty statements focused on the nature of this commitment to students in their programs, as Ben Thompson observed: "The unique part about our faculty—and this program—is that they care about our students, we 'mother-hen' them right through. We start when they are *freshmen*, and we advise them through their senior year."

A sense of caring was reflected at the large institutions, such as MSU, as well. One student, for example, compared MSU to Central Michigan and noted that MSU is at least twice as large. But, he continued, "My classes are so much smaller because of the different programs. I think recruiters for prospective teachers like that—that we have so much attention given to us. Our largest class is about twenty-five to thirty people." The same student observed that he thought the faculty in other schools he had experienced were more aloof.

At Ball State University, Ann Williams, a faculty member in elementary education, characterized the distinctive nature of the elementary program at Teachers College as "the intimate relationship with our students." A student there stated, with an obvious sense of pride that she had easy access to Chairperson Kay Stickle: "where else can you make an appointment with the chairperson—as a student—almost anytime you want to?

Faculty Collegiality

We also documented a visible sense of collegiality among the faculty in these elementary programs. At MSU, faculty clearly coalesced around a set of common values in the evolution of their program. Faculty throughout the program attested to their professional affinity with a particular strand including the collegiality which exists in the program emphases.

The size of the institution can also contribute to a sense of collegiality, as Tom Kraabel, vice president and dean of Luther College acknowledged:

> We are a community and, for whatever reason, the linkages in our faculty community are there. When we have a faculty meeting as we did yesterday, they are all there. I never went to a faculty meeting at my previous institution. It took me a while to get used to the fact that faculty know each other very well, and your friends are not necessarily people in your own department. They could be professors completely across campus and in different disciplines, because your neighbors or your daughters are in the high school swim team or something like that.

A similar illustration of UW-Eau Claire comes from Ben Thompson:

> I think what they'll tell you, what they've told me anyhow, and what really surprised them when they came here—is that we all work together; we help one another. We don't have such an ego that we won't share our tricks-of-the-trade and our syllabi and our materials. I think we're all happy together. We're typical people—just normal people getting along—doing the job.

INQUIRY INTO FACULTY ROLE IN PROGRAM

We have addressed faculty involvement in the development of curricular innovations, including their contribution to the scope and sequence of the curriculum, and its integrative nature. Here we review related issues, including diversity of instruction, faculty involvement in the schools, and perspectives on faculty research and development initiatives.

Diversity of Instruction

Clearly, diversity of instruction exists, sometimes manifested in team teaching or interdisciplinary approaches to teaching. Team teaching, for example, has, over time, been heavily embedded in the competency-based program at the University of Toledo. As Jim Johnson recalled:

> We put together the program years ago, and we made a commitment to interdisciplinary team teaching. We thought it was a good idea. We still believe it's a good idea. . . . Math, science, English, and social studies majors are all assigned to the same course, and both general and content specific methods are addressed. . . . It's been a big blend.

A professor at Ball State University, for example, noted the difference between her teaching of a math *content* course as opposed to a math *methods* course. Even in the content course we observed were multiple references of how that content could be adapted to the elementary teaching roles the young people in her class would assume. In her methods course, however, she indicated that specific laboratory activities would be built in and that she would work firsthand with students in the laboratory school setting. We were impressed by the variety of options made available to the Eau Claire students; it was not unusual, for example, to see within the space of a one-hour session a lecturette, some visual presentation, a structured written assignment, and small-group activities, such as a problem-solving exercise.

Faculty Involvement With the Schools

Several illustrations capture the nature of faculty involvement in the schools. A faculty member from Ball State University stated: "All of us are very much involved in the schools. We go out regularly and teach demonstration lessons. It isn't as if any of us haven't taught an elementary-age child in the last twenty years as is the situation in so many institutions."

At the University of Toledo, Professor Wilhoyte, a professor in Philosophy of Education, observes that he has spent a great deal of time in recent years in schools. Said Wilhoyte, "This is my ninth year having worked in the schools, and I can't tell you how much I've learned. It was a humbling experience for me to go out there and go through the same process to see that I'm not doing anything as well as the cooperating teacher."

At the University of Wisconsin-Eau Claire, the emphasis on faculty involvement in the schools is also clear. As Ben Thompson, Chairperson of the Department of Elementary Education, observed: "The students have specific assignments to do. . . . But it's not just a matter of placing them and forgetting them. The cooperating teacher does not merely deal with the students as they can. No! We won't put students out there unless we can supervise them."

In summary, the portrait of early and continuous field experience and the interactive nature of didactic experiences with field experiences is supported by faculty members who are knowledgeable about these experiences, supervise the students, and, in several instances, even teach in field sites themselves.

Research and Development

This category represents a pivotal point in our faculty profile. Thus far, we have characterized the faculty with whom we interacted as considerably committed to their students and programs and who spend considerable time perfecting their own teaching and working in the field. Such a role appears to leave little time in many instances for the reflective or inquiry-oriented life. In each of the teacher education programs we studied, some familiarity with recent research germane to teacher education was found, but evidence of these findings in the curriculum in several institutions was more problematic. With the exception of those institutions with a research orientation, especially MSU, actual inquiry *into* programs was noticeably absent. What faculty found useful from the knowledge base on teaching varied, as well, among institutions. We felt a particular lack of attention to research with regard to the courses concerned with the general aspects of teaching. The fragmented nature of the foundations and introductory courses generally was also a problem in this regard. General methods courses were typically skill-based, focusing on the nature of planning, classroom management, and organization for and individualization of instruction. Certainly, we can recite instances where individual faculty member or faculty collectives attempted to embed or integrate research knowledge into their teaching and at MSU this is the norm. Also, the efforts are ongoing, such as that by Ed Epperly, to organize a consortium in Iowa to bring his faculty and faculty in similar institutions in closer contact with research findings.

Therefore, while there are efforts to become more familiar with relevant research, there was not the kind of embeddedness in some instances necessary for scholarly inquiry to have a major impact on the nature of teacher education curricula. When research is centrally embedded in the curriculum, as is the situation at MSU, the impact is readily observable in students. Henrietta Barnes describes the way teacher canidates acknowledge these forms of scholarly inquiry with which they come into contact in the alternative programs:

> The difference is that they come to believe that there is professional literature, that there is professional knowledge, and that they have acquired some of it. That

seems to be what they tell us. They feel confident and competent, they know that they have some knowledge they can draw upon, and they attribute that knowledge to the program.

There was unevenness, as well, across institutions with regard to R&D efforts devoted to program evaluation and research. Most notably, institutional initiatives were limited as they are nationally (Zimpher and Loadman, 1985) to follow-up studies of graduates, usually the assigned responsibility of one or more faculty members on a rotated basis, with little input from the faculty with regard to questions asked or with little effort toward program change as a result of student feedback. This is not to say that student feedback is not solicited. Given the highly interpersonal orientation of most of these institutions, feedback is acquired from students in a variety of ways. Also in many instances faculty appear to know where many of their graduates are and have continuing contact with those who supervise and assess these students as teachers. This is to say that systematic frameworks for the *overall* evaluation of *programs* are not common.

Here, again, MSU stands in some contrast to the norm. In our portrayal of the alternative programs, we describe the efforts of Don Freeman, director of evaluation for the college, and Cass Book, the associate dean, to actually study differences in program strands. They have done so in part by looking *within* the program, not just at student satisfaction or performance after the program has been completed. To do so, MSU has attached, as a faculty role, a program evaluator to study students and outcomes by strand. Here alone are indices of various competencies and qualities students enter with calibrated with what could be determined as to the effects of program as an intervention. Still, much remains to be done at MSU and the other institutions.

CAUTIONS AND CONCERNS

The role of faculty in teacher education has captured the attention of a number of scholars nationally in recent years. As such, it is useful here to comment briefly on the demography and responsibilities of the education professoriate from several data bases to place our findings in perspective.

Faculty Demography

Fuller and Bown (1975) characterize the low status of teacher educators generally with this observation:

> Teacher educators have, by and large, humble social-class origins and low status in comparison with their academic colleagues. They more often hold paying jobs while working toward a degree, enter the faculty later, perhaps with the Ed.D., and so are less likely to have acquired the scholarly credentials valued by acade-

micians. Their work is likely to be conative rather than the cognitive pursuits esteemed by other faculty. Worst of all, the knowledge base of education is considered by academicians to be largely exogenous. These personal and occupational differences compound the historical problems of status experienced by normal schools turned colleges of education. (p. 29)

Ducharme and Agne (1982) summarize dimensions of this demography: more than 60 percent of their sample of more than 1,000 are the first generation to be college educated; 38 percent of their fathers had less than a high school education; approximately 30 percent of their mothers had less than a high school education; and 77 percent went to a college at an institution fewer than 300 miles from their homes. More recently, the RATE (1987) project study of a stratified random sample of AACTE institutions, their faculty and students, provides this demographic profile of the professors in this study: 64 percent of the faculty are male and 36 percent female; 8 percent are minority (5 percent black and 3 percent Hispanic).

Others are troubled by the general demography of education faculty, especially their conception of "scholarly" productivity as "work in the field," as reflected in this synthesis statement of Lanier and Little (1986):

A disproportionately large number of faculty teaching teachers most directly have come from lower-middle-class backgrounds. It is very likely that they obtain conformist orientations and utilitarian views of knowledge from their childhood experiences at home, educational opportunities in school, and restrictive conditions of work as teachers before coming to higher education. Thus the teacher educators closest to schools and prospective and practicing teachers often assume professional work assignments and routines that demand minimal intellectual flexibility and breadth and require, instead, conformity and limited analysis. (p. 535)

With regard to scholarship, 60 percent of the faculty in the RATE study (1986) do 100 percent of the publishing; 67 percent report supervising student teachers, while only 16 percent report conducting research in schools.

We need to define more precisely who is included in the definition of a teacher educator in order to ascertain if the social class origin hypothesis holds up across different types of programs, disciplines and departments. There might also be differences across rank. Then, where the profile holds up, effects of class could be more systematically examined as mediated by a number of key variables demonstrated as important to studies of the broader professoriate including differences in institutional mission, differential assignments and self-expectations for how they distribute their time and effort.

Faculty Identity

The education professoriate has been portrayed as caught between a clash of cultures institutionally, where expectations drawn from the normal school mentality contrast with more regular views of academe. Schwebel (in press), in his explanation of role confusion, distinguishes between the historical expectations that teacher educators focus their time on the *reproduction* of teachers to new post-World War II priorities when *production* of new knowledge began to overtake the reproduction mode. Ultimately he posits the dilemma. Does the press for new knowledge necessarily have to be gained at the expense of separating ourselves as practitioners from the field? Here Raths, Katz, and McArinch (in press) posit that teacher educators must "pass" in both cultures, carrying the "clinical mentality" of practice and the "scientific mentality" of the mind. These authors suggest that: "teacher education faculty need to communicate in the cultures of both mentalities, respecting the norms and customs of both" (p. 208). We are particularly concerned with the notion of balance or integration; that is, how can the manifestation of one culture work productively to meet the criteria for excellence in another?

Teaching Effectiveness

Studies of the effects of teacher education faculty instruction are rare. What exists now relies on perceptions and is equivocal. For example, in a study by Katz and Raths (1982) of methods professors (in this case of social studies), they found that they used a rather narrow range of instructional technologies, that what the professors said about teaching and their own goals for effective teaching were not manifested in their own classroom instruction. The 1987 RATE study, however, reflects a somewhat more optimistic profile of faculty instruction. Secondary education faculty who teach methods courses and their students alike depicted their methods courses as focused and well-designed. Students perceive their secondary methods course to be helpful in contributing to good teaching. Both faculty and students reported that a variety of instructional methods are used in secondary methods courses. Obviously much more research is needed here.

Supervising Student Teachers

Much has been said already about the labor intensive nature of being a college of education professor concerned with teacher education. Demands on faculty's time are even greater when they are expected to supervise teacher education students in the field. With the commonly mandated increases in field experiences prior to student teaching, the demands for field contact have nearly doubled as typical field experience hours (including student teaching) across campuses approximate 600 clock hours. Thus, the central question arises: do faculty who spend time with their students in field settings positively influence the teaching behaviors of their proteges? In a synthesis of research on the role of the university supervisor (Zimpher, 1987), several studies cite the inconsequential role of the university supervisor. Yet many of these studies can be criticized for limits in their designs. More naturalistic studies are needed if for no other reason than the obvious complexities involved in attributing appropriate influence. Initial findings from a handful of more qualitative studies suggest that were it not for the presence of the university supervisor in field settings, there would be little substantive criticism, direction, or goal-setting in the experience. More thoughtfully developed models for offering critical feedback and a more carefully shared role with clinical teachers in field settings is needed generally. The questions of just how much time professors should spend in these settings, what they should be doing, and how much preparation consonant with the best of what we know about learning how to teach is needed for them and for veteran teachers, who might more fully assume these roles, need to be more fully addressed.

Leadership in Program Renewal

We culminate this brief analysis of characteristics of the general education professoriate with an observation about the nature of leadership in the institutions included in this set of case studies. Clearly, leadership existed at all levels across the teacher education programs we studied: in the deanship, in chairs and program coordinators, and among the faculty in program groups. We found leadership critical to serious program design and maintenance. As Ed Dickson reflected: "I think good deans ought to be people who are looking for opportunities to develop educational ideas and programs. And there are always possibilities that you can find good ideas and you can engage in development work." As Phil Rusche, his successor, thinks about his opportunities, he has a bold vision of the future, even though the University of Toledo was not selected to be a part of the initial consortium of Holmes Group institutions.

Certainly, though, the leadership role of a dean can be a precarious one as Morsink (1987) illustrates:

> Leadership in an SCDE is management without top-down authority. Its decision base is colleagial. There is little authority to delegate and monitor responsibility. The college unit is a loose confederation that consists of independent scholars, each tied to an external academic discipline. Moreover, many SCDE administrators are untrained, 'talented amateurs,' who lack management expertise.
>
> The collegiate 'system' is cumbersome. It is over-regulated and dependent upon permission from external bodies, which make change and innovation slow or nearly impossible. There is little accountability, little budget flexibility, and little latitude in personnel decisions, especially after tenure.
>
> The unit does not exist as an organization with a uniified purpose. It exists to transmit knowledge, to encourage ideas and inquiry, to allow people to think and explore. At the same time, it owes expertise to the state that supports it and to the profession that depends on it for the improvement of practice. (p. 25)

Effective leadership is shared and emanates from a variety of sources. Particularly, recall the leadership at the program level at MSU. For each of the alternative programs, there is a program area coordinator. Their leadership appears critical to "developing and refining a focus for these programs." As Perry Lanier observed:

> There are some frustrations in that you're not in an administrative role where you can assign people, yet these classes need to be covered. So, you negotiate with particular individuals informally. . . . The quasi-administrative role I have as a coordinator gives me more degrees of freedom then I had when I was in the administrative chain because I can go directly to faculty members and their respective chairs. . . . I enjoy the latitude I have.

Leadership was also exhibited by several faculty members, including those chairing a program. Certainly, a leadership role was manifested by Kay Stickle, as chair of elementary education at Ball State University, by Ben Thompson at the University of Wisconsin-Eau Claire, and by Ed Epperly at Luther College.

Although these are only glimpses of leadership exhibited at the six institutions, they are evidence of what is needed to sustain coherent programs of teacher preparation on these campuses. We need to attend more closely to how leadership focused on *programs* and the collective efforts of faculty is fostered, shared, and maintained, or be correctly judged as Clark (1986) cautions: "The indictment of teacher education is that the consensus among well-informed observers about problems and solutions has been evident for so long and the movement to reform has been so miniscule" (p. 5). These concerns apply to the larger institutional setting as well.

Leadership also exists in the broader institutional context and we were able to visit with central administration personnel about the nature of the teacher education programs. In these institutions, teacher education was invariably acknowledged as an important endeavor of the university, more so in some institutions than in others. Certain administrators spoke to the importance of the teacher education program in the history of their universities and, in some instances, how those institutions evolved from primarily teachers colleges to more comprehensive colleges or universities. This rhetoric, however, seemed to depart from resource allocations we observed for the schools and colleges of education.

Most of the teacher education programs were extremely labor-intensive in nature, and invariably the resources necessary to support these programs adequately were not forthcoming from central administrations. At times, there was almost a sweat-shop mentality to teacher preparation. As well, the missions of some institutions are shifting toward an increased capacity for knowledge production and utilization which, for institutions like Ball State University and the University of Toledo, represents a considerable change in orientation from the teaching and service models many faculty embrace. Without stable funding or even an increase in funding, innovations in teacher education, long a characteristic of these institutions, are at risk!

INQUIRY ABOUT STUDENTS

Given profiles, generated from a national survey (RATE, 1987) of students who pursue education degrees, a perspective for viewing students observed and interviewed in these case studies can be provided. There are well over two million classroom teachers in public elementary and secondary schools. Surprisingly, the composition of this workforce over the past three decades has remained relatively stable in terms of gender and race. Feistritzer (1983) characterized the typical teacher as a woman approaching her fortieth birthday, married, the mother of two, and white. In 1984, Howey profiled the demography of the current teaching population as 91 percent white, 6 percent black, and 1.7 percent Hispanic. Yarger et al. (1977) portrayed the current teacher as provincial, coming from a small city or rural community and monolingual. In contrast, Haberman (1983) characterized our pupil population as one out of every six pupils being poor and one out of every four being a minority. By 2000, most schools will have substantial minority, low-income, and handicapped populations. Spanish-speaking students will predominate public education in Texas and New Mexico, as will Asiatics and Haitians in California, New York, and Florida. By the turn of the century, every city in excess of 500,000 will have what Hodgkinson (1988) called a "minority majority" population of poor and ethnically diverse students.

The RATE study (AACTE, 1987) provides an updated demographic profile of the pipeline; that is, those student in their junior year of teacher preparation. Students were identified in the institutions drawn from the stratified random national sample. At each institution, a maximum of four methods courses were identified and the names of five students were drawn alphabetically from a class roster to complete the RATE survey. As noted earlier, these studies identified respondents initially from secondary methods courses, then foundations courses, and most recently from elementary education. Although the data on elementary students are not yet available, the composite of foundations enrollees represents both elementary and secondary future teachers (Zimpher, 1988).

The demographic characterization of the 729 students polled in this second-year survey of foundations students reflects a slightly older population of students (almost twenty-five years old) who are largely female (76.3 percent; up 1.5 percent from the prior year), a fourth of whom are married, with a large percentage of the student population white (91 percent), with no blacks in the entire baccalaureate-only institution sample. Furthermore, most students, nearly 70 percent, travel fewer than 100 miles from home to attend college, with 50 percent traveling fewer than 50 miles. Most students grew up in suburban or rural communities and nearly one-half of the population of teacher education candidates surveyed speak no language other than English. Students pay about $5,600 to attend college (up 10 percent from last year); are generally full-time residential students on campuses; and seek most of their financial support for college from family finances, loans and grants, and their own paid employment.

The career preferences of these students suggest a considerable degree of interest in the social service of teaching. Students report their primary motivation for selecting teaching is helping children grow and learn, followed by the challenge of the field, and the sense of vocation and honor of teaching. Rather surprisingly, more than 50 percent were "somewhat" or "a great deal" influenced by the working conditions of teaching. Students are extremely positive about their feelings toward teaching as a career, and 87 percent report that they intend to go into teaching directly after graduation and more than 63 percent report that they expect to stay in teaching five years or more. They indicate that a teacher's salary is adequate for supporting an individual (although not a family), and they like their community roots and they wish to return to suburban and rural areas to teach, with fewer than 16 percent of the population interested in urban or major urban locales, down 4 percent from the prior year. They are also hesitant to travel anywhere nationally to take a teaching position. They prefer to teach average-ability students at a slightly higher rate than the gifted and talented, and their preferences for handicapped or learning disabled students is quite low. Finally, more than 80 percent of the population prefer middle-income settings as opposed to high-income or low-income settings.

Well in excess of one-half of the students begin college in the institution from which they ultimately matriculate. Of those who transfer, they bring approximately one and one-half years or more of credit with them, and they come mostly from community colleges, extension colleges, or state public institutions. They expend about seventeen hours per week on school work. Regardless, most students are able to maintain a B or 3.04 grade point average. These students also have average SAT scores and were in the top one-third of their high school graduating classes.

Already shared are student views on the degree of instructional diversity that is modelled for them by their methods professors. As well, both faculty and students were asked to assess the general rigor of the education courses in the professional sequence compared to courses students enroll in outside of the college of education. Nearly 70 percent of both the faculty and the students viewed the education courses as about as rigorous or more rigorous than other courses they had taken. As well, courses in the foundations were contrasted with courses at the same academic level in English, history, foreign languages, science, and mathematics. About two-thirds of the students rated their foundations course to be about as intellectually rigorous—however that term was interpreted by them—as English and history, although the majority of the students reported foundations courses as slightly less rigorous than those in math, science, and foreign languages. Both students and faculty view education courses as more time-consuming than other courses, in part due to the numerous field-based assignments.

These data have been highlighted in order to compare these responses to the observations made and data collected during our case studies. Generally, the demographic data referenced above was reflected in the populations of students at each of the six sites we visited. As well, we observed a degree of cultural insularity generally in the students and, to some extent, in the college environment into which they entered. We look closer, as well, at expressions of rigor in the elementary programs studied, as these reflect particular cautions and concerns.

The Lack of Cultural Diversity in Teacher Education

Students in the programs we visited appeared typical of those we have presented as the national composite. Students are largely white, middle- or working-class, frequently first- or second-generation college students, and often from small-town or rural backgrounds. As elementary majors, they are typically female and have had limited exposure to cultural diversity. Although the elementary education students in these institutions are generally between nineteen and twenty-three, the general teacher education population could be characterized as somewhat older, often married and with families and, in many instances, working full- or part-time to sustain their college educations. Not only do these students come from small towns in rural, midwest America, they intend to return to these sites to assume teaching positions. The standard characterization of these students at Ball State University was reflected by a veteran professor as follows: "They are first-generation college enrollees. They have limited travel and, in many ways, limited cultural experiences. They are not very sophisticated, but they are very good students, and they are hard-working, polite, and courteous."

The University of Wisconsin-Eau Claire campus serves a state and resident student body. It does draw a substantial number of its students from Minnesota, whose eastern border is sixty miles from campus. As a faculty member observed, the university, the community, and the elementary program all tend to be rather conservative. Another faculty member at Indiana University characterized education students as conservative but open-minded. One-half of the students at Luther College are residents of Iowa, 56 percent are women (much higher in elementary education), 3 percent are black, 2 percent are foreign nationals, and most of the students from Luther College beyond Iowa come from the three-state area of Minnesota, Illinois, and Wisconsin. The MSU and University of Toledo scenarios approximate the same white, middle-class, close-to-home profiles.

This limited cultural milieu and frequently conservative orientation re-flects a somewhat closed-loop problem at some institutions, reflected in the following observations. A local principal working with students from UW-Eau Claire indicated that for him, one of the appealing qualities of the educa-tion students, in addition to their apparent confidence and ability initially, was their conservative attitudes about education. The principal underscored that Eau Claire was a conservative community and "that's why people like to bring their children there to raise them." When asked whether he thought there were professors on the faculty or student teachers from the University of Wiscon-sin-Eau Claire whom he would characterize as radical, he indicated that they hire students from Eau Claire because they are *not* radical. At Ball State Uni-versity, Dean Kowalski indicated that he understood the need for the univer-sity to broaden the horizons of these young people, but he reflected:

> I'm not so sure how well our students would fare in many of these school systems if they had been exposed to more radical thinking. If you take students who come from families with a long history of a certain value system and they're first-generation college students, they aren't rebellious people; they are very coopera-tive and they tend to do what they are told. Superintendents and principals love them.

We observed this closed-loop perspective, as well, in the observations of both Judith Smith and Ed Epperly at Luther College. Smith was asked what the institution does for the character of the students, looking particularly at the parochial as opposed to the liberalizing influence of an institution like Luther on its students, and she responded:

> Parents send their children here because of the inculcation of values they hope they'll come out with and, in most cases, they're ones the parents believe in themselves, whether they went to Luther or not. They see a set of values here that, to them, mean something, and they're willing to pay for that. I'm not at all convinced that the teachers that we prepare at Luther College will cut it on 49th and Halstead, in the meat-packing section of Chicago. . . . You've got to value Luther College and what it represents. . . . which to me is a solid, conservative, liberal arts background.

We did find some countervailing influences attempting to create a more culturally diverse population of teacher candidate graduates, particularly in the cultural diversity presented in Jim Mahan's planned cultural experiences at Indiana University and through MSU's Heterogeneous Classrooms pro-gram. As one student characterized the latter program, "I think that the people in our program are more aware of our differences. They're not so quick to stereotype things. People in our program are more aware of biases and how they can challenge them, even if they have biases themselves, they can change them." This theme of equity and diversity is integrated into a series of on-campus and field experiences students enroll in sequentially. Still and all, there are problems associated with this culturally-diverse program, as Navarro cautioned. They have to move from preparing people who have some knowledge and background about different learning styles of a diverse group of students—to a program which can have significant impact on underrepresented populations who are truly at risk academically.

Navarro and his colleagues shared some frustration that even the students who are engaged in this intensive program focusing on equity and children at risk too often do not take positions in culturally diverse settings. The cultural limitations of students in the teacher education programs we visited in the Midwest contrasted with the growing cultural diversity in our schools, and our global society suggests a problem of major proportions. Notwithstanding attempts by two of the institutions to introduce cultural diversity, to counter parochialism and to open up the closed-loop of conservatism in preparing teachers to meet new challenges in the schools, much more work needs to be done in this regard, both in general education and professional studies.

Concerns for Rigor in the Program

The rigor generally perceived by faculty and students in each of the programs emanates from an intellectual challenge but also from the degree of hard work expected of and by the students in the programs as we indicated. For example, we asked students at the University of Wisconsin-Eau Claire to compare the rigor in the elementary education program to other students' majors. One student observed:

> When you're going through the program you're thinking 'why do we have to do all these papers and stuff,' but I think the idea is to discipline you, to get you to do those things and make you so busy that when you get out there and do student teaching, you sort of have an idea how it feels, how much you have to be dedicated to what you're doing. Some of it is busy work . . . maybe . . . but it really makes you discipline yourself, I think.

Thus, while the rigor, the intellectual character, and academic standards of the programs reviewed here and across the country, as surveyed in the RATE studies, appear higher than many suggest, there is little doubt that rigor is often confused with effort or demand and the nature of the effort demanded is still questionable. Certainly, more research into the character of programs is needed.

CONCLUDING OBSERVATIONS ON STUDENTS

Here we summarize observations and data drawn from our six cases regarding students, which are complemented by data in the RATE study of students from secondary courses who responded to the survey.

Common Demographic Characteristics

We suggest a portrait of the elementary education student as typically white and female, from a rural small town or suburban home community, matriculating in a SCDE fewer than 100 miles away from home. The profile further suggests a student who has selected an institution close to home, not particularly based on the institution's reputation or peer influence, but perhaps more plainly stated, "because it's there." Students matriculate through these programs they thought they could most likely be admitted to at a fairly continuous pattern without dropping out of school and in most cases plan to take a teaching position. The teacher candidates we interviewed suggest a higher retention in the profession, as well, because many indicated they expect to teach for some time, contrasted to the 50 percent drop-out rate during the first five years reported elsewhere (Schlechty, 1983). They enroll in courses as required, appear to work hard in the classes, accept the assignments proposed to them, often work *collectively* to complete assignments, respect their instructors, and feel they have completed a rigorous program. These sentiments are echoed by the faculty.

Limited Horizons

The career view of these students appears to be somewhat limited. Most students plan to stay very close to their home institutions or their hometowns, and certainly within the state, for their first teaching positions. Even at MSU and Indiana University, where cultural diversity was a central focus of the programs, professors expressed concern that graduates of these programs were not going to take positions teaching the at-risk populations they had been prepared to serve. This rather localized view was in some ways encouraged by the faculty; they feel some responsibility for staffing the local and regional schools served by their institutions.

Altruism

The profile drawn from our observations suggest that these students are eager to enter teaching, selecting this profession as one which would allow them to help children grow and learn and would engage them in a challenging field. They recognize the probable low remuneration, but seemed to view their incomes as a complement to their spouses' incomes. (Most students were female and assumed they would be married.) When asked if they, as women, were concerned they they would in all likelihood be working with a male principal, no complaints were registered.

Technical-Craft Orientation

As students spoke of the experience of learning how to teach, they essentially validated the views expressed by their professors in such areas as a vision of effective teaching, the nature of schools, and how one prepares to teach. At MSU, the experience of learning how to teach held a strong inquiry base. Students acknowledged and were able to articulate codified knowledge about teaching. They believed themselves to be well-perpared to teach. Others dispute this view. For instance, a self-portrait of the Luther College student suggests a bright person, fairly well-read and well-studied, who respects the liberal arts tradition, but who is somewhat uninformed about the corpus of research about teaching. Their encounters with learning how to teach seem to be more with regard to curricula (textbooks and materials) and workable methods. At other sites, the process of learning how to teach was highly experiential (this is how it works for me and can for you) and technical (teaching is largely a function of planning; first, one lesson; then, a day; and then, a unit). Consequently, students felt well-prepared. They have the skills and the experience to "put it all together."

In this chapter, then, we have reviewed promising practices and commendable conditions as well as concerns and problems attached to the programs we studied. We augmented our observations across institutions with analyses and informed opinion from related studies of programs, faculty, and students conducted by other scholars. We have attempted in this cross-institutional analysis to provide a more balanced description both of strengths and weaknesses than we did in the individual descriptions of programs where we emphasized examples of good practice. It is obvious that much can be done to improve the general state of teacher education, and in our final chapter we offer several suggestions for doing this with a particular emphasis on better defining the nature of programs of teacher preparation.

8

Toward Coherent Programs
and Improved Practice

In this final chapter, we address three major goals. First, we attempt to develop further the concept of a *program* of teacher education by drawing upon observations made in these cross-institutional case studies. We do this by identifying what appear to be attributes or characteristics—beyond what occurs at the individual course level—that contribute in positive ways to the education of beginning teachers. In this regard, we differentiate between *program* and *curriculum*.

Next, we briefly share some recommendations for the further improvement of preservice or initial teacher preparation. Tentative understandings from our study guide these suggestions, but we employ, as well, the wisdom and insights of several others. In this regard, we are neither so disenchanted with present efforts nor divorced from the realities of how changes tend to occur that we call for total reconstruction.

Many of the suggestions we make are probably all too familiar, although some bold new directions are invoked. Our view is that moving in future directions appears tied as much to more focused leadership, to setting priorities, and to more attention to corporate, institutional, or program considerations as they do to the assimilation of new ideas. Forward movement, in many respects, is a matter of our collective will. Finally, and most assuredly, more research into programs of teacher education is needed. Multiple forms of inquiry ranging from historical analyses, to conceptualization, to descriptive and ethnographic studies, to quasi-experimental and well-designed experimental efforts are needed. Thus, we conclude by sharing from our modest efforts a few questions that are especially troublesome to us and some hypotheses that we believe warrant testing.

PROGRAMS

We first address what we mean by *programs*. We have attempted to differentiate between the terms teacher preparation *programs* and *curriculum* in our cross-institutional analysis. Admittedly, these are not mutually exclusive categories. When referring to *curriculum*, we refer basically to courses and the laboratory and field experiences affiliated with study occurring largely in college classrooms. *Programs* for us, however, represent more than the sum of these courses and related experiences.

Programs have one or more frameworks grounded in theory and research as well as practice; frameworks that explicate, justify, and build consensus around such fundamental conceptions as the *role* of the teacher, the *nature* of teaching and learning, and the *mission* of schools in this democracy. These frameworks guide not only the nature of curriculum as manifested in individual courses but, as well, questions of scope; developmental sequence; integration of discrete disciplines; and the relationships of pedagogical knowledge to learning how to teach in various laboratory, clinical, and school settings. Programs embedded in such frameworks clearly establish priorities in terms of key dispositional attitudes and behaviors enabled and monitored in repeated structured experiences. Programs reflect consideration of ethos and culture building; to the critical socialization of the prospective teacher. The nature and function of collegial relationships is considered both between and among faculty and students as well as with those who assume responsibilities for teacher preparation in K-12 schools. Conceptually coherent programs enable needed and *shared* faculty leadership to engage in more generative and continuing renewal by underscoring collective roles as well as individual course responsibilities. Programs also contribute to more mutual endeavors in research and evaluation beyond the individual course level. Various student cohort arrangements and other temporary social systems such as inquiry teams, cooperative learning structures, or political action committees would be considered. Finally, programs provide considerable guidance both in terms of the nature and pattern of *pre*professional or *pre*education study and also to extended experiences in schools in the nature of induction programs.

Program approval is the primary means by which institutions are legally authorized to prepare teachers. Yet, in general, little careful thought appears to have been given to the concept of program beyond whether legally-mandated and faculty-endorsed knowledge, skills, and attitudes are embedded in a set of courses; courses reflecting a number of credit hours limited, or assumed to be limited, by regulation. We can do better than this. A major intention of our study is to provoke more attention to the nature and definition of program, and to this end we now offer some tentative attributes of what we believe to be programs. However, before we share what we believe to be conditions, policies and practices, enabling programs and attributes of program, a review of our original research questions about programs is in order. A major interest was to examine the extent to which programs of teacher preparation are conceptualized and implemented and reflect attributes of a cohesive design. The questions we generated were:

1. To what extent do the curricula reflect not only relatedness across courses and experiences in the preservice program, but also articulation with the institution's general studies/arts and sciences curricula?
2. To what extent are explicit conceptions of teaching and learning, and the mission of schooling filtered throughout the totality of the students' preservice degree experience?
3. To what extent are courses and experiences provided for students structured in a developmental sequencing of more complex or extended concepts and functions viewed as central to program conceptualization?
4. To what extent does the program accommodate faculty collegiality and student cohort groups?
5. How are schools and supervising teachers selected and prepared? To what extent are their philosophies about teaching and learning and schooling consonant with that of the programs?
6. What has been the extent of change over time in the programs, and what are their sources of leadership for development and maintenance?

CONDITIONS AND PRACTICES THAT APPEAR TO ENABLE PROGRAMS

A probable response to the question of what does a program of teacher preparation consist, is that it is a set of courses and attendant field activities a prospective teacher must satisfactorily complete in order to obtain certification. When one probes further, however, to ascertain what the specific attributes or characteristics of *program* might be, answers are not as quickly forthcoming. If one had asked what an effective school was a decade ago, we doubt very much that one would get the kind of response that most informed educators would provide today. It is clear today, based on several recent studies, that specific conditions and characteristics differentiate schools from one another in terms of desired student "outcomes" including academic achievement, school attendance, and interpersonal attitudes. Our initial hypothesis was that when we examined programs we identified as exemplary or at least distinctive in some way, we might well find characteristics and attributes parallel to those identified in the "school effectiveness" literature. Attempts to synthesize research studies of effective schools have identified numerous organizational, structural, and climate variables that distinguish more effective from less effective schools such as these identified by Purkey and Smith (1983):

1. instructional leadership;
2. curriculum articulation;

3. faculty collegiality;
4. clear goals;
5. high expectations;
6. maximized time for learning; and
7. recognition of academic success.

We were, in fact, able to identify similar attributes manifested to various degrees across the programs we studied and which were viewed favorably by faculty and students alike. We were able to identify additional distinguishing characteristics of programs, as well. We underscore, as we do in terms of the school effectiveness literature, that caution is in order. Our work is heuristic and hypothesis-setting in nature.

We should be critical in interpreting the way these attributes of effective schools were identified, thoughtful in more fully defining them, and wary in terms of how "reformists" suggest they are best achieved. The same applies to our own work. Romanish (1987) made the point well:

> School effectiveness researchers assert that an effective school has a strong leader (Fraser and Shoemaker, 1981), but doesn't the research point to this because the system has given inordinate decision-making authority to building principals? If authority rested with a team of researchers, students, parents and administrators, the research perhaps would show that an effective school has an effective leadership team. In that case, researchers would have to frame their hypotheses in entirely different terms, terms that so often are outside the dominant vision. For instance, Waldorf schools, which are progressive institutions based on the ideas of Rudolph Steiner and popular mostly in Europe, provide fertile ground for effective school research. Yet it would be impossible to demonstrate that a strong leader is necessary in Waldorf schools because those schools have no building principal at all. (p. 10)

We wholly concur with Romanish in this regard and have devoted our energies for some time to the evolution of more specifically defined leadership roles for teachers—roles embedded in the school site—and to programs that provide them with various kinds of leadership abilities beyond their knowledge of teaching, as such, and finally and most fundamentally, to altering their roles and role relationships with others. Our vision is one, two, three or more teachers—depending on the size of the school—engaged in teaching part-time and enabling the teaching of their colleagues at other times through such functions as collaborative action research, case studies of students, demonstration teaching, systematic observation and feedback, employing students creatively as informants and "coaching" or serving in advisory capacities to their colleagues.

Teacher preparation cannot advance without significantly altering conditions in schools as well in order that teaching can be a more civilized and enjoyable, let alone doable, endeavor. Obviously, no master plan exists for achieving these ends, but altering our basic conception of teacher roles and responsibilities in a variety of ways provides a needed launching pad for more organic growth and dynamic change in schools over time. As teacher educators concerned with the preparation of beginning teachers, we are committed to this mission of altering conditions in schools, as well. More thought must be given to conceptions of the broader *role* of teachers as well as to teaching itself. We ask many teachers to do more than they can do well, regardless of their preparation. As Nel Noddings (1986) has so poignantly argued:

> For the past few years, the blame for massive perceived failure in our schools has fallen on teachers and students, mainly on teachers. They must be brighter, more knowledgeable, more willing to change in whatever direction authority prescribes. We rarely ask how things might be changed so that teachers can accomplish the work they see as *teaching*, nor do we ask what this work is; nor do we ask how teacher educators might best educate people who are average in academic capability but superior in social commitment. (p. 502)

One further point about leadership should be made before we discuss tentative attributes. As we indicated, when some sense of programmatic coherence was achieved in the programs we studied, leadership was apparent; and this leadership was manifested in a variety of roles, more so than what appears to be the case in studies of school effectiveness. We clearly observed the pervasive influence of deans in each of the institutions visited. As well, in most instances, leadership was exerted by a specific individual at the program or departmental chair level to coordinate and sustain the efforts of faculty who invariably organized themselves around some shared values about teaching and how one best learns to teach. Beyond this, considerable leadership was exerted by various faculty members. At MSU, leadership roles for faculty were formalized and program coordinators identified for each of the alternative program strands. We examined at some length the role of Judith Lanier as dean; we could well have focused more extensively on Perry Lanier in his role as program coordinator. Henrietta Barnes underscored the critical role these program coordinators assume at MSU and called them the key to the development and maintenance of the planned variation which exists there.

We concur with her observations about the need for such a leadership role if more coherent programs are to be achieved. In our experience, when an obvious problem is not readily resolved, no one person seems to be specifically assigned to address that problem. It is a situation, too often, of everybody's concern, but nobody's particular responsibility. Thus, we argue here that key faculty members be identified, *prepared*, and *supported* to assume leadership roles for program development and renewal. We believe that considerable assistance can be provided to these program development leaders, and we are piloting such a program of technical support with key faculty in the nineteen institutions in the Midwest region of the Holmes Group.

At this point, we describe those conditions and practices that appear to contribute at the least to coherent programs of teacher preparation, because we cannot speak with any confidence about effectiveness, however defined. We believe program designers should attend to the following factors which, as we indicated are in some respects analogous to those characteristics identified in the effective school studies. Our list of fourteen such program attributes follows:

1. *Programs* of teacher preparation are driven by *clear conceptions of schooling/teaching*. This was perhaps best exemplified at MSU, but conceptions of teaching, while more implicit, also were the driving force for structuring and interrelating curriculum in the other programs we studied. Understandably, multiple perspectives could be brought to bear here, and we identified a number of these in chapter eight. We suggest that thoughtful conceptions grounded in theory, research, and practice can:

a. contribute to shared beliefs, faculty collegiality, and ongoing program renewal;
b. contribute to considerations of curriculum *scope, sequence, integration,* and *articulation*;
c. contribute clearly to what is valued in a teacher and what is expected of the prospective teacher (hopefully, more noble and less pedestrian visions of teaching would contribute in substantive ways to the socialization and professionalization of teachers);
d. contribute to a shared sense of reasonableness for what should be expected of a prospective teacher by identifying a limited number of core dispositional behaviors which emanate from the conception(s);
e. contribute to more realistic role definitions for teachers through conceptions of teaching that fully acknowledge the realities of schools as a workplace; and
f. contribute to an explicit, coherent design for programmatic research and evaluation.

2. Faculty appear to coalesce around experimental programs, planned variations and programs that have *distinctive* qualities and specific *symbolic* titles. Faculty did not identify themselves as the elementary faculty, per se, but rather as the faculty in *the* experimental elementary education program— EXEL. Such faculty collectives, as witnessed in the multiple strands at MSU, appear to meet more regularly, on both a formal and an informal basis, than faculty attached to a program certification area, as such. A sense of collegiality appears to develop over time. These clusters of faculty appear to achieve more of the psychic rewards and sense of efficacy which teachers can achieve in working with a class of students over a year's time or more in the public schools. Not only is there more of a shared agenda for instruction but a sense of joint ownership in and responsibility for the total program. We suggest that this shared responsibility could dispose faculty toward more concern for

research into and evaluation of the program. Research and evaluation of this type is challenging, often complex, and calls for a type of collaborative inquiry too uncommon in teacher education.

3. A sense of *reasonableness* and *clarity* are associated with the majoi goals of the program. One of the unanticipated findings in our discussions with students across these campuses was their ability invariably to share with considerable specificity what they believed to be the major goals of the program. Elementary teacher preparation programs especially are vulnerable to extended lists of rather disparate objectives given that they draw from a variety of disciplines. Again, Raths and Katz (1985) and their Goldilocks theory about "just the right size" in terms of the number of major goals set forth for students, especially in the form of dispositional behaviors, appear to have some validity in terms of programs we visited. The programs we selected for our study were viewed as distinctive; therefore this undoubtedly contributed to this phenomenon. At MSU, for example, students had to select from explicitly defined program options.

Achieving such clarity and a sense of reasonableness, especially while not detracting from intellectual challenge and rigor, is not a simple task. It understandably goes beyond written documents describing a program, its conceptual underpinnings, and the major goals for students. In the programs we observed, faculty consensus about program priorities allowed the revisiting of key concepts across courses and other structured experiences for students.

Howey and Strom (1986) go further in this regard and suggest that *selection* into programs be hinged on a series of diagnostic simulations, written inventories, and clinical observations early on in a program that are *explicitly* and directly related to a limited number of dispositions, in this instance desired human qualities of a teacher. They derive their dispositional behaviors from a conceptual framework embedded in related constructs of psychological maturity. Certainly, a basic moral issue is involved in the degree to which expectations are made clear and *justified*, if not negotiated, with these adult students.

4. That the program is *rigorous* and *academically challenging*, that students will have to work hard to achieve, is explicitly stated and eventually modelled. Raising admissions standards—which too often represent criteria that have limited predictive validity in terms of one's ultimate success as a teacher—speaks to the nature of students desired in the program, but indicates little about the nature and the rigor of the program itself. We invariably witnessed faculty, students, and supervising teachers who work with these students expressing their perception of considerable challenge in the program. While often these expectations were articulated in terms of the amount of time it took to be prepared to teach effectively, numerous references were made, as well, to the intellectual challenge students believe to be held out for them in their curriculum. Students routinely compared and contrasted their studies in

education with either their general studies, or with previous majors in which they had been involved and testified that at least as much rigor was found in the professional education curriculum. The recent RATE studies sponsored by AACTE, wherein comparisons by students and faculty with other types of courses in general studies were made, largely support our observations of the intellectual challenge perceived by students. Certainly, more study is needed here to examine a number of mediating factors, including student variables, different institutional contexts, and geographic region.

In summary, the emphasis at present in many institutions to upgrade standards for admission should be accompanied, as well, by standards in curriculum and instruction clearly communicating high quality and a needed commitment of much time and energy by students. Specific milestone points and benchmarks for success should be underscored and high achievement symbolically highlighted.

5. *Themes* run throughout the curriculum, like threads, in which key concepts, like buttons, are tied together throughout a variety of courses, practica, and school experiences. These themes can take on the nature of a primary conception of learning how to teach, as in the Academic Learning program at MSU, or they can be articulated more in terms of a basic respect for individual diversity or in the primacy of the pupil as a major source of the curriculum as exemplified in more than one program. Henrietta Barnes (1987) speaks with considerable experience about the nature and manifestation of themes:

> In short, the theme of the program is probably important, and perhaps only, if the program is also structured to help students develop schemata of teaching that are complete, well-organized, and stable. If this is true, then the program's theme must be more than rhetoric. It must provide clear direction for structuring the program so that agreement among faculty can be reached at a very specific level. Nominal agreement on the purposes and goals of the program is not sufficient. If all program courses, practices, and management strategies used in the program do not create and support a consistent image of what the philosophy of the program means in day-to-day classroom life, the program will not contribute to the schema development that is needed. For example, one of the program's themes [at MSU] emphasizes individual responsibility for decision-making. Students enrolled in the program are given reasonable program choices, must make their own decisions about meeting program requirements, and are confronted with the consequences of their choices as they proceed through the program. (p. 15)

Margaret Cohen (1985) provides a similarly cogent example, taking achievement-motivation as a key theme and illustrating how it was consistently manifested in prospective teachers' behavior throughout their program of preparation.

6. There is an appropriate *balance* and *relationship* between *general knowledge which can be brought to bear pedagogically, pedagogical knowl-*

edge, and *experience designed to promote pedagogical development*. In our study, we found among students (although they varied considerably) respect for content as well as experience in learning how to teach. Teaching is far more than technique. The wisdom of Harry Broudy (1980) bears repeating here:

> There is an important difference, however, between the intellectual base for the teaching profession and for the prospective engineer, physician, agricultural expert, or lawyer. These professions have their theory base in generalizations derived from empirical science or highly codified bodies of principles and precedents that are accepted by the members of the guild. This is not the case in education. In this field, the important empirical generalizations are very few. Education has to rely on a great variety of disciplines to provide contexts and perspectives for the human encounter we call teaching. For every item that we teach *to* the pupil, there are dozens of ideas, images, concepts, categories *with* which we teach but do not teach *to* anybody.
>
> Unfortunately, the nature of building is not clear, although the lack of facility on context building and context apprehension is quickly discernible. For one thing, the context-building resources furnished by the study of psychology, history, philosophy, and the arts operate tacitly more often than explicitly. Like good manners, they work best when one no longer has to pay attention to them. For another, the disciplines as learned in school are transformed in time into structure or schemata while many of the details are forgotten, so that tests of retention are not indicative of the presence of these interpretive structures. Yet a lack of such structures is far harder to remedy than a lack of specific items of knowledge or skill. (p. 8)

Narrower conceptions of method or technique, especially in elementary education programs, need to be kept in proper perspective.

7. In several of the programs we studied, student *cohort* groups were identified as a strength of the program. Multiple benefits were attached to this concept. A collective sense of pride and public accountability among students was obvious. The pride of a group in its accomplishments over time also appears related to sustaining high levels of expectation for one another. A sense of *public* accountability was found in these groups. Also, when these groups of twenty to thirty view themselves as the junior class and then the senior class, a greater sense of appreciation was apparent in terms of what they have accomplished in one year and respect for what they are entering into in another than is found when individuals must employ the total student population as a reference group in terms of where they are in the progression through their studies. These cohort groups appeared to enable one another not only in the academic but in a more personal and psychological sense, as well.

Finally, faculty appear to have benefitted from their interaction with cohort groups. Faculty indicated more of a sense of accountability in terms of their teaching when they were interacting with a group that they knew relatively well over a period of time. They indicated that this was quite a different situation than meeting with a group of diverse students who only came together at a particular point in time in a program.

Obviously, the transient nature of student populations at a number of institutions makes a cohort design difficult; but where it can be incorporated, it appears to have advantages for both students and faculty. As we indicated, several variations on the cohort theme exist, including inquiry teams, cooperative learning groups, and political action committees.

8. At some point in the program, the cohort or cluster of students invariably encounters a particularly challenging element, a *milestone* or *benchmark point*, which sociologists have identified as *shared ordeal*. In each of the programs, students were able to identify signal events to which they attached particular significance in terms of meeting the demands placed upon them and in terms of achieving a greater sense of status having met these challenges. Students, prior to entering this series of courses or activities, invariably expressed apprehension. Upon completion, however, an even greater sense of both individual and collective pride was evidenced than exhibited earlier and, as we have indicated, we were considerably impressed by the extent and degree of pride which we saw manifested across students and faculty. The actual curricular and instructional activities and events which defined the shared ordeal varied widely, and not all were designed with that intent. Yet, little doubt exists that the shared ordeal served a major function in the socialization of these young people in their programs of teacher preparation and in reinforcing their commitment to teaching as a career. We advocate that such milestone events or checkpoints be purposefully built into programs at key points. Schlechty (1985) points out with regard to effective induction programs:

> In an effective induction system, entry into the occupation is marked by distinct stages and statuses. The successful completion of each stage is accompanied by ceremony, ritual, and symbols. Each status carries with it a distinct set of performance duties, rights, and obligations. Recruits in the early stages clearly have lower status and fewer privileges than persons in later stages, and only after full entry into the occupation do they have all the rights and privileges available to full members of the occupational group. For example, first-year medical students are inferior in status to second-year medical students and first-year students in law schools and in the military academies have less status than second-year students. Thus, time, grade, and performance are related to status in fully developed occupations. (p. 39)

9. Organizational and structural features of the programs enable an *interdisciplinary* or *integrative approach to curriculum*, as seen in the curriculum in many elementary schools. Curriculum organized this way was invariably referred to as a "block," the primary effect of which was to allow students to address, repeatedly, core teaching functions and concepts such as

planning for instruction across different subject areas. Because the elementary school curriculum is multidisciplinary in nature, the premise is that an elementary teacher will often integrate concepts across subject matter in order to accommodate this broad curriculum. Thus, modelling such curriculum is important.

Several cautions should be noted here. First, knowledge of how specific knowledge matter is organized and how *conceptual* learning in specific subjects is acquired cannot be sacrificed. Second, integrated, interdisciplinary, or broad fields of curriculum design are not usually best taught across more than two or three subjects. More authentic team planning and actual team teaching, dialogue and dialectic among faculty, and less turn teaching is needed. As well, we believe there is a greater need for team teaching in elementary schools among teachers with greater knowledge of *specific* subjects complementing one another than currently exists. The impetus for more collaboration among teachers in elementary schools will come from preservice *programs* structured to promote such planning and teaching and specialization in the elementary teachers they prepare. There is still much to be done in this regard.

10. *Adequate "life space"* is found within the curriculum. Certainly, one of the primary issues debated in the Holmes Group is the notion of adequate time for assimilating needed learnings and abilities at the postbaccalaureate level. We found repeated instances of both faculty and students acknowledging that they had *time over a period of time* to acquire what were perceived as significant learnings. In some programs, students began their education studies in the freshman year. Students frequently spoke to the revisiting of key concepts over time in the curriculum and the clarity in understanding and ability and confidence to employ these that only came over time.

Norm Sprinthall and Lois Theis-Sprinthall, in their pioneer studies attempting to promote cognitive growth in teachers, underscore the need for *extended* periods of action and reflection. We heard repeated references by faculty to the "spiral" nature of their curriculum, and, in the best of these designs, key content and concepts appear to be, in fact, repeatedly revisited.

Scope as well as sequence is an important consideration in the design of programs and they are interrelated concepts. The question of how much study of different subjects, related or not, one can engage in productively at any given time should be considered in tandem with the ordering of a program's content, concepts, and activities. *Inadequate time collapses sequence and broadens scope.* The long-standing but rarely achieved value of inquiring and reflective teachers seems antithetical to a compressed curriculum. Earlier and better articulation with the arts, sciences, and humanities, as we outline shortly, appears in order.

11. Adequate curriculum materials, instructional resources, and information and communication technologies, and a well-conceived *laboratory component* are found in these programs. As we indicated, one of our primary concerns is the lack in teacher education of what other professions hold forth

as laboratory and clinical training. We saw some evidence of the latter, but these experiences were not organized in the way that laboratory and clinical opportunities could be structured to flow continually and centrally through a program. We elaborate on the nature of this laboratory and clinical training more fully in our recommendations which follow shortly. The boldness in vision attached to the Center for Excellence at Indiana University deserves emulation in terms of the use of our modern technologies. In terms of the use of more traditional curriculum materials, as well as teacher- and student-made materials, we can learn much from the best of our early teachers' centers in terms of the organization, display, and use of various curriculum materials and materials from which curriculum can be made. The physical presence of Workshop Center for Open Education at City College of New York is a classic example of how teachers, beginning as well as experienced, can be productively engaged in curriculum. We should not underestimate the nature and character of *physical environment* in learning how to teach. Again, much work must be done.

12. In these programs, we found numerous examples of *curriculum artic-ulation* between the activities which occurred on *campus* and those activities which occurred in *schools*. Usually, those supervising teachers whom we interviewed had a fair understanding of what student teachers who were placed with them were expected to do, and the RATE studies suggest, as well, that this is commonly the perception of students across the country. Nonethe-less, how such consonance, especially given evolving conceptions of how one learns to teach, can be better achieved than at present needs further attention.

But this is not the whole issue. While the extent to which programs of teacher preparation and the faculty within them model a critical pedagogy and a transforming role for schools in society is arguable, one plausible explana-tion for the present articulation or congruence could well be a common emphasis on the technical aspects of teaching and a pervasive conservative view of teaching and schooling. In our study we found exceptions and, in one instance, a program at MSU had this critical perspective as a major priority. Little dialogue, however, between college *faculty* and K–12 *teachers* appears to occur in terms of fundamental questions about the mission of schools and the nature of teaching.

There are other aspects of the field components which we found more laudable; for example, how program designs might address what is referred to as the "feed-forward" problem (Koehler, 1985) in teacher preparation. A common perception is that preservice students are engaged with concepts which they cannot internalize because of their lack of both more immediate and appropriate experience in classrooms. This is related to the "life space" problem just discussed. We found this problem challenged in programs whereby students dealt with pedagogical principles and curricular concepts in the college classroom in the morning and that very afternoon were able to practice—if not experiment—with them in cooperating classrooms.

Finally, we found examples of faculty providing some continuity and articulation in the curriculum not only through supervising students whom they had in class, but also through *teaching* on occasions in the schools and working closely with classroom teachers, at least, for brief periods of time. Recall the innovative mentoring program planned at MSU by Perry Lanier, which addressed quite a different view of learning how to teach than embraced by most teachers. If classroom experience in learning how to teach is viewed as a time for being more reflective about how pupils think and especially how pupils acquire basic concepts in different subject matter, then major conceptual shifts in how the teachers cooperating with the program view teaching are apparently needed. This calls for modelling of a different sort by college faculty as well.

In the final analysis, faculty in higher education can and should spend only so much time in schools; yet, on the other hand, it makes little sense for people who see themselves as expert in teaching methodology not to be intimately involved from time to time in the "real world" of schools and to be committed to a stronger partnership and better communication than typically exists between them and their colleagues in K–12 schools. An obvious strategy is to prepare jointly teacher leaders released partially from their teaching to assume broader roles in the clinical and student teaching or internship phases of teacher preparation.

13. Certainly, programs of teacher preparation should have some direct linkage with *research* and *development* into teacher education, as well as into the content that informs teacher education. While such efforts are most commonly manifested in the research-oriented university contexts, we found instances of cross-institutional linkage by institutions which do not have a research mission, such as that pursued at Luther College.

Schalock (1983) has treated extensively the methodological, political, and practical problems associated with research into *programs* of teacher education. He argues, as we have throughout this book, that more coherent *program development* has to occur in many instances before we can engage in well-conceived study of benefits and costs which accompany these model variations. Large-scale, long-term, well-funded developments accompanied by research are simply without precedent in teacher education. Surely a major long-range agenda for the Holmes Group should be the development of core, "standardized" curriculum and instructional artifacts which can contribute to the fuller delineation of similar programs across institutions and which in turn will facilitate replicable programmatic research and development.

14. A plan for *systematic program evaluation* exists. This is the last in this list of attributes which we have identified in terms of hopefully contributing to more coherent and well-conceived programs of teacher preparation. Generally, we found little evidence that systematic program evaluation occurred. Yet, its value cannot be denied; nor can our responsibility to engage in more than course evaluation or "follow-up" studies of our graduates' percep-

tions of the program from which they graduated. In each of these programs, with their highly personal nature, formative feedback of various types was provided to faculty on a continuing basis in terms of the effects of both the programs as a whole and of individual professors. We will not easily forget the large number of the students, for example, who said office hours were not necessary; if they had problems, they could always locate faculty with whom to share their concerns. We were impressed, even at large institutions, in terms of the personal regard for students and the multiple opportunities provided for formative feedback regarding the nature of the teacher preparation effort. Notwithstanding, there remains a need, just as there is in terms of research and development, to institute more comprehensive and formalized schemes of evaluation that critically examine key aspects of *programs* of teacher preparation. Hopefully, this initial list of program attributes can contribute to what these key aspects might be.

In summary, just as no simple formula is found for designing elementary and secondary schools that are more effective than others, no simple formula is found for designing *programs* of teacher preparation that might differentiate themselves as more effective than others. Identifiable conditions and characteristics have, however, been enumerated by faculty and students with whom we visited and observed that appear to contribute in substantial ways to the education of teachers, and we attempted to describe some of these. We realize much work remains to be done to validate their potency individually and in various combinations. More studies, such as the modest one which we pursued, are needed to provide further descriptions and to identify, increasingly, valid factors associated with effective teacher preparation. In this way, we can move to more scientifically based, effective preparation than currently exists in many institutions in what passes for approved "programs" of teacher preparation.

IMPLICATIONS FOR POLICY AND PRACTICE

We have summarized tentative understandings we derived from the six field studies. Here, we examine what these tentative understandings might imply for policy and practice. While we rely primarily on the data sources we accessed in these studies, we acknowledge at the outset that the suggestions we make relative to future directions for teacher preparation are buttressed both by the broader literature and our several years of experience in teacher preparation.

In looking here at implications for policy and practice, we first offer some general observations and limitations to our study; then following our previous pattern, we visit again specific curricular and instructional practices, followed by a review of conditions relative to faculty who teach in these programs and conclude with observations about students pursuing teaching as a career.

Clearly, high-quality teacher preparation programs can reside in a variety of institutions of higher education, ranging from small liberal arts colleges to schools and colleges of education embedded in a large university setting, albeit they draw to various degrees on different strengths. Likewise, teachers can be effectively prepared in a variety of structural variations, ranging from programs initiated, to some extent, in the freshman year, to those designed largely within the context of the final year of undergraduate study, to those basically postbaccalaureate in nature, although such variations were not the focus of our study.

We should reiterate that the programs we studied cannot be judged effective based on data that indicate that teachers graduating from them have acquired designed knowledge, skills, and dispositions at a specified criterion level or, beyond that, that teachers graduating from these programs have demonstrated themselves to be effective by enabling some set of goals for their pupils or by achieving specific pupil outcomes when they have assumed teaching positions. Our study was limited to attempting to capture the prevalent perceptions of the persons most closely involved in these programs; the faculty, the prospective teachers, and the supervising teachers and administrators in schools which cooperated with these programs. These perceptions, as we have shared, of both the programs and the teachers enrolled in them, were generally positive and were frequently offered with considerable enthusiasm and pride. The first two studies of the RATE committee, which also relies on the perceptions of students and teacher education faculty, tend to corroborate these perceptions (AACTE, 1987). We were also struck by the considerable force of conviction about the importance of preparing teachers, repeatedly demonstrated in all of the institutions we visited.

We contend neither that the programs we studied are representative of most programs nor that we can generalize from our observations. These programs were nominated from multiple sources which indicated that they were *distinctive and/or exemplary in some ways*. Further, our study was limited to six Midwestern institutions. Also, we focused our energies on programs preparing *elementary* teachers; programs which, historically, have received faculty attention in terms of curriculum innovation and program variation because of the need to bring together faculty from a variety of disciplines and perspectives.

While we designed our study carefully in order to examine specific conditions and practice and to observe instruction in a variety of contexts, we were also considerably limited by the brief time we were able to spend on each campus due to financial considerations. Thus, our study must be viewed as pilot in nature.

Therefore, we believe that the first major implication, given these tentative understandings, is that further case studies should be conducted. The National Center for Research on Teacher Education at MSU is conducting just such research, focusing particularly on how one learns to teach mathematics and writing in a variety of program alternatives and distinctly different contexts. More specifically, such inquiry should allow for more intensive and sustained field work at the sites, especially in terms of examining more actual instructional practice and how written curriculum is manifested by professors, prospective, and cooperating teachers. Beyond this, study must be extended beyond the preparation of elementary teachers and must look more closely at context differences across different types of institutions.

CURRICULUM

As we indicated, the educational value of studies in the arts, sciences, and humanities was not readily acknowledged by students with whom we visited. Beyond that, we found that the social, historical, and philosophical orientations to, or "foundations" of, education were given limited attention in several of the programs. When we did observe reactions by students to major societal issues and problems they tended to be visceral. We remain most concerned about the fuller articulation of the arts, sciences, and humanities with teacher preparation and Siegel and Delattre (1981) state well our concern:

> The jargon of studies intended to promote social reform—'appreciation of culture and world values,' 'exploring human nature,' 'ethnic heritage programs,' 'global perspectives'—conceals a shallowness in the resulting curricula. It is not likely that students will come to any real understanding of human nature without studying literature and history. It's not likely that 'global perspectives' will be informed if they are taught without geography and foreign languages. 'Relevant' contemporary issues can't be grasped in any depth without some background in the natural sciences, mathematics, and economics. Popular, contemporary treatment of social issues leads, at most, to shallow understanding of those issues. What is worse, it teaches that history, literature, mathematics, science, and languages are not really very important in dealing with contemporary issues. Such studies promote nothing but uninformed and undisciplined conviction, which, even if right, has no roots in knowledge or reflection. (p. 17)

In terms of achieving better articulation of teacher education programs with the arts and sciences, we suggest that there are three activities which could yield relatively immediate benefits. The first of these has to do with a revisiting of the question of the distribution requirements for different kinds of education majors. Such work would be facilitated by better baseline knowledge of what currently exists in this regard in different institutions which prepare teachers; perhaps through transcript analysis. We should add that we were pleasantly surprised by the general *scope* of courses which elementary education majors engaged in relative to their studies in the arts, sciences, and humanities. What we and others do not clearly understand, however, is the more exact nature of this curriculum and, most fundamentally, the instruction embedded within it. Sharing of such baseline information across institutions could serve as grist for needed curriculum and faculty development.

Second, and corollary to the above, is a facilitation of a dialogue regarding the nature of an academic major for prospective elementary teachers. This question should be addressed specifically within the larger question of whether schools might be better served by having more specialists in academic subjects teaching in elementary schools. In support of this idea, numerous scholars suggest that learning how to teach is very much intertwined with one's knowledge of the way concepts embedded in *specific* disciplines are accurately or inaccurately conceptualized by youngsters at various stages of cognitive development.

Third, we suggest the possibility of designing specific courses that directly link disciplines traditionally taught in arts and sciences with education. A portion of the distribution requirements in the arts and sciences and humanities could be satisfied by courses which, at the culmination of a preeducation major's work, would focus that discipline specifically on the nature of education and schooling. Recall Maxine Greene's illustration in chapter seven. Currently, the various branches of psychology appear to have almost exclusive rights in terms of study of their application to education. But other disciplines are equally suitable for such study. We suggest that many institutions could enhance their all-university commitment to teacher preparation by having faculty in arts and sciences together with faculty in teacher education jointly design courses in different core disciplines as preeducation or linking courses to education as articulated in the example below by Kneller (1985):

> Under any consideration I still would make room for courses in literature and education. The neglect of literature by educationists is incomprehensible. Like the historian, the philosopher, and others in humane studies, the creative writer gives us knowledge of how to live. The writer embodies knowledge of human beings and education in a tale that moves our imagination and emotions as well as our intellect. Writers make us see and feel what it is like to educate and be educated in different times and places. Charles Dickens, for example, portrays twenty-odd schools and refers to several more. He also depicts a dozen types of coercion in child training. In *Women In Love*, D. H. Lawrence, a former elementary school teacher, gives us a riveting portrayal of a lesson seen by a school inspector. Especially since World War II, education has become the central theme and setting of many novels. For portraits of teaching, learning, classroom interactions, and the joys and miseries of childhood and adolescence, we can do no better than study such works as Muriel Spark's *The Prime of Miss Jean Brodie*, John Horne Brown's *Lucifer With A Match*, Frances Patton's *Good Morning, Miss Dove*, Herman Wauk's *Marjorie Morningstar*, and many others I could name. (p. 19)

Such bridging courses could involve art, music, economics, and anthropology among others in terms of their application to education.

OTHER CURRICULAR CONSTRAINTS AND OMISSIONS

While we observed themes of various types in the programs of teacher education we visited, rarely did we see strands focused specifically on the *moral* and *ethical* dimensions of what is a highly moral endeavor. Again, the dominant emphasis in most institutions remains on the technical and communicative dimensions of teaching. Also, while we observed more diversity of instruction than we anticipated, attention to learning within *groups* and using classrooms to promote social development, as articulated in the works of such scholars as Robert Slavin, and David Johnson and Roger Johnson, was uncommon. The attention to interventions designed to alter the climate of the classroom and to promote various interpersonal dispositions and skills, was not readily apparent in programs of teacher education and this is especially difficult to understand given the social nature of schooling.

We have given several examples of the way research findings and faculty with research agendas have been integrated into programs of teacher education. Across institutions, a dominant emphasis was on research with general applicability in terms of managing and organizing classrooms and not so much research embedded in instruction within specific subjects as was exemplified for us in the Academic Learning program at MSU. Again, considerable variation was found. For example, research findings in the areas of reading and writing instruction appeared to receive attention across the programs while research pertinent to other subjects common in the elementary curriculum was less apparent to us.

We did observe some faculty in these programs thinking through carefully the nature of experiences in schools relative to the question of the way one best learns how to teach and how to study this. This is not entirely new. There has been dialogue for years around Dewey's (1904) notion that practical experience, especially at the outset of teaching, should be pursued primarily to make the teacher more thoughtful rather than gain some form of immediate proficiency. While this dialogue has been long-standing and advocates for more emphasis on reflection and studied action are found in the literature, nevertheless experiences we observed appeared heavily weighted toward practice and the efficient acquisition of teaching proficiency.

Since inquiries have recently evolved that address the question of what types of experiences create the necessary opportunities for learning to teach (Yinger, 1986; Koehler and Carter, 1986), the matter of the way experiences in classrooms are structured for beginning teachers and the way differences in the thinking of veteran and beginning teachers are accommodated (expert-novice studies) deserves more attention in preservice programs than it has received to this point. These topics should be a primary focus for dialogue in forums of teacher educators—both college and school-based—with further research in this area supported here as well.

These omissions or less-than-adequately-represented aspects of the curriculum need to be addressed. The professional education portion of the curriculum of teacher preparation should be revisited from multiple perspectives. The dominant source for designing teacher preparation programs currently appears to be the academic curriculum in K–12 schools as this is buttressed primarily by understandings derived especially from behavioral psychology and translated through the rules and regulations of legal authority at the state level. We recommend that various stakeholders in schools and in teacher education critically examine the nature of this curriculum through lenses which focus on political, social, aesthetic, moral, and ethical dimensions of teaching and schooling and with greater emphasis on developmental and cognitive psychology.

Relative to the relationship of theory and research to practice, we acknowledge the pervasive presence of this at MSU as an example of what can be accomplished in research-intensive institutions. Similarly, we applaud the initiatives taken at Luther College in terms of forming a confederation with an institution similar to MSU. Such consortia would have quite a different purpose than the Holmes Group, and we encourage establishing networks between research and nonresearch oriented institutions.

FACULTY: IMPLICATIONS

One of the more lasting impressions we have from this study is the labor-intensive nature of teacher preparation. We are both professors involved in teacher preparation in a higher education context ourselves. We have assumed responsibilities for research and service of various types and frequently have taken on administrative assignments of one nature or another in addition to teaching. We are hardly without the firsthand understanding of the nature of faculty workload. Notwithstanding, we were impressed by the very considerable investment which teacher educations across the sites appeared to put forth. It was so evident on one campus that the *work ethic* became the major characteristic in our portrayal of their program. We found faculty contributing in numerous ways to initial teacher preparation beyond their teaching and advisory functions. At MSU, for example, ample and sustaining evidence is found of how faculty centrally integrate research into these preparation efforts. Not only do faculty, in several instances, supervise students in a variety of school sites, but we found programs designed whereby faculty occasionally taught in elementary schools themselves and incorporated lessons learned from this teaching in a timely manner into their instruction on campus. Perhaps most unanticipated, however, was the considerable time faculty gave to students outside of *formal* instruction and supervision.

ADDRESSING WORKLOAD

Resolving concerns associated with faculty workload and the *work ethic* requires on the one hand an acknowledgement of the complexities associated with the self and external images conjured by the title "teacher educator"; and as well a consideration of how normative behavior of teacher educators can be restructured, given general university expectations of education faculty. With regard to the background and affiliation of education faculty, Lanier and Little (1986) have woven a provocative profile of what drives many teacher educators to labor as they do. In part, one must acknowledge the cultural context of the education professor: committed to work largely associated with women and children; coming to college as a first-generation postsecondary client; and selecting the education doctorate as a mode for upward social and cultural mobility. Such a vision reflects a labor-oriented family background. Second, as Broudy (1980) aptly observed, teacher educators tend to devalue abstract thought and decisionmaking in lieu of a busy practice-oriented focus. In short, the cultural- and school-based orientation to labor (and hard work) makes the socialization of this type of person into the abstract if not scholarly world of academe difficult (Ducharme and Agne, 1982). So, can we easily counter the sociocultural background of such faculty to the extent this exists and to the extent it has limiting effects? The first order of business might be to obtain fuller data and test this hypothesis especially across different institutions and programs. We saw in our study an aging faculty, in several instances representative of the image presented above. We certainly observed older faculty non-representative of this profile as well. In addition, we also met many younger, more academically oriented faculty coming into the ranks. We would also be well-advised to examine institutional factors which constrain faculty scholarship.

The second factor concerns external forces. For years institutions of higher education have held informally a set of expectations for education faculty, impacted to a considerable degree by a contextual (Clark, 1984) and resource environment (Orr and Peseau, 1979). Education faculty are expected to serve large numbers of students both on-campus and in field settings that do not approximate the norms or expectations of faculty members in other disciplines across campus. Not only is this apparent at the baccalaureate level, but observations at the graduate level suggest that faculty advising of graduate students in SCDEs far exceed average ratios elsewhere on campus.

We offer a few modest recommendations toward ameliorating the frantic, chalkdust image of the education professor. Certainly, one consideration is that we as professors aggressively acknowledge that we have taken on more than we can deliver in a quality manner at current resource levels. Second, programs could be developed with more cohesion and with a better differentiation of responsibilities with school personal with regard to responsibilities for clinical preparation. The notion of clinical professorships for school-based teacher educators, advocated for decades, might finally be within reach, and we elaborate on this shortly. Third, the development of somewhat standardized curriculum materials could help by reducing instructional demands on individual professors. Fourth, while we do not advocate any separation of the triadic roles of teaching, research, and service in research-oriented institutions, we do believe that faculty could *specialize* in some instructional areas; for example, as laboratory or clinical experts. This could be especially appropriate in what historically have been non-research oriented institutions.

Finally, our advocacy for changing the bootstrap mentality that surrounds resource allocations for education may find some responsiveness given the heightened attention and politicized context of teacher preparation. Some have posited, for example, that shifting teacher education to the postbaccalaureate level will increase funding and lead to an increased orientation to inquiry. Ultimately, however, changing funding formulas at the state level is needed to make the conditions of practice for the education professoriate more tenable.

ENABLING INSTRUCTION

What we observed relative to *formal instruction* offered by faculty appears to some degree to contradict conventional and collective observations about the nature of teaching in higher education. We observed and had repeatedly reported to us by students and faculty examples of considerable diversity in instruction. While the lecture/discussion format understandably remains a staple of instruction, the faculty and students whom we observed were involved in a range of other activities, as well, including peer and microteaching, engaging students in systematic observations and recordings in schools, involving them in diagnoses and studies of pupils and completing research reports. It may well be that in order to capture the richness and diversity of instructional activities in which students engage during their preparation for teaching, one has to spend considerable time with students and faculty in a variety of contexts and that practices reported in survey literature probably do not capture adequately what actually occurs. Again, we should underscore that we made no systematic effort to assess the appropriateness or efficacy of this instruction, however diverse.

While the nature of instruction was more diversified (and hopefully appropriate and effective as well) than generally acknowledged, and elementary programs might be richer in certain materials than other programs, it is nonetheless apparent that major problems exist. As we indicated, an unevenness is found across faculty within institutions as well as across institutions in terms of instruction. Some instruction is pedestrian, sterile, and, from our limited observation, misguided. Modern technologies to enable teaching were rarely observed.

Thus, on the basis of our observations we make four major recommendations. The first concerns the clear need to develop more robust and integrated
laboratory activities for pedogogical training which are largely embedded at
the college site in programs of teacher preparation. In this regard, we refer to
the concepts advanced by David Berliner (1985) who characterizes a laboratory component in teacher education as including computer simulation, videotape libraries of carefully chosen classroom interactions that students can
analyze and code from a variety of perspectives, protocol materials that allow
analyses of sophisticated concepts, viewing model lessons, analyzing standardized cases, microteaching, and other forms of mediated practice. His
contention is that findings from research often do not find their way into
college classrooms, and, when they do, they are not adapted into opportunities for learning how to teach. Thus, he calls for laboratory experiences such
as the above.

Our primary recommendation in this regard is that cross-institutional
confederations be formed whereby faculty from different institutions who
teach in the same disciplines and subjects (especially in the core and foun-
dational content of teacher preparation) are brought together periodically to
develop collectively a range of laboratory-type materials that could be tested
and employed eventually in *any* program of teacher preparation. These include numerous types of simulations, including computer simulations, case
studies, curriculum artifacts of various types, teaching protocols, especially
employing videotape, and any number of problem-solving activities, for
example, the problem-oriented, in-basket approach.

The second major recommendation concerns the development of technologies and facilities to facilitate networking among schools and colleges of
education with K–12 schools. Certainly, the vision of Howard Mehlinger, at
Indiana University, is instructive here. While the new facility envisioned at
this university, referred to as the Center for Excellence in Education, is
beyond the realm of possibility for most institutions, much of the technology
envisioned for this facility is not. Neither are the linkages which Dean Mehlinger has articulated.

A major insight which we gained in our several classroom observations
was the extent to which students reflected the instructional posture of their
professors. That is, if we were in a class in which the professor engaged
students in a very active and intellectually challenging type of dialogue,
students invariably were able to respond to this and, in fact, build upon and
further contribute to understanding the topic at hand. However, if students,
and in many instances the very same students, were in a situation where they
were placed in a relatively passive and noninitiating role, they behaved accordingly.

We should not be surprised at the changing roles students assume in
the classroom. Some of the more insightful studies of instruction in K–12
schools acknowledge students' ability early on to assume roles socially as

well as academically acceptable to their peers as well as their teachers. Thus, our third recommendation as a result of these observations is to focus professional development for professors on assuming a broader repertoire of activities designed to *actively* engage students. Exemplary efforts have been piloted in a number of higher education contexts focusing on "active student learning," and these should be built upon and tested more fully in schools and colleges of education.

Finally, we believe that much can be done to assist the best of teachers in K–12 schools to assume broadened responsibilities in the clinical component of teacher preparation and, as we suggested, this speaks to the workload problem as well. This could be done while maintaining some teaching responsibility or while on leave from their teaching responsibilities for, perhaps, two or three years. Both the increasing attention to career ladders for teachers and the Holmes Group's concern for the development of clinical professors lend themselves to this notion. The key here is to develop *high-quality* programs to develop these teachers further as clinical instructors. A growing knowledge base is concerned both with learning how to teach and with providing feedback about teaching that should serve as the foundation for such clinical training. We are currently piloting programs of leadership training for teachers in this regard, drawing upon related domains of knowledge critical to the preparation of teachers in these new roles, including: interpersonal and adult development; classroom processes and school effectiveness; instructional supervision; and finally, building a disposition among teacher leaders and those they assist toward reflection and inquiry about teaching practice.

STUDENTS

Just as with the faculty, we were pleasantly surprised in many respects with regard to the "profile" we developed of students in elementary education which emerged for us as we visited the six institutions. These students appeared to be academically able in the great majority of instances, dedicated to becoming effective teachers and most enthusiastic about assuming a teaching role. We did not anticipate the evident pride students generally exhibited in terms of their programs, the faculty with whom they worked, and the career in which they were about to embark. Teaching was presented to us in the nature of a secular calling in numerous instances. Also contrary to the existing evidence we have on the tenure of beginning teachers, the prospective teachers with whom we talked invariably indicated that they viewed teaching as a long-term career and appeared surprised when we shared data demonstrating that the majority of teachers are no longer teaching within five years after graduation. Doubtless, such enthusiasm and commitment will, as many studies have found, be tempered by actual practice in school settings. But to the extent that the seeds for socialization and professional image begin at preservice, we can be reasonably confident that professional esteem is being cultivated in these undergraduate programs.

COMBATING PAROCHIALISM

Major concerns were also evidenced in terms of the students we observed and as they were observed by others with whom we visited. As we indicated across each of our cases, we were struck by the parochial, often conservative nature of these students. Only rarely did the students indicate to us that they wished to teach in urban settings or with at-risk learners. There seemed to be, almost without exception, a relatively unthinking acceptance of current school policy and practice. Examples of the moral and ethical consequences of teaching were rarely volunteered or well-responded to when we probed. The dominant conception of teaching these prospective teachers embraced was technical in nature, albeit embedded in very real personal regard for their pupils. Commonly, students described their general education as not that helpful and not instrumental enough in preparing them for teaching. Exceptions were found with regard to acknowledging the general educational value of the arts, sciences, and humanities, and especially in those institutions where this orientation is dominant.

We wrote earlier of the way better linkages might be made between professional studies and general studies and the way more thought might be given to the nature of general studies as well. Earlier in this chapter, we wrote of the need for a critical cultural prespective to be embraced as one of the *themes* running through a program of teacher education, if not serving as a primary framework for a program.

Even if major program revisions were made, the demography of prospective teachers (including those whom we observed and interviewed) stands in sharp contrast to the diverse population of students in K–12 schools, thereby causing concern. The problems of teacher recruitment and selection are hardly limited to attracting enough academically able students into teaching positions. We need to address, centrally, how more cultural diversity can be achieved in the teaching force. While no simple solutions are evident, we offer some suggestions.

First, we found two examples of programmatic efforts which addressed this problem, albeit on a relatively modest scale in one instance and with but limited success in terms of placing graduates in settings reflecting considerable cultural diversity in the other. We refer to the yeoman efforts of James Mahan at Indiana University in the former instance and MSU's Heterogeneous Classrooms program, which is guided by Richard Navarro, in the latter. Efforts such as these, however rare, need to be described more fully, especially in terms of their potential adaptability by others. Both the program design at MSU and the intensive field experience sustained over the years by

Mahan at Indiana University appear replicable. Other instances of "best practice" should be identified and held up for example.

Second, Angene Wilson (1982) provides a thoughtful developmental model for educating the culturally insular student which she refers to as cross-cultural experiential learning. This framework guides prospective teachers, whatever their ethnicity and culture, through rather natural cross-cultural encounters, from self-development activities to cross-cultural experimental learnings and finally to teaching from a global perspective. Thoughtful treatises such as this one can help guide program design which has multicultural development as a priority.

Third, a specific focus in the many *entry-year* or *induction* schemes evolving across the country for new teachers—often mandated and funded at the state level—should be on providing special support for teachers willing to work in urban and remote rural areas and with at-risk students. Perhaps many beginning teachers who are not disposed to work in these settings would be more inclined to do so if there was the support of a formal induction or entry-year assistance program wherein they could work with a mentor, or perhaps better a team of experienced teachers. In this way they could receive specific and continuing support while working with culturally diverse and at-risk students. Given such policies, more teachers might pursue such positions. We suggest that state policymakers consider how these evolving entry-year arrangements could attract able beginning teachers into urban settings with appropriate support for what are admittedly challenging assignments.

Ultimately, however, this lack of cultural diversity in the teaching force has to be addressed early. We need to implement programs to recruit able young persons from minority cultures into teaching while they are still in high school. Secondary school minority students could be assigned to experienced elementary teachers for focused teacher aide roles as they proceed through high school, and receive some financial support and academic credit, similar in some ways to the Career Opportunities Program sponsored in the late 1960s and early 1970s by the federal government. This would be the first type of incentive. Next, those who develop and maintain an interest in teaching and who were successful could be provided forms of financial assistance as they enter into their college years with a declared major in teacher education.

There is considerable rhetoric across the country today regarding career ladders. Political and economic reality suggests to us that such career variation will be enabled by teaching aides, such as those outlined above, assigned to lead teachers who are released partially from some of their teaching responsibilities. Conceptually and politically, career ladders and lattices cannot be based primarily on a teaching meritocracy. Rather they need to be embedded in a concept of continuing *teacher education* that allows some teachers, partially released, to work with other teachers through expert roles in curriculum, instruction, inquiry, and professional development. In this manner conditions in schools can over time be altered as well, not only to provide higher-quality instruction but to create more dynamic, fluid, and civilized conditions for teaching and for continuing to learn how to teach.

Thus, we suggest that career ladder models should also include assignments below what we typically construe as entry level: that is, well-conceived auxiliary roles which can eventually culminate in initial certification. This concept has manifold implications for institutions of teacher education as well as for K–12 schools. Not only can aide roles help balance the costs of teachers in leadership roles, they help provide these teachers in leadership roles various legitimate responsibilities. This could also be one way to address a major social problem as well, through focusing on minority students who wish to explore teaching by providing them paraprofessional roles.

Finally, if we are successful in attracting more minorities to teaching, we must also look carefully at the selection criteria typically in force in SCDEs. The context for teacher recruitment and selection is greatly effected by a move toward higher standards and selectivity in teacher education. The range of initiatives to increase the quality of the teacher pool has spawned proposals for teacher competency testing, mandated higher grade point averages for entrance to and exit from teacher education programs, tested program graduates, and defined higher institutional standards (Zimpher, 1987). These initiatives constitute a sequence of points where standards for selection can profoundly effect the teacher population, particularly with regard to minority recruitment.

By far, the most popular new admissions screens are a number of teacher competency testing programs. Sandefur (1984) presents data reflecting high percentages of failure by blacks and Hispanics. Some would argue these reflect linguistic and cultural bias suspected in most standardized testing formats. Thus, we suggest a closer look at criteria that extend the variables against which selection considerations for teacher education programs could be made, not to undermine the continuing need for academically able teachers, but to enhance selection by looking at other important characteristics which might have predictive validity in terms of teaching success, such as those posed by Howey and Strom (1986). In this way, we might expand our attention in selection beyond results of standardized testing to qualities which characterize good teachers as adaptive, problem-oriented, and altruistic. This posture, in combination with increased attention to early career identification will, we hope, allow us to attract an increased minority population to teaching.

SOME TROUBLESOME QUESTIONS WHICH CALL FOR FURTHER STUDY

What remains in extending our study further is to test a series of assumptions with regard to the nature of attributes which guide effective programs. We evolved a set of understandings that appeared in the six sites studied to contribute to distinctive, if not exemplary, programs of teacher education. Yet these attributes remain to be confirmed, especially at other sites. Stated below are the kinds of questions that call for extended investigation:

1. How does the nature of teaching, the role of teachers, and the mission of schooling as viewed across faculty and by students define and impact the nature of the preservice program?

2. To what degree are clear and reasonable goals or dispositions found, with regard to faculty and students? Are the goals or objectives of the program attainable? And if so, what are the measures for successful completion of the program?

3. To what extent are discernible themes identified that run throughout the program and are manifested in curriculum materials, professors' instruction, and laboratory and clinical activity? To what extent are developmental progressions found in the themes, such as moving from relatively simple to increasingly complex notions of teaching or rather, moving from modest observatory initiatives in the school to ultimately more sustained teaching?

4. To what degree are provisions for concept or schema development by students found; that is, the extent to which students are made aware of certain conceptual frameworks guiding our understanding of pedagogy and our understanding of the way children learn and teachers facilitate that development in schools?

5. What explicit considerations guide the nature of curriculum design, such as the scope, sequence, and degree of integration and articulation?

6. To what degree does a characterization of the nature of the curriculum itself exist that can be explicated, understood, and known among faculty and students?

7. To what degree does a recognizable sense of distinctiveness by faculty and students exist with regard to the nature of the preservice program and what contributes to this?

8. What are the matriculation patterns of the students and does a structured pattern exist in which students take first one course and then another, ultimately deriving from that matriculation pattern a sense of program?

9. What forms and degrees of faculty collegiality exist both within the program and outside the program to other parts of the university and elementary and secondary schools, and in what ways do these degrees of collegiality contribute to effective programs?

10. To what degree does articulation exist between the general studies (arts, sciences, and humanities courses) on the one hand and articulation between the program and school-based experience on the other? To what extent do these articulations enhance the degree of program effectiveness?

11. To what extent do designs exist for actually studying the process of learn-

ing how to teach and the impact of the program in encouraging whatever conceptions of good teaching exist in the program?

12. To what extent do designs exist for comprehensive program evaluation beginning with an assessment of specific qualities students enter programs with and then following students through initial years of teaching to ascertain program effects?

These, then, suggest extensions of the kinds of attributes that were apparent to various degrees in the programs studied herein. They represent not only a potential set of parameters for defining *programs*, but also for ascertaining the degree to which robust programs of preservice preparation exist. These are, from our perspective, critical questions in determining ultimately how to assess preservice teacher education as an intervention and the efficacy of those interventions from one campus to another. We share them as a heuristic for further study and subsequent writing which will build on this work.

Bibliography

American Association of Colleges for Teacher Education. (1987). *Teacher education policy in the states: Fifty-state survey of legislative and administrative actions.* Washington, DC: American Association of Colleges for Teacher Education.

American Association of Colleges for Teacher Education (1987). *Teaching teachers: Facts and figures.* Washington, DC: American Association of Colleges for Teacher Education.

Apple, M. (1987). Will the social context allow a tomorrow for tomorrow's teachers? *Teachers College Record, 88*(3), 330–37.

Barnes, H. (1987). The conceptual bases for thematic teacher education programs. *Journal of Teacher Education, 38*(4), 13–17.

Berliner, D. (1985). Laboratory settings and the study of teacher education. *Journal of Teacher Education, 36*(6), 2–8.

Bloom, B. S. (1981). *All our children learning.* New York: McGraw-Hill.

Bogdan, R. C. & Biklen, S. K. (1982). *Qualitative research for education: An introduction to theory and methods.* Boston: Allyn and Bacon.

Broudy, H. S. (1984). The university and the preparation of teachers. In L. G. Katz and J. D. Raths (Eds.), *Advances in teacher education* (Vol. 1, pp. 1–8). Norwood, NJ: Ablex.

Broudy, H. S. (1980). What do professors of education profess? *The Educational Forum, 44*(4), 441–51.

Carr, W. & Kemmis, S. (1983). *Becoming critical: Education, knowledge and action research.* London: Falmer Press.

Clark, D. L. (1984). Transforming the structure for the professional preparation of teachers. In J. D. Raths and L. G. Katz (Eds.), *Advances in teacher education* (Vol. 2, pp. 1–20). Norwood, NJ: Ablex.

Clark, D. & Guba, E. (1977). *Research in institutions of teacher education* (RITE Occasional Paper Series). Bloomington: Indiana University College of Education.

Cohen, M. W. (1985). Enhancing motivation: An application to the preservice experience. *Journal of Teacher Education, 36*(4), 40–45.

Combs, A. W. (1974). *The professional education of teachers* (rev. ed.). Boston: Allyn & Bacon.

Dewey, J. (1904). The relation of theory to practice in education. In C. McMurray (Ed.), *Third yearbook of the national society for the study of education*. Chicago: University of Chicago Press.

Ducharme, E. (1987, April). *A national study of professors of education: Data and reflection*. Paper presented at the American Educational Research Association, Washington.

Ducharme, E. & Agne, R. (1982). The education professoriate: A research-based perspective. *Journal of Teacher Education, 33*(6), 30–36.

Feistritzer, C. E. (1983). *Profile of teachers in the U.S.* Washington, DC: National Center for Education Information.

Fenstermacher, G. D. (1986). Philosophy of research on teaching: Three aspects. In M. C. Wittrock (Ed.), *Handbook of research on teaching* (3rd ed). New York: Macmillan.

Fraser, H. W. & Showmaker, J. (1981). What principals can do: Some implications from studies of effective schooling. *Phi Delta Kappan, 63*, 178–82.

Fuller, F. & Bown, O. (1975). Becoming a teacher. In K. Ryan (Ed.), *Teacher education NSSE yearbook*. Chicago: University of Chicago Press.

Grant, G. & Riesman, D. (1978). *The perpetual dream: Reform and experiment in the American college*. Chicago: University of Chicago Press.

Greene, M. (1986). In search of a critical pedagogy. *Harvard Educational Review, 56*(4), 427–41.

Griffin, G. (1983). *Student teaching and the commonplace of schooling*. Paper prepared for the annual meeting of the American Educational Research Association, Montreal.

Guba, E. G. & Clark, D. L. (1978). Levels of R & D productivity in schools of education. *Educational Researcher, 7*(5), 3–9.

Haberman, M. (1983). Research in preservice laboratory and clinical experiences: Implications for teacher education. In K. R. Howey and W. E. Gardner (Eds.), *The education of teachers*. New York: Longman.

Hodgkinson, H. (1988). *Ohio: The state and its educational system*. Washington, DC: Institute for Educational Leadership, Inc.

Holmes Group. (1986). *Tomorrow's teachers: A report of the Holmes group*. East Lansing, MI: Holmes Group.

Howey, K. R. (1988, February). *AACTE RATE project national study for teacher preparation, year two: Foundations courses*. Paper presented at the annual meeting of the AACTE, New Orleans.

Howey, K. R. & Zimpher, N. L. (1986). The current debate on teacher preparation. *Journal of Teacher Education, 37*(5), 41–50.

Howey, K. R. & Strom, S. (1986). Teacher selection reconsidered. In L. G. Katz and J. D. Raths (Eds.), *Advances in teacher education* (Vol. III, pp. 1–34). Norwood, NJ: Ablex.

Howey, K. R., Matthes, W. S. & Zimpher, N. L. (1985). *Issues and problems in professional development*. Elmhurst, IL: North Central Regional Educational Laboratory.

Johnson, R., & Johnson, D. (1985). Student-student interaction: Ignored but powerful. *Journal of Teacher Education, 36*(4), 22–26.

Katz, L. G., & Raths, J. D. (1982). The best of intentions for the education of teachers. *Action in Teacher Education, 4*(1), 8–16.

Kennedy, M. (1988, February). *Does teacher education make a difference?* Paper presented at the annual meeting of the AACTE, New Orleans.

Kirst, M. W. (1986). Sustaining the momentum of state education reform: The link between assessment and financial support. *Phi Delta Kappan, 67*(5), 341–45.

Kneller, G. F. (1985). The proper study of education, in J. Denton, W. Peters, and T. Savage (Eds.), *New directions in teacher education: Foundations, curriculum, policy* (pp. 13–24). College Station, TX: Instructional Research Laboratory.

Koehler, V. R. & Carter, K. (1986). The process and content of initial year of teaching programs. In G. A. Griffin and S. Millies (Eds.), *The first years of teaching: Background papers and a proposal.* Chicago: University of Illinois at Chicago.

Koehler, V. (1985). Research in preservice teacher education. *Journal of Teacher Education, 36*(1), 23–30.

Koff, R. (1986). The socialization of a teacher: On metaphors and teaching. In *Tension and dynamism: The education of a teacher.* Conference proceedings, University of Michigan, School of Education, Ann Arbor, MI.

Krathwohl, D. R. (1985). *Social and behavioral science research: A new framework for conceptualizing, implementing, and evaluating research studies.* San Francisco: Jossey-Bass.

Lanier, J. E. & Little, J. W. (1986). Research in teacher education. In M. C. Wittrock (Ed.), *Handbook of research on teaching* (3rd ed., pp. 527–69). NY: Macmillan.

Lincoln, Y. S. & Guba, E. G. (1985). *Naturalistic inquiry.* Beverly Hills: Sage.

Liston, D. P., & Zeichner, K. M. (1987). Reflective teacher education and moral deliberation. *Journal of Teacher Education, 38*(6), 2–8.

Morsink, C. (1987). Critical functions of the educational administrator: Perceptions of chairpersons and deans. *Journal of Teacher Education, 38*(5), 23–27.

Noddings, N. (1986). Fidelity in teaching, teacher education and research for teaching. *Harvard Educational Review, 56*(4), 496–510.

Orr, P. & Peseau, B. (1979). Formula funding is not the problem in teacher education. *Peabody Journal of Education, 57*(1), 61–71.

Purkey, S. C. & Smith, M. D. (1982). Effective schools: A review. *The Elementary School Journal, 83*(4), 427–52.

Raths, J. D., Katz, L. G. & McAninch, A. (In press). A plight of teacher educators: Clinical mentalities in a scientific culture. In R. Wisniewski and E. R. Ducharme (Eds.), *The professors of teaching: An inquiry* (pp. 105–118). Albany: SUNY Press.

Raths, S. D. & Katz, L. G. (1985). *Teacher dispositions as goals for teacher education.* Paper presented at the annual meeting of the American Educational Research Association, Chicago.

Robinson, W. S. (1951). The logical structure of analytic induction. *American Sociological Review, 16*, 812–18.

Romanish, B. (1987). A skeptical view of educational reform. *Journal of Teacher Education, 38*(3), 9–12.

Sandefur, J. T. (1984). *Standards for admission to teacher education programs.* Issue paper prepared for the Minnesota Higher Education Coordinating Board. Bowling Green, KY: Western Kentucky University.

Scannell, D. P. (1984). The extended teacher education program at the University of Kansas. *Phi Delta Kappan, 66*(2), 130–33.

Schalock, D. (1983). Methodological considerations in future research and development in teacher education. In K. R. Howey and W. Gardner (Eds.), *The education of teachers* (pp. 38–73). New York: Longman.

Schlechty, P. C. (1985). A framework for evaluating induction into teaching. *Journal of Teacher Education, 36*(1), 37–41.

Schlechty, P. C., & Vance, C. (1983). Recruitment, selection and retention: The shape of the teaching force. *Elementary School Journal, 83*(4), 469–487.

Schwebel, M. (in press). The new priorities and the education faculty. In R. Wisniewski and E. R. Ducharme (Eds.). *The Professors of Teaching: An Inquiry* (pp. 52–66). Albany: SUNY Press.

Shulman, L. (1986). Paradigms and research programs in the study of teaching: A contemporary perspective. In M. C. Wittrock (Ed.), *Handbook of research on teaching* (3rd ed.). New York: MacMillan.

Siegel, J. S. & Delattre, E. J. (1981, April). Blackboard jungle. *The New Republic, 17,* 17–18.

Slavin, R. (1983). *Cooperative learning.* New York: Longman.

Smith, D. C. (1984). PROTEACH: Teacher preparation at the University of Florida. *Teacher Education and Practice, 1*(2), 5–12.

Sprinthall, N. A. & Theis-Sprinthall, L. (1983). The need for theoretical frameworks in educating teachers: A cognitive-developmental perspective. In K. R. Howey and W. E. Gardner (Eds.), *The education of teachers: A look ahead* (pp. 74–97). New York: Longman.

Tom, A. (1987). The Holmes group report: Its latent political agenda. *Teachers College Record, 88*(3), 430–35.

———. (1986). *The case for maintaining teacher education at the undergraduate level.* Paper prepared for the Coalition of Teacher Education Programs, St. Louis.

Wilson, A. (1982). Cross-cultural experiential learning for teachers. *Theory Into Practice, 21*(3), 184–92.

Yarger, S. Howey, K. & Joyce, B. (1977). Reflections on preservice preparation: Impressions from the national survey. *Journal of Teacher Education, 33*(6), 34–37.

Yinger, R. J. (1986). Learning the language of practice. Implications for beginning year of teaching programs. In G. A. Griffin and S. Millies (Eds.), *The first years of teaching: Background papers and a proposal.* Chicago: University of Illinois.

Zeichner, K. (1987). The ecology of field experience: Toward an understanding of the role of field experiences in teacher development. In M. Haberman and J. M. Backus (Eds.), *Advances in teacher education* (Vol. 3, pp. 94–114). Norwood, NJ: Ablex.

Zimpher, N. L. (1988, February). *1987 national survey of students in teacher education programs: Preliminary findings.* Paper presented at the Annual Meeting of the AACTE, New Orleans.

——— (1988). A design for the professional development of teacher leaders. *Journal of Teacher Education, 39*(1), 53–61.

& Yessayan, S. (1987, Fall). Recruitment and selection of minority populations into teaching. *Metropolitan Education*, 5.

——— (1987). Current trends in research on university supervision of student teaching. In M. Haberman and J. M. Backus. *Advances in teacher education* (Vol. 3, pp. 118–50). Norwood, NJ: Ablex.

Zimpher, N. & Loadman, W. E. (1985). *A documentation and assessment system for student and program development* (Teacher Education Monograph No. 3). Washington, DC: ERIC Clearinghouse on Teacher Education.